HEALTH TECHNOLOGY ASSESSMENT AND HEALTH POLICY TODAY: A MULTIFACETED VIEW OF THEIR UNSTABLE CROSSROADS

SERIES ECONOMÍA DE LA SALUD Y GESTIÓN SANITARIA
Edited by **Vicente Ortún**

HEALTH TECHNOLOGY ASSESSMENT AND HEALTH POLICY TODAY: A MULTIFACETED VIEW OF THEIR UNSTABLE CROSSROADS

Directors

Juan E. del Llano-Señarís
Director, Gaspar Casal Foundation
President, Spanish Association for Healthcare Technology
Evaluation (AEETS)

Carlos Campillo-Artero
Clinical and Health Services Evaluation, Health Service,
Palma de Mallorca
Associate researcher, Research Center on Health
and Economics, University Pompeu Fabra, Barcelona

Series *Economia de la salud y gestión sanitaria*
Edited by *Vicente Ortún, CRES-UPF*

Health Technology Assessment and Health Policy Today: A Multifacedted View of their Unstable Crossroads
ISBN 978-3-319-15003-1   ISBN 978-3-319-15004-8 (eBook)
DOI 10.1007/978-3-319-15004-8

Springer Cham Heidelberg New York Dordrecht London

Springer International Publishing AG Switzerland is part of Springer Science+Business Media (www.springer.com)

This book was supported by an unrestricted educational grant from Celgene.

Table of contents

PART II: ISSUES

Authors

José Mª Abellán-Perpiñán

José María Abellán is Professor at University of Murcia, Spain. He is Head Researcher of the Health Economics and Economic Evaluation Research Group of the same University, Coordinator of the Economic Evaluation Group of the *Spanish Health Economics Association/ Asociación de Economía de la Salud (AES)* and Vice President of this Association. His primary research interests are Health Economics, Behavioural Economics and Experimental Economics. He has published different papers about QALYs and health state utility measurements in leading journals such as *Health Economics, Journal of Health Economics, or Management Science*. One of his articles was awarded as the best paper in Health Economics published by a Spanish researcher in 2012. At present, he is working in the development of methods that help to minimise psychological biases that distort preference elicitations.

David Banta

David Banta was born in the United States of America. He was awarded an MD degree from Duke University, and MPH and MS degrees from the Harvard School of Public Health. In 1975 he joined the Congressional Office of Technology Assessment (OTA) where he headed the health activities group. During his 8 years with OTA, his team defined the basic methods and strategies for health technology assessment (HTA). In 1985, Dr Banta moved to the Netherlands, taking Dutch citizenship in 1993. Dr Banta headed the first European project aimed at coordinating HTA in Europe, EUR-ASSESS. During these years, Dr Banta travelled to many countries to consult on HTA, spending considerable time in China, Malaysia, Poland, Romania, Latvia and Brazil. Dr Banta is Professor at Maastricht University and has published extensively on HTA, including its international aspects, health technology diffusion and health policy.

CARLOS CAMPILLO

Dr Campillo-Artero holds a PhD in Medicine (University of Barcelona), an MPH (The Johns Hopkins University School of Public Health, Baltimore, MD, USA) and is a specialist in preventive medicine and public health. He works in clinical, health services and health policy research for the Balearic Health Service. Dr Campillo-Artero was a former staff member and current consultant of the World Health Organization (in Washington, DC), and is a current member of the Technical Committee on Clinical Safety of the Spanish Minister of Health, Social Services and Equity. Professor and tutor in several master programmes in clinical, health services evaluation and pharmacoeconomics. He is associate editor and referee of several national and international medical journals and associate researcher at the Centre for Research in Health and Economics, Pompeu Fabra University (Barcelona, Spain).

ANTHONY J. CULYER

Tony Culyer is a professor of economics at the University of York, UK and Senior Fellow at the Institute of Health Policy, Management and Evaluation at the University of Toronto, Canada. He was the founding Organiser of the Health Economists' Study Group. For 33 years he was the founding co-editor, with Joe Newhouse, of the *Journal of Health Economics*. He was founding Vice Chair of the National Institute for Health and Care Excellence (NICE) and chairs NICE International's Advisory Group. He is Editor-in-Chief of the on-line *Encyclopaedia of Health Economics*. Dr Culyer was responsible for the 1994 report that led to the redesign of the NHS's system for supporting R&D. For many years he was chair of the Department of Economics & Related Studies at York University and, for six of these years, was deputy vice-chancellor. In Canada he was Chief Scientist at the Institute for Work & Health. He helped to found the Citizens' Council and the Occupational Cancer Research Centre. The third edition of his *The Dictionary of Health Economics* (Edward Elgar) has just been published. A collection of his non-technical essays called *The Humble Economist* is available on-line free of charge.

MICHAEL DRUMMOND

Michael Drummond, BSc, MCom, DPhil, is Professor of Health Economics and former Director of the Centre for Health Economics at the University of York, UK. His particular field of interest is in the economic evaluation of healthcare treatments and programmes. He has undertaken evaluations in a wide range of medical fields including care of the elderly, neonatal intensive care, immunisation programmes, services for people with AIDS, eye healthcare and pharmaceuticals. He is the author of two major textbooks and more than 600 scientific papers, and has acted as a consultant to the World Health Organization and the European Union. He has been President of the International Society of Technology Assessment in Health Care, and the International Society for Pharmacoeconomics and Outcomes Research. In October 2010 he was made a member of the Institute of Medicine in the USA.

GLYN ELWYN

Professor Elwyn is a physician-researcher, professor and senior scientist at The Dartmouth Health Care Delivery Science Center and The Dartmouth Institute for Health Policy and Clinical Practice, USA. He leads a research group with an interest in implementing and measuring shared decision making, user-centred design of patient decision support tools and their integration into healthcare delivery systems. His current focus is on option grids and measurement of their impact on practice. He also holds the following additional position: Chair at the Scientific Institute for Quality of Healthcare, Radboud University Nijmegen Medical Centre, Netherlands.

STUART W. GRANDE

Dr Stuart Grande is a postdoctoral fellow at the Dartmouth Center for Health Care Delivery Science in Hanover, New Hampshire. Stuart holds a PhD in health behaviour and an MPA in public management from Indiana University, where he received the Keller Runden Fellowship for his work in community-based conflict resolution. Dr Grande's research broadly explores shared decision making and innovative methods of patient engagement. More specifically, he explores the social effects of new technologies on patient-provider communication and peer support among disenfranchised groups. He also leads an interdisciplinary qualitative research group at Dartmouth College whose remit is to support novel methods that leverage the patient voice across healthcare systems and stakeholders.

Juan Ernesto del Llano

Dr. Juan Ernesto del Llano Señarís, Physician (1981) and PhD in Medicine (1990) from Complutense University, Madrid. Specialist in Preventive Medicine and Public Health (MIR 1982–84, La Paz Hospital, Madrid). MSc in Community Health, Usher Institute, University of Edinburgh (1985–86). European Healthcare Leadership Program, INSEAD (1999–2000). Senior Management of Healthcare Institutions Program, IESE, Navarra University (2004). Advanced Health Leadership Forum, Universitat Pompeu Fabra (UPF), Barcelona and University of California, Berkeley (2005). General Director, Gaspar Casal Foundation (FGC). Academic Director and Professor of Public Health and Health Service Management, Master of Health Service Administration and Management (MADS), University Pompeu Fabra and Gaspar Casal Foundation. Associate Researcher, Centre of Health Economics Research (CRES), UPF. President, Spanish Association for Healthcare Technology Evaluation (AEETS). Associate Editor, *Gestión Clínica y Sanitaria* Journal. Biomedical Reviewer, National Agency for Assessment and Prospective (ANEP). Assistant Professor, National Agency of Evaluation, Quality and Accreditation (ANECA). Author of more than 50 peer-reviewed articles and twelve books.

Ricard Meneu

Dr Ricard Meneu is Vice President of the Instituto de Investigación en Servicios de Salud (Institute of Health Services Research) in Spain. He is a physician specialised in preventive medicine and public health and holds a PhD in economics (University of Valencia). He works in healthcare management for the Valencian Health Service. Former Head of Service of Health Technology Assessment and Head of Service of Quality in Health Care, he was member of the Technical Committee on Clinical Safety to the Spanish Minister of Health, Social Services and Equity. Editor in chief of the quarterly *Gestión Clínica y Sanitaria*, author of more than one hundred articles and book chapters, and also referee of several national and international medical journals. Professor and tutor in several master programmes in health economics, health services management and pharmacoeconomics, is associate researcher, Centre for Research in Health and Economics, Pompeu Fabra University (Barcelona, Spain).

VICENTE ORTÚN

Vicente Ortún is Dean and Professor of the School of Economic and Business Sciences, University Pompeu Fabra of Barcelona, Spain. He is founder, former director, and member of the Center for Research in Economics and Health (CRES), University Pompeu Fabra. Author of 400 articles and books. Director of the book series on Health Economics and Health Management, with 30 titles published by Springer and Elsevier.
MBA by ESADE (1969), Master of Science from Purdue University (1970), BA and PhD in Economics by University of Barcelona (1990). Doctoral studies in Public Health at Johns Hopkins University and Visiting Scholar (2009) in the Department of Economics at the Massachusetts Institute of Technology (MIT).
Business and public policy experience at regional, national and international levels.
Former president of the Spanish Society of Public Health and Health Administration (SESPAS), former president of the Association of Health Economics (AES), former secretary of the European Public Health Association (EUPHA) and merit member of CAMFiC.

JOAN ROVIRA

Dr Joan Rovira Forns is Professor Emeritus at the Department of Economics, University of Barcelona, Spain. Associate Professor of the Andalusian School of Public Health. Senior Health Economist for Pharmaceuticals at the Department of Human Development of the World Bank, Washington (2001–2004). Short-term professional at the WHO European Office in Copenhagen, as acting Officer for Health Economics (1989), consultant on health policy and economics for the WHO, the PAHO, the IDB and the European Commission. Editor-in-Chief of the journal *Cost-Effectiveness and Resource Allocation*. His present areas of interest include economic evaluation of health technologies, optimisation of clinical trials, modelling disease processes, health systems financing, intellectual property policies, pricing and reimbursement, generic drug policies, and other topics related to the accessibility to medicines.

Foreword

A foreword is meant to lend credibility to a book. In this case, it's the other way around: the book gives credibility to the foreword, since it has been written by distinguished and well-known practitioners and academics of health technology assessment, among them some of the founding fathers who have contributed to the consolidation of this multidisciplinary endeavour during the last 40 years and keep showing here how aware they are of the many challenges to overcome: David Banta, Anthony Culyer, Michael Drummond and Joan Rovira.

A foreword should deal with the genesis and purpose of the book. I acknowledge my indebtedness with my two distinguished colleagues, friends and long-time partners, Carlos Campillo and Juan del Llano, when they proposed to publish the book in the collection Health Economics and Health Services Management. A collection promoted by the Research Center on Health and Economics at University Pompeu Fabra (CRES-UPF) during the last 15 years with its titles published by Masson, Springer-Verlag, Elsevier and, lately, by Springer Ibérica under a Creative Commons license. I can't imagine a better and more relevant book for this 30th title, an auspicious milestone.

To the best of my knowledge, Carlos Campillo and Juan del Llano, have successfully developed what they stated as the intention of the book about one year ago:

"A sweeping wealth of documents dealing with HTA has been published over the last three decades. HTA allegedly is one of the bedrocks of regulation and medical decision making. However, countervailing visions contend that geographical variations in the role that HTA is actually playing among countries pinpoints specific room for improvement.

Given our social preferences, cherry-picking HTA's features and successes over the last decades moves it away from its possibility frontier. The time has come for it to take a renewed stronghold. Insufficient resources, delays in assessment, inadequate priority setting, regulatory capture, public distrust, actual influence on regulatory decisions, the need for strengthening international cooperation and harmonisation, and lack of assessments of surgical innovations stand as some of the most salient hindrances that HTA faces in several countries to make headway toward its consolidation as an efficient tool for regulation and decision making." Progress has been made, but there are still obstacles, circumstances and economic, social and political conditions that have irreversibly changed in many areas. The book tries to flee from both conformist approaches, not uncommon and useless, and maverick positions. HTA itself is just another technology that shall be scrutinised. "This book disentangles these and other issues in connection with the advancement of HTA and its interface with health policy. It highlights the factors that should shape its progress in the near future. Interdisciplinary and critical views from a number of professionals are put together in a prescient order to cast some light and make recommendations as to the next steps HTA should take to fit for purpose."

Each of the nine chapter titles accurately describes its content and scope and each text closes with conclusions or wrap-ups and advancement proposals. The title of the third chapter, "The wisdom tooth of HTA", is more intriguing until you start reading it (no clues here) and realise its contribution in helping to obtain the greatest health gains within financial constraints, and informing decision makers on how to balance the pressures of demand and supply for new technologies within a health-system budget by grounding decisions in a clear, transparent and coordinated process. Or shall we let the individual alone in a stratified society where the few – those that can afford it – would pay for any technology without considerations of effectiveness, and the rest will remain in the outer darkness? The book's authors recognise the difficulties of making decisions in the midst of conflict, but they teach us how to deal with the fog of war at any stage: the intelligence phase, universal and falsifiable knowledge on HTA, the decision phase, contingent policy decisions, the implementation phase – requiring soundness and legitimacy – and the evaluation phase, where population again has the last word. Prevention of bad health and inefficiency does not depend on increased regulation, but on better regulation.

All chapters are policy oriented and addressed to an international audience of health authorities, regulators, policy makers, health service professionals and managers, and healthcare industry stakeholders, particularly those of the medical devices and pharmaceutical sector, where the full blown value-based pricing should be fostered without forgetting any longer diagnostic tests and surgical innovations. Every reader has their own point of view and preferences – chapters can be read in any order – and everyone would pick their favourite but would surely appreciate all. Enjoy!

Vicente Ortún
Dean School of Economics and Business and Research
Center on Health and Economics (CRES)
University Pompeu Fabra, Barcelona

PART I: CRITICAL OVERVIEW

CHAPTER 1

Health Technology Assessment and its Interface with Regulation, Policy and Management

Michael Drummond

Introduction

The purpose of health technology assessment (HTA) is to assist those who make key decisions regarding the allocation of scarce healthcare resources. However, although considerable attention has been paid to developing appropriate methods for conducting HTA, much less attention has been paid to ensuring that those conducting HTA are sufficiently well-connected to, and perceived as being relevant by, those making the resource allocation decisions. Therefore, this chapter explores how those conducting HTA can interface better with the key decision makers. Three groups in particular are discussed: *regulators*, such as the US Food and Drug Administration (FDA) and the European Medicines Agency (EMA), who give approval for new health technologies to enter the market; *policy makers*, who influence the diffusion and use of health technologies by providing reimbursement or issuing guidance; and *health service managers*, who are responsible for implementing policies and managing the day-to-day use of health technologies.

Health Technology Assessment and Regulators

It is important that those conducting HTA have a good interface with regulators, since the clinical evidence generated during the regulatory process is often used in the subsequent health technology assessment. This is particularly true in the case of pharmaceuticals where, in order to obtain approval to market, the manufacturer must undertake at least two well-controlled clinical trials. These will normally be randomised controlled trials (RCTs), comparing the new drug with a placebo, or other active therapy.

The situation is more variable in the case of medical devices and procedures, where the level of clinical evidence required depends on the level of risk associated with the device and the jurisdiction. In general, the evidence requirements tend to be lower for devices, partly because of the relative difficultly in conducting RCTs and other key differences

© Springer International Publishing Switzerland 2015

J.E. del Llano-Señarís and C. Campillo-Artero (eds.), *Health Technology Assessment and Health Policy Today: A Multifaceted View of their Unstable Crossroads*,
DOI 10.1007/978-3-319-15004-8_1

between devices and drugs. For example, because of the 'learning curve' associated with devices used as part of a surgical procedure, it may be more relevant to collect data on the clinical outcomes obtained in regular clinical practice after the device is marketed, as opposed to the sometimes artificial environment of many RCTs [1]. In general, clinical studies tend to be formally required only for higher risk devices, such as implantable devices. Even here an RCT is not required in all cases or in all jurisdictions and an observational study, such as a registry, may be all that is required. In addition, in some jurisdictions a new medical device can claim 'substantial equivalence' to a device that is already on the market, obviating the need for a new clinical study

For all health technologies, whether RCTs are required or not, it is possible that the clinical data obtained as part of the regulatory process may not suffice for an HTA. This is because the regulatory requirement is merely to demonstrate that the technology is efficacious and safe. In contrast, for an HTA it is necessary to compare the outcomes obtained for the new technology with those obtained using the current standard of care in the jurisdiction where the reimbursement decision is being made. Indeed, the current standard of care may be a mixture of existing technologies and these could vary from jurisdiction to jurisdiction. Therefore, it is unlikely that all these options would have been examined as part of the regulatory process. In addition, those conducting HTAs favour clinical studies that have been conducted in a 'real world' setting, measuring clinical outcomes of direct relevance to the patient. However, as mentioned earlier, RCTs conducted for regulatory purposes may have been conducted in a highly controlled setting, measuring intermediate, or 'surrogate' outcomes such as biomarkers. These may be considered sufficient to demonstrate a beneficial change to show efficacy, but may not be related to outcomes experienced by the patient such as reductions in quality of life, or related to hard clinical endpoints such as fatal and non-fatal myocardial infarctions. This potential miss-match of evidence requirements has led to several initiatives exploring the difference of perspective between regulators and 'payers', with the objective of harmonising evidence requirements.

It has been common practice for several years for the developers of new health technologies (primarily new pharmaceuticals) to engage in early dialogue with regulators, such as the FDA. The reasons for this are self-evident. Given the large and costly investment in clinical research and development to establish the efficacy and safety of a new product, it is important for the company to be reasonably certain that, if research of an adequate quality is conducted, approval to market will be granted if the net clinical benefit is considered to be positive. Therefore, technology developers often present their proposed clinical trial designs to regulators in order to obtain feedback and to receive suggestions on their improvement.

A more recent development is that in several jurisdictions, including Australia, Canada, the Netherlands, Sweden and the UK, a health technology assessment, including an economic evaluation, is now required as part of the processes for determining the price and reimbursement status for new technologies. In these jurisdictions the process is that the sponsor of a new technology prepares a submission containing such an evaluation, according to an agreed set of guidelines [2]. Although the published guidelines give some clues as to the required scientific quality of clinical and economic evidence that may be required, they do not provide sufficient detail to answer important strategic questions such as 'to obtain reimbursement for first-line use in a given category of patients, precisely what evidence should be submitted?' This is understandable, given that they are not written for this purpose; they are written to help potential applicants prepare a submission from the evidence that has already been generated rather than specifying, before the event, what evidence should be generated.

Although the requirements for the submission of evidence to pricing and reimbursement agencies are not usually backed by legislation in the same ways submissions to regulators to obtain a licence, they are gaining increasing importance, since they are critical for market access for a new product. Since market access, not product licensing, is the ultimate goal, technology developers are increasingly viewing the clinical development programme as providing data for market access, as well as product licensing. It is therefore important that the developers of new technologies are aware of this, since they would like to generate data from their clinical development programme that will address the needs of both regulators and pricing and reimbursement agencies.

Therefore, a growing number of technology developers have realised that a dialogue on evidence requirements may be beneficial with pricing and reimbursement agencies before their clinical trial designs are finalised with regulators [3]. Therefore, a pilot project was conducted by a manufacturer, to explore the evidence requirements of a number of HTA agencies and to compare these with the requirements of the FDA and EMA [4]. The project demonstrated that a feasible process of early dialogue with HTA agencies could be established. Although there was some variation in the advice obtained from the various agencies, the similarities far outweighed the differences. Several important conclusions were reached about the viability of the company's aspirations for product positioning, the desirability of particular treatment comparisons, the outcomes to be used in trials, and the length of trial follow-up.

This raises the question of whether early dialogue should be sought with regulators and payers in parallel (i.e. tripartite advice). It could be argued that, through the growing interest of regulators in 'relative efficacy', some convergence is already taking place [5]. If tripartite meetings could facilitate this process they may be beneficial. For example, the pricing and reimbursement agency might suggest a non-trivial change to proposed clinical trial design; in a tripartite meeting, the developer of a new technology would be able to get a response on the proposed change from the regulator in real time. Another pilot study took place in Sweden, where companies could have a joint meeting with the Medical Products Agency (Lakemedelsverket) and the Dental and Pharmaceutical Benefits Agency (TLV) in order to obtain parallel advice [6]. In addition, within the context of an EU financed joint action, the EUNetHTA project, several initiatives involving regulators and payers have been undertaken within the work package dealing with 'relative effectiveness' [7].

Although these initiatives are promising, to date they have mainly focused on pharmaceuticals. Non-pharmacological technologies pose additional challenges because of the lower evidence requirements for market approval [8]. These challenges are currently being examined through another EU funded research activity, the Medtechta project (www.medtechta.eu). In the work package dealing with the current state of medical device regulation, Ferré et al. [9] argue that, given the lower evidence requirements for market approval, post-marketing surveillance is especially important, not just for safety monitoring, but also to assess effectiveness in regular use, given the device/user learning curve and the organisational impact of medical devices.

They also point out that although all the major jurisdictions they studied relate evidential requirements to the level of patient risk associated with the use of different categories of device, there are slight differences in the requirements across jurisdictions and in the balance between pre-market and post-market controls. These are mainly reflected in slight differences of medical device classifications between countries, such as which devices are classed as 'high risk'. In the light of potential harmonisation of regulatory requirements, more effort should be made developing a set common classification standards.

Ferré et al. [9] also argue that more debate is required regarding the nature of the clinical data required for different categories of medical devices, with the objective of developing international standards. In most of the jurisdictions studied, there were ongoing debates about the need to reform regulatory processes for devices. It is important, in the context of these discussions, to consider the need for improved clinical data for HTA, alongside other important needs such as safety and rapid patient access.

Finally, Ferré et al. [9] recognised that there were several innovative models of collaboration between regulators, reimbursement agencies and manufacturers taking place in some jurisdictions (e.g. the EXCITE programme in Canada), with the objective of speeding up the process of assessment, thereby securing faster patient access for those devices that can be shown to be cost effective. On the one hand, more efficiency in the process can be seen as a great advantage for the producers of medical devices since it would allow for a quicker entrance in the market, and, on the other hand, public institutions would have the possibility of having more say on the type of evidence needed to be produced in order to allow them to make regulatory and reimbursement decisions.

Health Technology Assessment and Health Policy Makers

Although the interface between those conducting HTA and regulators is important, probably the most important interface is with health policy makers, since these are the major audience for HTAs. Therefore, in this section several aspects of the interface with health policy makers are explored, including the development of key principles for conducting HTA for resource allocation decisions, the extent of the current evidence of the impact of HTA on these decisions, and whether, on balance, this has led to improved efficiency in health-care provision.

Key principles for health technology assessment

HTA is a dynamic, rapidly evolving process, embracing different types of assessments that inform real-world decisions about the value (i.e. benefits, risks, and costs) of new technologies, interventions and practices. In addition, the landscape for HTA is changing rapidly, particularly in the US, Eastern Europe and parts of Asia and Latin America. Drawing upon the substantial body of existing experience with HTA around the world, several groups have identified examples of good and bad practice and proposed recommendations to guide the conduct of HTAs [10–12]. Building upon these and other previous efforts, Drummond et al. [13] proposed a set of 15 principles that can be used in assessing existing or establishing new HTA activities, providing examples from existing

HTA programmes. The principal focus was on those HTA activities that are linked to, or include, a particular resource allocation decision. In these HTAs, the consideration of both costs and benefits in an economic evaluation is critical. In addition, it is important to consider the link between the HTA and the decision that will follow. The principles are organised into four sections: (i) 'Structure' of HTA programmes; (ii) 'Methods' of HTA; (iii) 'Processes for Conduct' of HTA; and (iv) 'Use of HTAs in Decision Making' (see Table 1-1). It can be seen that several of these, most noticeably Principles 1, 10, 12, 13, 14 and 15, seek to improve the interface between those conducting HTA and health policy makers. The same group of researchers has also examined the extent to which the key principles were followed by different HTA organisations [14] and have proposed audit criteria that could be applied by organisations wishing to assess the extent to which their practices were consistent with the various principles [15].

Table 1-1. Key principles for the conduct of health technology assessment (HTA) for resource allocation decisions.

Principle 1. The goal and scope of the HTA should be explicit and relevant to its use.
Principle 2. HTA should be an unbiased and transparent exercise.
Principle 3. HTA should include all relevant technologies.
Principle 4. A clear system for setting priorities for HTA should exist.
Principle 5. HTA should incorporate appropriate methods for assessing costs and benefits.
Principle 6. HTAs should consider a wide range of evidence and outcomes.
Principle 7. A full societal perspective should be considered when undertaking HTAs.
Principle 8. HTAs should explicitly characterise uncertainty surrounding estimates.
Principle 9. HTAs should consider and address issues of generalisability and transferability.
Principle 10. Those conducting HTAs should actively engage all key stakeholder groups (e.g. professional bodies, patient organisations, manufacturers).
Principle 11. Those undertaking HTAs should actively seek all available data.
Principle 12. The implementation of HTA findings needs to be monitored.
Principle 13. HTA should be timely.
Principle 14. HTA findings need to be communicated appropriately to different decision makers.
Principle 15. The link between HTA findings and decision-making processes needs to be transparent and clearly defined.

Adapted from Drummond et al.[13]

Impact of the use of health technology assessment for reimbursement decisions

There have been a number of studies of the impact of the use of HTA on the reimbursement decisions reached. These mostly related to the reimbursement of pharmaceuticals and have recently been reviewed by Drummond [16]. Clement et al. [17] compared the decisions by the National Institute for Health and Care Excellence (NICE) in the UK, the Pharmaceutical Benefits Advisory Committee (PBAC) in Australia and the Common Drug Review (CDR) in Canada up until the end of 2008. Overall, the percentage of drugs listed (unrestricted or with restrictions) was 87.4% for NICE, 54.3% for the PBAC and 49.6% for the CDR (the corresponding figures for the sub-set of drugs considered by all three agencies were 84%, 73.6% and 52.6%). In general, the restrictions imposed limit the use of the drug to sub-sets of the licensed population, for example, to those patient sub-groups in which it can be demonstrated to be cost effective. In some cases (e.g. NICE) the definition of 'cost effective' relates to an explicit cost-effectiveness threshold of GBP20,000 per quality-adjusted life-year (QALY) gained. In most other jurisdictions the threshold is not explicit, but the same logic is being applied.

Clement et al. [17] discuss the potential reasons for these differences and argue that the high rate of listing by NICE resulted from the agency being more willing to explore patient sub-groups for which the drug was cost effective. On the other hand, in contrast to the two other agencies, the PBAC was more willing to negotiate, allowing resubmissions at a lower price, or more willing to recommend risk-sharing arrangements. Since the time period studied by Clement et al. [17], the UK appears to have followed the PBAC's lead on price negotiation, through its greater use of 'patient access schemes'. In these schemes a drug that is facing possible rejection can be given positive guidance if a financially attractive deal is offered to the Department of Health. This can be to offer some courses of therapy free, to cap dosing, or to give refunds in situations where the patient does not respond to therapy. Implicitly, many of these schemes represent price reductions.

Another study, by Mason et al. [18], compared the coverage decisions for cancer drugs made by several organisations in the US and UK. Their results are shown in Figure 1-1. It can be seen that the two UK organisations, NICE and the Scottish Medicines Consortium (SMC) were applying considerably more restrictions than the three bodies in the US (the Centers for Medicare and Medicaid Services, the Veterans Affairs and Regence, a Blue Cross Blue Shield plan). In addition, NICE and the SMC had not reached decisions on several of the drugs, reflecting the time that it took to undertake the assessments.

This study gives a reasonable indication of the absolute impact of undertaking HTAs with an economics component, since the application of these methods was either absent or very low in the US organisations studied. However, it should be noted, that does not fully identify the extent of rationing in the two jurisdictions concerned, since some of the drugs may have been made available through other schemes, such as the Cancer Drugs Fund, in the UK, and access may have been limited by ability to pay in the US, where patient co-payments can be between 20–50%. In an editorial commenting on the differences between the US and UK, Malin [19] observed that two quite different rationing processes were being applied, the one in the US being driven by co-pay as opposed to central direction. She remarked, "We have a choice. Do we use science to help us reach consensus on what we are willing to pay for new therapies and innovation, or do we leave individual patients to wrestle with the skyrocketing costs of cancer care and treatment determined by their ability to pay?"

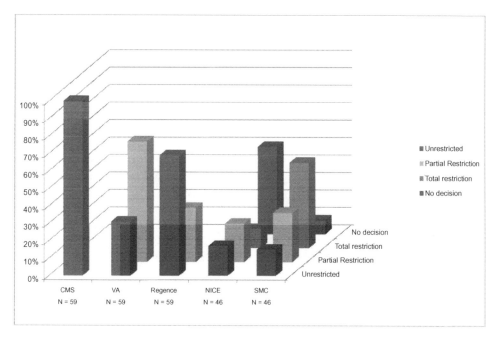

Figure 1-1. Coverage restrictions for eligible anticancer drugs, US Food and Drug Administration (FDA) approved 2004–2008. CMS, Centers for Medicare & Medicaid Services; NICE, National Institute for Health and Care Excellence; SMC, Scottish Medicines Consortium; VA, Veterans Affairs.
Source: Mason et al. [18].

Other studies have sought to estimate the relative importance of economic criteria in the reimbursement decision, as compared with other factors. In an early quantitative study, using multivariate regression, Devlin & Parkin [20] estimated that the probability of a technology being rejected by NICE greatly increased if the incremental cost-effectiveness ratio (ICER) was above GBP30,000 per QALY. A later study, Dakin et al. [21] showed that interventions supported by more RCTs were more likely to be recommended for routine use. Higher ICERs increased the likelihood of rejection, but did not affect the decision between routine and restricted use. More recent research has shown that cost effectiveness alone (as measured by the size of the ICER) correctly predicted 82% of NICE's decisions [22].

In addition, several qualitative studies have involved interviews with decision makers, asking them about the reasons for their decisions. A stated preference binary choice experiment with members of the same committee suggested that increases in the ICER, economic uncertainty, and the availability of other therapies were associated with a statistically significant reduction on the odds of a positive recommendation [23]. Similarly, a study of the preferences of Dutch healthcare professionals, using a discrete choice experiment, showed that severity of disease, cost per QALY gained, individual health gain, and budget impact were the most important decision criteria [24].

A study by George et al. [25] of decisions made by the PBAC in Australia showed that, whilst there was a clear relationship between the ICER and the likelihood of a drug being rejected, or being recommended only if the manufacturer was willing to lower the price, there were several outliers (i.e. drugs that appeared not to be very cost effective, yet receiving a positive recommendation, and *vice versa*). They argue that, in its deliberative decision-making process, the committee was giving consideration to issues such as the seriousness of the health condition the drug was indicated for, the existence (or not) of alternative therapies to the drug under study, the affordability of care to patients if the drug was not reimbursed and the overall budgetary impact of the decision to list the drug.

However, although it is possible to identify a number of examples of HTA influencing reimbursement decisions, it is noticeable that these originate from a relatively small number of jurisdictions, mainly from northern Europe, Canada and Australia. There are still many jurisdictions where HTA has not made much of an impact, most noticeably the US and Japan. This suggests that there are still some barriers that HTA has found difficult to overcome.

Impact of health technology assessment on healthcare provision

Of course, the ultimate test of incorporating economic evaluation into the reimbursement process is whether it has improved healthcare provision (e.g. has it made the provision of healthcare more efficient, more equitable, or both?). The first problem in addressing this question is that there are often difficulties in implementing the decisions made by reimbursement agencies, particularly in the case of 'mixed' decisions (i.e. where the drug is recommended for use, but only for a subset of the patient population). In different jurisdictions various mechanisms have been used to enforce adherence to the decisions or recommendation of the agencies. These include making guidance mandatory on the healthcare system, designating treatments to be 'on authority' (i.e. allowed only when the physician verifies that the patient meets the eligibility criteria), the use of prescribing incentive schemes, audit of local practices/decisions and the use of 'risk sharing schemes'.

The second problem is that, in most healthcare settings, very little is known about the range of options facing physicians, or other decision makers, when considering the implementation of the reimbursement agency's decision. For example, if a decision maker in the UK operating under a fixed budget, decides to make a given treatment available in accordance with NICE guidance, what is actually displaced? It could be a highly cost-effective service, but one which had not been assessed by NICE, or it could be another treatment option for which there was no reliable evidence. One function of adopting a cost-effectiveness threshold would be to reflect this opportunity cost, but for most jurisdictions either no explicit threshold exists, or the basis for establishing the threshold is inadequately researched. As to whether or not an explicit threshold can be determined, more research is required on the nature of the disinvestments that occur as a result of implementing the recommendations of HTAs.

Finally, in common with the evaluation of most policy changes, it is difficult to specify the counterfactual. Namely, how would decision-making processes in the various jurisdictions have developed if economic evaluation had not been incorporated into the reimbursement processes. Of course, bearing in mind the variations in the state of the world prior to the incorporation of economic analyses, the counterfactual may be different for different jurisdictions.

Some commentators have argued that there is no evidence that the application of economic evaluation in reimbursement processes has improved healthcare resource allocation and may have made matters worse [26]. On the other hand, Drummond [16] argues that there is evidence that expensive therapies have been targeted towards their most cost-effective uses and that, depending on local arrangements, price reductions have been secured in some instances, such as in the case of 'Patient Access Schemes' agreed between manufacturers and the Department of Health in the UK. In addition, the application of economic evaluation in the reimbursement process has influenced the production of clinical evidence on health technologies in the direction of measuring outcomes of more relevance to patients, comparing the therapy of interest with the relevant treatment alternatives

Health Technology Assessment and Health Service Managers

The research on the interface between HTA and health policy makers shows that there is another important interface, which is often overlooked, namely the interface with health service managers. This is important since, although policy makers can make reimbursement decisions at the national or regional level, the services that are actually provided within the healthcare system are also partly under the control of managers at the local level. That is, recommendations made as a result of HTAs conducted at the national or regional level may not necessarily be implemented.

There has been some research into the implementation, or lack of implementation, of recommendations based on HTAs. For example, Sheldon et al. [27] investigated the implementation of 12 pieces of guidance for the use of technologies produced by NICE in the UK. They found that implementation was very variable. In addition, they argued that guidance was more likely to be adopted when there was strong professional support, a stable and convincing evidence base, no increased or unfunded costs, a good system for tracking implementation, and no isolation of the professionals involved. At the time of this study, guidance produced by NICE was voluntary, but subsequently adoption of the recommendations from NICE technology appraisals was made mandatory for the National Health Service (NHS) in the UK.

It is likely that local implementation of the recommendations does partly depend on the mechanisms available to health policy makers to encourage their adoption. Apart from making recommendations mandatory, it is sometimes possible to link funding to adoption of the recommendations, by giving access to additional funds or establishing a new fee code. This choice of mechanism will depend on the type of technology. For example, the use of a new device could be encouraged by establishing a procedure code for its use; use of a new vaccine could be encouraged by providing funding to include it in the vaccination schedule.

Several HTA agencies have considered ways of encouraging the adoption of their recommendations. For example, in the UK, NICE has developed several implementation tools for health service managers. These include commissioning guides, costing tools, a forward planner and a 'how to' guide to implementation. (http://www.nice.org.uk/using-guidance/implementationtools/implementation_tools.jsp).

Another approach is to give more consideration of the challenges faced by health service managers in implementing the recommendations of HTAs. Some researchers discuss the notion that some technologies may be particularly 'disruptive' [28]. The characteristics of disruptive technologies in healthcare include the following: large budgetary impact (especially within year), the need for re-alignment, or creation, of new budgets, the need for organisational adjustments (e.g. investment in new facilities or re-deployment of staff), the need for re-training or acquisition of new skills, the requirement for change in existing clinical roles or responsibilities and requirements for change that run counter to existing incentives. The interface between HTA and health services managers would be improved if these challenges were more often recognised and programmes put in place to tackle them.

Finally, in some settings initiatives have been taken to shift the focus of HTA activities from the national to local level. One example of this is the growth of hospital-based HTA. This is also the subject of an EU funded research project, AdHopHTA (www.adhophta.eu).

Conclusions

The methods and practice of HTA have advanced considerably over the last 30 years. Arguably it has been one of the most successful multidisciplinary activities in the healthcare field, particularly in respect of its increasing influence on decision making. The central theme of this chapter is that, in order to continue this success, those conducting HTAs need to pay attention to the interface with key stakeholders in the process, including regulators, health policy makers, clinicians, patients and health services managers. This chapter focused on the interface with three of these stakeholder groups. In each case the key challenges have been outlined and some of the current initiatives to overcome them have been outlined. Suggestions for other initiatives have also been given.

This book was supported by an unrestricted educational grant from Celgene.

REFERENCES

1. Drummond MF, Griffin A, Tarricone R. Economic evaluation for devices and drugs. Same or different? Value in Health. 2009;12(4):402-4.
2. International Society of Pharmacoeconomics and Outcomes Research. Pharmacoeconomic guidelines around the world. www.ispor.org (assessed May 9, 2014).
3. Backhouse ME. Raising the standards of trial-based economic evaluation: the devil is in the detail. Value in Health. 2005;8(5):519-20.
4. Backhouse M, Wonder M, Hornby E, Kilburg A, Drummond MF, Mayer FK. Early dialogue between the developers of new technologies and pricing and reimbursement agencies. Value in Health. 2011;14(4):608-15.
5. Eichler H-G, Bloechl-Daum B, Abadie E, Barnett D, Konig F, Pearson S. Relative efficacy of drugs: an emerging issue between regulators and third-party payers. Nature Rev Drug Discovery. 2010;9(4):277-91.
6. Ljungberg B. Presentation at the Health Technology Assessment International (HTAi) Annual Conference, Dublin, June 2010.

7.   Berntgen M, Gourvil A, Pavlovic M, Goettsch W, Eichler H-G, Kristensen FB. Improving the contribution of regulatory assessment reports to health technology assessments — A collaboration between the European Medicines Agency and the European network for Health Technology Assessment. Value in Health. 2014. Published online 25 June 2014. In press http://dx.do.org/10.1016/j.jval.2014.04.006

8.   Tsoi B, Masucci L, Campbell K, Drummond MF, O'Reilly D, Goeree R. Harmonization of reimbursement and regulatory approval processes: a systematic review of international experiences. Expert Rev Pharmacoecon Outcomes Res. 2013;13(4):497-511.

9.   Ferré F, Torbica A, Tarricone R, Drummond M. Regulatory framework for medical devices. Workpackage 1, Deliverable D 1.1, August 2013. www.medtechta.eu.

10. Busse FR, Orvain J, Velasco M, Perleth M, et al. Best practice in undertaking and reporting health technology assessments. Int J Technol Assess Health Care. 2002;18:361-422.

11. European Federation of Pharmaceutical Industries and Associations. The use of health technology assessments (HTA) to evaluate medicines:EFPIA key principles. EFPIA Position Paper. 2005. Available at:www.efpia.org/Objects/2/Files/HTAprinciplesEPIApositionpaperfinal.pdf.

12. Emanuel EJ, Fuchs VR, Garber AM. Essential elements of a technology and outcomes assessment initiative. JAMA. 2007;298:1323-5.

13. Drummond MF, Schwartz JS, Jönsson B, Luce BR, Neumann PJ. Key principles for the improved conduct of health technology assessments for resource allocation decisions. Int J Technol Assess Health Care. 2008;24(3):244-58.

14. Neumann PJ, Drummond MF, Jönsson B, Luce BR, Schwartz JS, Siebert U, Sullivan S. Are key principles for improved health technology assessment supported and used by health technology assessment organizations? Int J Technol Assess Health Care. 2010;26(1):71-8.

15. Drummond MF, Neumann PJ, Jönsson B, Luce BR, Schwartz JS, Siebert U, Sullivan S. Can we reliably benchmark health technology assessment organizations? Int J Technol Assess Health Care. 2012;28(2):159-65.

16. Drummond MF. Twenty years of using economic evaluations for drug reimbursement decisions. What has been achieved? J Health Polit Policy Law. 2013;38(6):1083-104.

17. Clement F, Harris MA, Li JJ, Yong K, Lee KM, Manns BJ. Using effectiveness and cost-effectiveness to make drug coverage decisions: a comparison of Britain, Australia, and Canada. JAMA. 2009;302:1437-43.

18. Mason A, Drummond M, Ramsey S, Campbell J, Raisch D. Comparison of anticancer drug coverage decisions in the United States and United Kingdom: does the evidence support the rhetoric? J Clin Oncol. 2010;28:3234-8.

19. Malin JL. Wrestling with the high price of cancer care: should we control costs by individuals' ability to pay or society's willingness to pay? J Clin Oncol. 2010;28:3212-14.

20. Devlin N, Parkin D. Does NICE have a cost-effectiveness threshold and what other factors influence its decisions? A binary choice analysis'. Health Economics. 2004;13:437-52.

21. Dakin H, Devlin ANJ, Odeyemi IAO. "Yes "No" or "Yes, but"? multinomial modelling of NICE decision-making. Health Policy. 2006;77:352-67.

22. Dakin H, Devlin N, Feng Y, Rice N, O'Neill, P, Parkin D. The influence of cost-effectiveness and other factors on NICE decisions. HERC Research Paper 05/14, Health Economics Research Centre, University of Oxford, 2014.

23. Tappenden P, Brazier J, Ratcliffe J, Chilcott J. A stated preference binary choice experiment to explore NICE decision making. Pharmacoeconomics. 2007;25:685-93.

24. Koopmanschap MA, Stolk EA, Koolman X. Dear policy maker: have you made up your mind? a discrete choice experiment among policy makers and other health professionals. Int J Technol Assess Health Care. 2010;26:198-204.

25. George B, Harris A, Mitchell A. Cost effectiveness analysis and the consistency of decision making – evidence from pharmaceutical reimbursement in Australia (1991 to 1996). Pharmacoeconomics. 2001;19:1103-9.

26. Birch S, Gafni A. Economists' dream or nightmare? Maximizing health gains from available re-
     sources using the NICE guidelines. Health Economics Policy and Law. 2007;2:193-202.
27. Sheldon T, Cullum AN, Dawson D, Lankshear A, Lowson K, Watt I, West P, Wright D, Wright J.
     What's the evidence that NICE guidance has been implemented? Results from a national evalua-
     tion using time series analysis, audit of patients' notes and interviews. BMJ 2004;329:999.
28. Christensen CM. The innovator's dilemma. New York, Harper Collins, 1997.

CHAPTER 2

Health Technology Assessment (HTA) and the Incentives to Innovation in the Life Cycle of a Health Technology

Joan Rovira

Introduction

The objective of this chapter is to explore how health technology assessment (HTA) can best be used to steer socially needed innovation in health technologies. To that end it is essential to analyse the driving factors in the life cycle of health technologies, i.e. the factors that determine how they are created, developed, regulated, used and, eventually, finally discarded, as well as the roles and motivations of the key stakeholders in this process. The next step is to design and implement the appropriate policies and institutional arrangements that provide the incentives required to ensure that the right amount and distribution of resources is applied to promote the development and use of new technologies that efficiently and equitably address existing social health needs. In order to do so, it is important to take a holistic approach that acknowledges the interactions between stakeholders and external factors in making the relevant decisions in the innovation process.

Innovation is a contentious topic, especially in the health technology sector, where availability and access to innovative treatments is a high priority for most people and sometimes a matter of life or death. In countries with universal health systems, public financing of health services removes the individual budget constraint of the consumer, making the demand for healthcare technologies very rigid, i.e. insensitive to its price. A similar phenomenon occurs in the context of voluntary and mandatory insurance systems in what is known as the *moral hazard* effect of insurance and third-party paying. As a result, the demand and supply of health technology innovations has grown steadily over time in spite of the increasingly higher prices, while the benefits of innovations in terms of health improvements to the users do not seem to grow at the same rate. To the frequently posed question "Has technological change in medicine been worth what it costs?" Garber [1] suggests that in most industries, the market would answer the question. "If too few consumers believe that a new detergent, toaster, or television is 'worth it', it will fail. But a medical product or service can succeed even if it is worth only a fraction of its cost that insured patients pay out of pocket". This is because healthcare often is either free or highly subsidised for the consumer at the time of delivery.

© Springer International Publishing Switzerland 2015
J.E. del Llano-Señarís and C. Campillo-Artero (eds.), *Health Technology Assessment and Health Policy Today: A Multifaceted View of their Unstable Crossroads*,
DOI 10.1007/978-3-319-15004-8_2

Societies positively value the overall effects that the evolution of health technology has had on health and wellbeing and expect R&D to bring new treatment options for diseases that still have no cure, as well as improvements in existing treatments. On the other hand, the introduction of new health technologies is regularly blamed for being one of the main causes of the rise in health expenditure. The problem for society, and more specifically for health system managers and policy makers therefore, is to promote innovation, while at the same time ensuring the value for money of new technologies and of health expenditure, in general, and ultimately the financial sustainability of the health system. HTA certainly has a key role to play to this end, namely to provide the information required for decision makers to take the right decisions in order to promote the right type and amount of innovation in health technology.

But before trying to find out how to best promote innovation in health technology it is necessary to clarify what this term means.

The Meaning of Innovation

Innovation is a value-loaded term. In the economic literature innovation is assumed to be a key driver of productivity and economic development; innovation is hence associated with progress and prosperity, two concepts that most people value as positive and desirable. The economist Joseph Schumpeter [2] has been one of the most influential authors in the analysis of innovation and its effect on economic development. Interestingly, his central concept of "creative destruction", the process by which new technologies entering the market make the older ones obsolete or redundant, highlights the point that innovation often has negative effects as well, as it renders valueless the tangible and intangible assets on which the substituted technologies worked.

Innovation has been defined as the "successful introduction of something new and useful, for example, introducing new methods, techniques, or practices or new or altered products and services"[1]. This definition is however very vague and does not have a precise meaning, either in the technical or in the common language. Innovation is a complex, multifaceted and elusive concept that deserves a close analysis and discussion in order to fine-tune its meaning for analytical purposes.

The *Oslo Manual Guidelines for Collecting and Interpreting Innovation* is one of the key references in the analysis of innovation [3][2]. The main purpose of the Oslo manual is to provide a framework with standardised definitions and methods to measure and collect information on innovation in a rigorous and comparable way.

The Oslo manual states that "An innovation is the implementation of a new or significantly improved product (good or service) or process, a new marketing method, or a new organisational method in business practices, workplace organisation or external relations". It goes on to define four broad types of innovations: 1) product innovations[3], 2) process innovations, 3) organisational innovations and 4) marketing innovations.

---

1   http://en.wikipedia.org/wiki/Innovation.
2   The first edition of the manual was issued in 1992 and the second edition in 1977.
3   The development of a new use for a product is also included in the definition of product innovation.

How is innovation related to invention and to research? Innovation and invention are distinct things. An invention is a technical solution to a need or problem. In order to become an innovation, an invention has to be put into practice or implemented: in the case of products it must be introduced to the market, i.e. a manufacturer has to turn the invention into a final consumer product and produce it at a cost that is attractive for consumers to buy a large enough volume that makes production profitable and feasible; consumers – or third-party payers – have to be convinced that the innovation is effective and justifies the price they are asked to pay for it; otherwise the would-be innovation will end up in a museum of failed inventions. In the other categories – process, organisational and marketing innovations – they must be given actual use in the firm.

Research and development (R&D) defines the set of activities carried out by companies that intend to innovate. R&D often is a requirement for inventions, but a large volume of expenditure in R&D does not guarantee that inventions will follow or that inventions will find their way into the market and become commercially successful products. On the other hand, a brilliant simple idea that took little time and cost to formulate and develop, may become a breakthrough and bring large revenues to the smart innovator.

An authoritative source of definitions and analysis relevant to the topic of R&D is the Frascati manual, *The Measurement of Scientific and Technological Activities Proposed Standard Practice for Surveys on Research and Experimental Development* [4] a piece of work with a similar purpose and approach to the Oslo manual in its specific field. The Frascati manual states that "Research and experimental development (R&D) comprises creative work undertaken on a systematic basis in order to increase the stock of knowledge, including knowledge of man, culture and society, and the use of this stock of knowledge to devise new applications" and indicates that R&D – both intramural (in-house) or extramural (acquired) – is only an input to the process of innovation.

What is Innovation in Health Technology?

As could be expected, innovation is by no means a univocal concept in the context of health technologies any more than in other areas of technology. Neither the Oslo, nor the Frascati manuals pay much specific attention to the health sector[4]. They nevertheless make some relevant and interesting remarks. The Oslo manual highlights, for instance, that in the services sector – which includes healthcare – production and consumption occur simultaneously and the distinction between product and process is often blurred. This remark applies to medical services and procedures, but not to medicines and other health products: they are obviously not being produced and consumed simultaneously. In the case of medicines, the so-called innovative firms seem to concentrate on developing new, more effective medicines, with limited concern for improving the production processes and reducing their cost. This is probably due to the limited impact that direct

---

4   The Frascati manual does not address many health-specific issues, except for some remarks on clinical trials. After mentioning the four standard phases of clinical research, it states that for the purposes of international comparison, by convention, clinical trial phases 1, 2 and 3 – which take place before permission to manufacture is accorded – can be treated as R&D, while phase 4 clinical trials, which continue testing the drug or treatment after approval and manufacture, should only be treated as R&D if they bring about a further scientific or technological advance.

manufacturing costs have on the total costs of the industry in relation to R&D, marketing and other general expenses. Reducing the manufacturing cost seems to be mainly a task for the generics industry, which is forced to do so in order to make its way in a market environment characterised by aggressive price competition.

The analysis of innovation might be better addressed if the concept can be properly contextualised and more narrowly defined and restricted in its content, for instance, if we restrict the analysis to innovation in health products (medicines and devices), rather than to the broader range of health technologies that are included under the standard definition, i.e. to entities such as medical equipment, surgical treatments, public health programmes, etc.

In order to facilitate our task, we will restrict our analysis to medical products, such as medicines, diagnostic tests, medical devices and the like. It must however be noted that in spite of its similarities, the feasibility and actual practice of technology assessment varies remarkably across medical products. Huot et al. [5] aimed to ascertain the level of evidence available for implantable medical devices (IMDs) access to reimbursement in France and concluded that IMDs are far less investigated than drugs. In the USA the situation is similar: Feldman et al. [6] state: "This drug/device split in testing extends throughout the healthcare system to health plans and hospitals, as formulary committees for drug coverage have few device-coverage correlates". The authors urge independent HTA organisations and other stakeholders to address this situation and support HTA of medical devices. There does not seem to be theoretical justification for the less frequent evaluation of health devices in relation to medicines, but rather practical and historical reasons. As mentioned above, the early occurrence of some fatal episodes in the consumption of unsafe medicines prompted a reaction in the form of conditioning market entry to the requirement of submitting evidence of safety based on clinical trials, the oldest form of HTA, and the generalisation of drug regulatory agencies in most countries, which, until recently, did not address the need to request a similar control of other medical products. Moreover, the methodology of randomised clinical trials (RCTs) has been developed for medicines and is less appropriate for medical devices and other health products.

Van Nooten et al. [7], while acknowledging that payers are increasingly interested in innovative products, recognise that definitions of "innovation" vary among stakeholders, but it can generally be defined as improvement in relative efficacy and/or efficiency compared with the current standard of care[5]. This means that innovation could be measured as an improvement in efficacy, and hence in any indicator of health outcome, such as, diseases averted, life-years gained or increase in life expectancy; total quality-adjusted life-year (QALYs) gained could be a general indicator of innovation in absolute terms, which could be standardised by cost in the form of the compound indicator "QALYs gained per additional dollar spent on a new technology". Such an indicator would recognise the time-related nature of innovation, as it would measure the improvement it meant at the time the technology was introduced, irrespective of whether it was later overcome and made obsolete by the next technology.

---

5   However, in the same article the authors seem to adhere to another definition of innovation, when they state that a "valuable innovation" is defined as something that "truly fills an unmet need"; they also mention that according to NICE in the UK "an innovative product is one that is new, offers an improvement compared with existing therapies and provides "a step-change in terms of outcomes for patients". In fact, all these definitions reflect quite different criteria.

The Kennedy Report's [8] main target was to assess whether other factors than the cost per QALY framework and the related threshold criterion should inform National Institute for Health and Care Excellence (NICE) decisions, particularly, whether innovation-related benefits should be considered. Kennedy made 25 recommendations, several of them specific to the issue of innovation. One of the recommendations was that NICE should establish an explicit definition for innovation in the context of health technologies (specifically, for pharmaceutical products). As Green [9] ironically commented, "Kennedy found that whilst everyone was content to use the word "innovation" and everyone agreed it was a good thing (referring to the consultation process), it was not easy to identify what was being discussed". Kennedy accepted NICE's view that innovation is supposed to meet three criteria: a) novelty, b) improvement over existing interventions, and c) providing a "step change in terms of outcomes to patients".

He went further to suggest that NICE consider the following as being possible criteria of a "step-change", and of the need for properly articulated criteria to recognise this value:

- The product significantly and substantially improves the way that a current need (including supportive care) is met
- The need met is one which the National Health Service (NHS) has identified as being important
- Where appropriate, research on stratification … has identified the population(s) in which the product is effective
- The product has been shown to have an appropriate level of effectiveness – for example, benefiting 70% of the intended target group. This may be all of the population with the condition or just a subset, and
- The product has marketing authorisation for the particular indication.

The Kennedy report globally supported the general framework used by NICE as the best tool available, but stated a certain lack of transparency in the way social value judgements were considered in the decision-making process.

He also mentioned that the contribution of the pharmaceutical industry to the wider UK economy should also be somehow considered.

The response by NICE did not suggest that likely dramatic changes would follow, in the way of making the innovation criteria more explicit, but rather that NICE would use flexibility and discretion to accommodate new relevant criteria into the incremental cost-effectiveness ratio (ICER)/QALY approach[6].

Finally it is worth presenting here the results of an exercise carried out in the context of the EU Pharmaceutical Forum meetings. Pricing and reimbursement officials from EU member states were asked to identify the types of benefits they would consider worth paying for a new medicine: "This report is a bottom-up exercise, based on discussions and collection of views from the relevant member state authorities on how to recognise, assess and reward valuable innovative medicines. This exercise covers valuable innovation in

---

6   NICE response to Sir Ian Kennedy's report: Appraising the value of innovation. http://www.nice. org.uk/aboutnice/howwework/researchanddevelopment/KennedyStudyNICEResponse.jsp.

three main areas: 1) therapeutic/clinical benefits regarding the disease, 2) quality-of-life benefits for the patient, and 3) broader socio-economic benefits. The table below summarises the results of the exercise."

Table 2-1.   Potential benefits from innovative medicines.

Therapeutic/Clinical	Quality of Life	Socio-economic
Higher probability of full recovery	Higher physical self-sustainability/ self-management at home	Avoiding pandemics (vaccination, ...)
Faster partial or total recovery	Higher psychological self-sustainability	Dealing with resistance (HIV, antibiotics, ...)
Slower progression of diseases	Higher social self-sustainability	Reduced total cost of medication
Increased ability to cope with disease symptoms (e.g. analgesic)	Higher convenience/comfort for the patien and his environment	Reduced total cost of treatment
Higher probability of preventing the (re-)emergence of a disease		Reduced non-healthcare spending
Survival rate, life expectancy		Reduced cost of sick-leave
Fewer or less severe side effects		Higher productivity of the citizen
Fewer or less severe interactions with other medicines		
Higher tolerability		
Broader/easier dosing, improving compliance		
Easier administration schedule, improving compliance		

Source: European Commission, Enterprise and Industry. Working Group on Pricing and Reimbursement, Characterisation of the Value of Innovative Medicines [10]. © European Union, 1995–2014.

Aggregate innovation has been usually approximated by intermediate indicators, such as number of patents granted, number of new chemical entities (NCE) registered, etc. For instance, in trying to assess the assumed superiority of the US over the EU in pharmaceutical innovation claimed by Grabowsky & Wang [11], Light [12] reanalyses a set of aggregate indicators of research productivity proposed by the former, that basically rely on the number of NCEs that are classified as 1) global[7], 2) first-in-class, 3) biotech, and 4) orphan. Such indicators are not very valid and sensitive, as they assume that all NCEs are innovative and homogenous, i.e. that they have the same innovative value. This certainly is a strong assumption that makes them useless to assess the degree of therapeutic innovation of single medicines. The number of patents granted is also taken by some authors as an indicator of the degree of innovative activity. But similar to the variable "NCEs marketed",

---

7   Global was defined according to various criteria: introduced into four or more of the G7 (Group of 7) countries.

patents are not unambiguously associated with therapeutic advances. A larger number of patents might just mean that innovators are more likely to submit patent applications, or that patent offices maintain lower patentability requirements for granting a patent. Finally, patents are as heterogeneous as NCEs as indicators of the degree of innovation.

Motola et al. [13] developed an algorithm to assess the degree of therapeutic innovation of new therapeutic agents by evaluating a) the seriousness of the disease, b) the availability of previous treatments, and c) the extent of the therapeutic effect. The combination of these three variables yielded three scores of therapeutic innovation: A, important, B, moderate and C, modest.

The authors applied this score to all medicinal products approved by the European Medicines Agency (EMA) between January 1995 and June 2003, and later [14] to the products approved between January 1995 and July 2004; the second study included 227 medicinal products corresponding to 209 active substances. Among all therapeutic agents, only 28% were classified in category A, although most of the substances were claimed as innovative by the respective manufacturers.

As in any other domain or field of technology, there are diverging interpretations of the meaning of innovation and of the way to assess and measure it: right holders and producers usually pretend that any new product or procedure that is different from existing ones is an innovation, quite irrespective of how it works and of the contribution it makes to health outcomes. However, innovation is increasingly defined in the healthcare sector as added value, which is generally identified with therapeutic added-value or utility, i.e. a health innovation would be any new technology or new application of an existing technology that provides a better health outcome than existing technologies in the same application.

Morgan et al. [15] found that between 1996 and 2003 the Patented Medicines Pricing Review Board (PMPRB) of Canada classified 68 (5.9%) of the new products as "breakthroughs", while for the remaining 1005 new products, the PMPRB did not find any evidence of therapeutic advantage over existing treatments and were classified as "me-toos". The result was that the share of "me-toos" increased from 41% in 1996 to almost two-thirds in 2003, accounting for about 80% of the increase in expenditure, which seems a high price for society to pay for the social benefit added by these drugs.

Innovation may also have detrimental effects for the consumers, due, for instance, to the occurrence of unexpected or hidden negative effects. A recent analysis of the Canadian market [16] showed that of the 528 new drugs approved in Canada between January 1990 and December 2009, a total of 22 (4.4%) were withdrawn for safety reasons until October 2013. The median time to withdrawal was 1271 days, which according to the author "emphasizes the need to be particularly cautious in prescribing new drugs early in their life cycle".

If only health benefits for the patient are considered, innovation could be defined and measured as a health gain, by means of a measure of health such as the QALYs; whereas, if changes in resource use and other effects are to be included in the impact, innovation could be measured by an improvement in the net social benefit. In both cases innovation should be measured against the most effective or the most efficient existing technology, respectively, and be preferably standardised by its additional costs.

Anyway, even if we could agree on a general definition of innovation in terms of added value, it is obvious that the precise content of this term is subjective and dependent on each individual's values and perceptions. The long debate between welfarists and extra-welfarists is proof of the subjectivity of the issue, which cannot be solved with exclusive recourse to objective and scientific arguments: all we can expect is to reach increasingly larger consensus in value judgements.

Definitions of innovation might be unclear, and inconsistent across laws, regulations and policies, but the request for demonstrating evidence of product innovation is likely to rise in the future as a condition for a medical product to attain market access and premium pricing.

Key Decisions in the Life Cycle of Health Technologies: Do the Present Institutional Arrangements Provide Appropriate Incentives for Socially Needed Innovation?

Innovators must take multiple decisions along the life cycle of a health technology. Some decisions are of a scientific or technological nature and are related to the R&D process itself. Other decisions are related to the institutional, economic and legal aspects of the product development and marketing[8].

First the innovator must select the objective of his innovative activity. It might decide to advance its own resources, or look for either public or philanthropic funding to develop its own idea[9]. It can also apply for philanthropic or public funds, which are earmarked for a given innovation selected by the funding organisation.

Later in the life cycle of the innovation it will have to decide whether, when, where and how to look for intellectual property (IP) protection, which type of claim to make (broad or narrow), etc.

When the invention is ready for consumer use, the innovator might have to obtain a marketing authorisation. Obtaining a marketing authorisation[10] is a necessary step for a medicine to legally enter the market in most countries. Again, the innovator will have to decide when and where to make a submission, for which indications, specify conditions or restrictions of use (e.g. hospital use only), etc.

The role of publicly funded research & development

Publicly financed R&D usually concentrates on basic research, but it does also address clinical research. A debate has been going on with inconclusive results on the complementarity of public and private research. Toole [17] found strong evidence that "public basic and clinic research are complementary to pharmaceutical R&D investment and thereby stimulate private-industry investment". The influence of public research is determined by the degree to which industry scientists draw from and add to public scientific knowledge. Basic research opens new lines to therapeutic outcomes by accepting a high degree of uncertainty in the feasibility of obtaining results and on its likely market applicability. It has also been suggested that publicly financed research

---

8   The following list of questions does not pretend to be exhaustive, but only illustrative of some of the main decisions the average innovator will face.

9   An intermediate option is to look for partial grants and subsidies or tax breaks.

10   Also referred to as licensing or registration.

plays an important role in finding new applications for older, off-patent drugs. In a posterior article Toole [18] found that public basic research has its main impact in the earliest part of the drug discovery stage of industry research, the concept phase. He concludes that the investment in basic research by the National Institutes of Health (NIH) influence pharmaceutical innovation 14 to 20 years prior to the drug application and that a 10% increase in public investment in basic research leads to a 6.4% increase in the number of drugs in the market.

The World Health Organization (WHO) has been supporting meetings and debates for several years in order to explore mechanisms to improve coordination in research for neglected diseases and more specifically, to explore interventions that delink the cost of R&D from final price in order to improve affordability.

"A Consultative Expert Working Group on R&D Coordination and Financing (CEWG) was established to analyse various proposals for innovative mechanisms. The WHO working group through a process of public consultations has received various proposals from WHO member states, civil society, academics, industry and other stakeholders. Proposals that have been considered include: innovation inducement prizes (both prizes for final products as well as milestone prizes); open source R&D models; priority review vouchers; new indirect taxes; medicines patent pools; equitable and humanitarian licenses; biomedical R&D treaty; pooled funds related proposals; advanced market commitments, Health Impact Fund, Green Intellectual Property." After a hotly debated process of selection, the 67th World Assembly in May 2014 considered the following proposals: a global R&D and access initiative for visceral leishmaniasis by the Drugs for Neglected Diseases *initiative* (DNDi); an international open-source collaboration to accelerate drug development in addressing diseases of poverty by the Medicines for Malaria Venture (MMV); and the development of easy to use and affordable biomarkers as diagnostics for the neglected tropical diseases by the African Network for Drugs and Diagnostics Innovation (ANDI). Finally the Special Programme for Research & Training in Tropical Diseases (TDR) suggested the creation of a new pooling funding mechanism.

Patents and other exclusivity rights

Patents, intellectual property rights (IPR) and other exclusivity rights provide financial incentives – a potential monopoly – to rights holders. They allow the appropriation by the innovator of the commercial value of the innovation market demand, by selling either a) the IPR itself, b) voluntary licenses, or c) the final products, which, thanks to market exclusivity, can be sold at higher prices than under competition and allow for extraordinary profits.

IPR always had strong critics, the earliest ones being the most liberal, pro-market economists, who found IPR were in conflict with the principles of competition. Criticisms to the present patent system ranges from technical topics that the authors think can be fixed with reforms that do not essentially question the principles and main practices of the system (Federal Trade Commission, 2003), to authors who ask for deeper reforms [19] up to those who claim that the system is "broke" and think that it requires radical changes [20].

The more radical approaches claim that a reward is needed for innovation, but not necessarily the present type of patents and other types of monopolistic, exclusive marketing rights, such as test data protection, which allow the right holder to exclude potential competitors and lead to high prices that make medicines unaffordable for a large part of the population. Property rights could take the form of a fixed royalty, or a right to a defined amount of money. Lexchin [12] claims that there is enough evidence to state that lower prices would not necessarily jeopardise drug research.

Licensing

Licensing, also known as registration or marketing authorisation, is the first institutional test hurdle, according to industry, that a drug has to overcome in its life cycle in most countries. However, it does not pose very strict requirements in relation to efficacy, as regulators usually grant the licensing of new drugs if they show either non-inferiority to an existing one or superiority to placebo. None of these two alternative criteria ensure that the licensed drug brings a therapeutic added value. Moreover, the weak transparency requirements on the results of clinical trials have for many years allowed clinical trials to be simply withdrawn when the results were not favourable (enough) for the new product. Together with the lack of a requirement for standardised reporting and transparent and comprehensive disclosure of trial results – often in the name of patient confidentiality and other fundamental rights – they question the validity of any systematic review of the evidence based on RCTs. If researchers do not have access to all the clinical trials that involve a given product, there is no way to guarantee that the most systematic literature reviews and meta-analyses will yield valid, unbiased and reliable aggregate results.

Pricing and financing

Pricing systems are increasingly aimed at rewarding therapeutic added value. It is becoming customary not to accept a premium price for a new drug over that of existing alternatives unless the new drug can provide evidence of adding some therapeutic advantage or added value to the existing treatments, what is generically known as value-based pricing. As Rai [21] indicates, "the use of QALY based analysis by payors is an indirect mechanism for channelling biomedical innovation in a direction that maximises QALY" that "does not involve intellectual (IP) policy per se at all". Although the use of value-based pricing indirectly involves IP policy[11], the author is right when he states that "A more IP-based approach to maximising QALY might involve a patent prize system that calibrated rewards based on the number of QALYs produced by the technology" [21].

VBP uses HTA to address the conflict between setting prices low enough to be affordable and high enough to incentivise companies to develop new, effective treatments and signalling the companies that society is willing to pay for good value, i.e. innovative pharmaceuticals.

---

11 Because it is precisely the market power granted by patents and other exclusivity rights allows the regulator to steer the incentives of innovators by allowing market power to materialise in certain directions.

Options and Proposals for Using Health Technology Assessment to Assist Policy Practices Aimed at Promoting Socially Needed Innovation in Health

Several authoritative sources have expressed their concerns about the capacity of the market to efficiently allocate resources to innovation in health. The reasons are manifold: the diverging interests of innovators – especially commercial ones, on one hand, and health systems and society at large, on the other; lack of adequate information to consumers and their agents (health professionals); moral hazard; externalities; and above all, the market failure of biomedical knowledge and information being global public goods.

The Kennedy report highlighted that there is an inevitable conflict between individual interests (e.g. pharmaceutical industry interests) and the perspective of NICE, which is concerned with the collective needs of all patients [9]. Adang [22] also points to the obvious conflicts of interest at stake: "The firm adheres to the firm perspective, which is maximising shareholders' wealth by following the net present value rule (choosing those projects with the highest net present value). CEAs in healthcare usually follow a societal perspective maximising societal health using the incremental cost per quality-adjusted life years rule." It is not clear how the imperfect health markets can reconcile these conflicting positions in selecting objectives and allocating resources to innovation.

It is therefore legitimate and relevant to analyse the way the present innovation processes operate, how far and efficiently they satisfy society's innovation needs (or desires) and whether and how changes can be introduced to improve the said processes. Some authors have reviewed and summarised the proposed alternatives to the present system of incentives to medical innovation. Nathan [23] and Rovira [24] provide global overviews of proposals and suggestions for improving the impact of pharmaceutical research, development and utilisation on global medical need; Mueller-Langer [25] makes a similar exercise but focusing specifically on neglected infectious diseases.

The role of health technology assessment as a tool for efficiently promoting innovation

HTA has been proposed as a tool to improve the relevance of future research by identifying gaps in evidence and improving research design. One way to attain this goal is to meaningfully involve all relevant stakeholders (patients, clinicians and payers) in the process of defining future research needs and designing studies to address these needs [26].

Ladabaum [27] suggests that by assessing the relative clinical value of interventions we could unleash market forces to develop the kind of cost-saving innovations that have been typical in other industries, but rare in healthcare. But providing information in itself might not lead to a change of behaviour if there are no incentives – financial or otherwise – to do so.

Health technology assessment in public funding of research & development

Funding biomedical R&D would certainly benefit from some form of priority setting among disease areas. Cost and burden of disease studies can provide a first approximation to the social need and to potential social benefits of R&D and innovation by disease or disease area. QALYs or disability-adjusted life-years (DALYs) lost due to premature – i.e. potentially avoidable – mortality and morbidity can be weighted by other criteria to account for social values or preferences for certain conditions – rare diseases, children's diseases, unavailability of treatment, end of life or life-threatening conditions, etc., – could be allocated a higher weight if these are society's preferences.

Of course, the choice of disease and of specific health problem for R&D should not take into account only the potential benefits of finding a solution, but also of the likely additional effort required to reach the solution. Moreover, an integral view of the problem should take into account not only the estimated costs of finding the solution, but also the estimated cost of providing it to those in need. In practice however, it might be difficult to make even rough credible estimates of any of these future costs. But making these estimates and taking the respective risks is anyway part of the task of innovators and policy makers. The need for an integrated incentives policy has become evident in the field of rare diseases. Companies receive substantial public subsidies to R&D in orphan drugs, but health authorities often do not reimburse later the new drugs because they feel the price is too high; if the product is not reimbursed, the subsidies to R&D turn out to be a waste! It would probably make more sense to jointly negotiate the subsidies to R&D and the future price of the expected drug – as a package of public financing – and condition the subsidies to R&D to a previous agreement on the price of the product.

Health technology assessment by innovators during the process of research & development

Innovators are increasingly requested by payers to prove not only safety and efficacy, but also effectiveness, relative effectiveness and cost effectiveness of their products in order to get reimbursed at a favourable price. For innovator companies it has become a current practice to develop effectiveness and economic evaluation studies as a complement of its clinical research programme. Initially, these studies were done independently from the clinical research programme, often when the indications and even the price of the new product had been already decided. Economic evaluations were considered part of the marketing of a new product. But it later became clear that it was more efficient to plan real world and economic evaluation studies simultaneously and in coordination with the clinical research programme. One should expect that innovator companies progressively start the cost-effectiveness assessments at an earlier phase of the product development and that the early estimates of the cost effectiveness of products on the R&D pipeline increasingly become a criterion for continuing or dropping the development process of a product.

Health technology assessment and intellectual property rights policies

One of the traits of patents in the case of medicines is that they are granted at an early stage of the life cycle of a technology, when there is little or no evidence on the safety and efficacy and much less on the effectiveness of the new product[12]. As a consequence, from the point of view of patent law, innovation in the field of health technologies has little to do

---

12 This is done in order to prevent that relevant information is disclosed to other parties before the invention is duly protected.

with the concept of added therapeutic value, a criterion that is however increasingly used at the pricing and reimbursement phases. The patent holder is given an exclusivity right, which often amounts to an actual monopoly, on a product that might not bring to the patients any benefit over existing treatments. Moreover, there is a strong asymmetry of information that allows the patent holder to market the product with an aura of superiority over existing products. One way to overcome this undesirable situation would be to turn the patent right into a provisional exclusivity right that would be confirmed at the time of registration only if the patent holder could provide evidence of relative effectiveness or added therapeutic value over the most effective product existing at the time the patent was submitted. In case the added value could not be shown, the innovator would still be allowed to market the product, but not under exclusivity. A similar approach would be to modulate the patent duration according to the degree of innovation estimated through HTA studies at the time of licensing.

Several authors have proposed a flexible drug patent term as a mechanism to stimulate innovation and health [28]. This option might address the problems of the uncertainty on the future benefits of a new drug at the time the patents are granted and the convenience of being able to provide different financial stimulus for different degrees of innovation. However, it is not clear that modulating the patent term has any theoretical or practical advantage over the use of pricing and reimbursement policies as a means to attain the said objective, i.e. to reward the innovator according to the added value of the innovation.

HTA could also be used to determine the royalty paid to the patent holder in case of compulsory licensing (CL). Patent laws usually state that a fair compensation has to be paid to the patent holder, but they do not specify the criteria to calculate the amount of the compensation or royalty and leave this decision to the courts. Should a fair and efficient compensation not be somehow proportional to the added value of the innovation that is the target of a CL?

Other authors support the idea that in some cases the government should buy the patents and make them available to manufacturers in order to reduce the price and improve accessibility [29]. Again, setting a fair price for a patent is not an easy exercise, but it would probably make sense that it had some relationship to the benefits of the product concerned, no doubt a task for HTA.

Under the Trade-Related Aspects of Intellectual Property Rights (TRIPS) agreement, countries are free to define innovation almost as they like. Most countries do not identify innovation in health with therapeutic added value or relative effectiveness. One interesting exception is India, and example that shows that a country can use its right – accepted under TRIPS – to define innovation, to protect their national interests. Section 3 (d) of India's patent law prohibits granting patents to new forms of known substances unless it results in enhanced efficacy over the known substance. Under this provision, Novartis lost protection on its blockbuster drug Glivec® last year and recently the Indian Patent Office has refused a patent on US firm Abraxis BioSciences' anti-cancer drug Abraxane®, paving the way for domestic companies to launch affordable versions in the local market. The application was refused on the grounds of the US firm's claims lacking of inventive step, not being patentable and insufficiency, legal sources say[13].

---

13   According to a story of the *Times of India* quoted in IP-health by James Love on June 24, 2014.

Prizes and health innovation funds

A new idea that has been proposed to substitute or complement the incentives provided by patents is paying directly for innovation instead of granting innovators the privilege of exclusivity, which often becomes a monopoly. Once the innovation is adequately rewarded it would become public domain and the final products (medicines and other health goods) would be produced under competitive conditions, as generics.

This approach is usually referred to as delinking. Incentives for innovation from prizes, implies the separation of the innovation and the products markets [30]. The rationale behind that approach is that research-based pharmaceutical companies carry out two separate activities, namely R&D and manufacturing medicines. Under the present IPR system there is only one form of rewarding the two activities: the sale of the final products. A prize system would allow to pay independently for the two activities and to avoid the problems associated with the monopolisation of the product market and the deadweight loss of monopolies.

Stiglitz [31] is one of the best known economists who advocates the use of prizes instead of IPR to promote pharmaceutical innovation. While acknowledging that innovation is at the heart of the success of a modern economy, he raises the question of how best to promote it, pointing at the negative effects of IPR and claiming that "TRIPS imposed a system that was not optimally designed for an advanced industrial country, but was even more poorly suited to a poor country". He proposes a prize fund paid for by industrialised nations that "would provide large prizes for cures and vaccines for diseases such as AIDS and malaria that affect millions of people". In his opinion this would provide appropriate incentives for research without the inefficiencies associated with monopolisation.

But the person who has more intensively lobbied for alternative non-monopolistic mechanisms to incentivise innovation in the biomedical field and has been more influential with his proposals of prizes, health innovation funds and an International Treaty for Financing Biomedical Research certainly is James Love, director of Knowledge Ecology International[14] [32]. The idea behind a health innovation fund is that all innovators would register their innovations at a certain office, but instead of an exclusivity right, they would receive a right to a part of the fund, which would be proportional to some measure of the benefits of the innovation (e.g. total QALYs gained or total net benefit). Each innovation is allocated an individual score (e.g. based on cost-effectiveness criteria) and will receive a reward from the fund over a number of years. The points accumulated by the innovation in a given year are the cost-effectiveness score times the number of treatments consumed in the year. The annual fund is distributed among innovators according to the points (scores) accumulated during the year by the products introduced in the current or in the previous X years. Such a fund turns out to be a fixed prospective budget for innovation.

HTA would certainly have a key role to play in this new approach, either in assessing the maximum appropriate amount for a prize according to a willingness to pay (WTP) estimation or in calculating the innovation scores to apportion the annual health innovation fund compensation among all entitled innovations. Hollis [33] made a concrete proposal for the creation of a fund for pharmaceutical research where the prizes are determined with the help of economic evaluation analyses.

---

14 See, http://keionline.org.

Health technology assessment in licensing medicines and other health products

HTA – basically, RTCs – is already used at present for licensing medicines. The questions under discussion are whether a) the assessment and the decision to authorise the product should be more restrictive, by requesting evidence of superiority – or at least, non-inferiority – over the most effective alternative available, and b) the same criterion should be extended and generalised to other, or to all health products and technologies; Feldman et al. [6] urged independent HTA organisations and other stakeholders to address this apparently anomalous situation and support HTA of medical devices.

The possibility of requesting comparison and superiority of existing treatments in order to grant a marketing authorisation might have a risk, namely that of "killing" potentially useful new products that cannot provide evidence of superiority at the time of licensing, but could attain it later through the learning process involved in its use in clinical practice. Theoretically, this risk could be reduced by some form of initial controlled or conditional use scheme, such as a risk-sharing agreement or a patient access scheme. But the problem is that once a new technology is licensed, it might become politically difficult to stop or control the diffusion, even if evidence shows later that it is clearly not cost effective, nor even effective[15].

Ben Goldacre [34], a practising doctor, wrote an angry article to *The Guardian* expressing his frustration with the way he was misled by the partial information he had received on the effects of reboxetine. He concludes: "Drugs are tested by the people who manufacture them, in poorly designed trials, on hopelessly small numbers of weird, unrepresentative patients, and analysed using techniques that are flawed by design, in such a way that they exaggerate the benefits of treatments. Unsurprisingly, these trials tend to produce results that favour the manufacturer. When trials throw up results that companies don't like, they are perfectly entitled to hide them from doctors and patients, so we only ever see a distorted picture of any drug's true effects. Regulators see most of the trial data, but only from early on in a drug's life, and even then they don't give these data to doctors or patients, or even to other parts of government. This distorted evidence is then communicated and applied in a distorted fashion."

In the first months of 2014 there have been important initiatives at the EU level in favour of improving the transparency of clinical trials, which has been supported by strong citizen pressure; now EU member states have to negotiate the final text with Parliament. There is a Parliament opinion that post-market authorisation clinical trial data should be public, but Big Pharma is lobbying against it on the grounds of commercial confidentiality[16].

Health technology assessment in pricing and financing health products

Relative effectiveness and cost effectiveness are two key criteria increasingly requested as part of the procedures for the adoption, financing and pricing of the technologies. In fact, here is where HTA is more used at present to ensure the effectiveness and cost ef-

---

15 If the technology is in the market, and the innovator aggressively advertises and promotes its use, it might be difficult to keep it outside public reimbursement and/or to force a cost-effective reduction of the price, especially in countries where HTA is not well established.

16 Clinical Trial Vote: the good, the bad, the uncertain, Posted by David in uncategorised, http://tacd-ip.org/archives/date/2013/05

fectiveness of the new technologies and where it does simultaneously serve to incentivise innovation: if potential innovators consistently observe that authorities are more likely to adopt, reimburse and accept a relatively high price or a price premium over existing alternatives to technologies which are able to show added value according to transparent and predictable methods, they get a clear signal of the type of innovation the health system and regulators are prepared to pay for.

Pricing based on economic evaluations with some explicit or implicit threshold to somehow define the criterion for reimbursement or refusal of new medicines and other health technologies has been increasingly applied since the early 1990s in Australia, Ontario (Canada), the UK, the Netherlands, Sweden and other countries. This approach, with some variations and modalities, has come to be known now as value base pricing (VBP). NICE is one of the clearer and most transparent examples of this approach, and it has issued guidance to approve the routine use of a health intervention, reject it or recommend use within a research programme [35]. NICE has also established a formal process for the consideration of patient access schemes (PASS), which aims at linking access to improving cost effectiveness with evidence generated after licensing. Reimbursement decisions are linked with recommendations for further research, meaning that HTA is clearly influencing – or at least trying to influence – innovation.

VBP has been practised too in Sweden for patent-protected drugs since 2002. The system attempts to set prices on the perceived value, rather than on the "actual cost". The authors of a recent article [36] claim, however, that the system can be improved, by addressing its main present shortcoming, namely, "the conflict arising when the national agency makes decisions about pricing and reimbursement while the budget responsibility for drugs is with the health providers at the regional level". The modification suggested is to split the payment of medicines: the county councils would pay the marginal cost of production while the state would pay for the innovation. This proposal seems to follow the rationale of delinking the incentives for innovation from the prices of the products.

Countries that use external reference pricing (ERP) – maybe because they are not able to apply HTA and VBP – could still promote innovation by using a basket of reference countries that properly use VBP to reward innovation, and adjust the average price of those countries by means of a relative average income or PPP index.

Health technology assessment and competition policy

Innovators should be adequately rewarded for socially needed innovation. But, as long as the reward and the incentives rely on exclusive property and marketing rights, public authorities should ensure that these rights are not misused or abused. Right holders must be credibly convinced that the temporary exclusivity will effectively finish when it is due to finish. If they feel that it is feasible to extend the period or the scope of exclusivity beyond the limits set, they might probably be more interested in spending their money in trying to extend as long as possible their temporary position, than in finding new, innovative technologies. From a commercial, profit-seeking perspective, it is perfectly rational for a company to spend the money where it is likely to produce more profits. Strategies such as *evergreening*, defensive patenting, agreements with generic competitors to delay the market entry of generics, aggressive advertising and marketing to ensure brand loyalty once the patent expires, discrediting good quality generics and many other strategies may increase corporate profits, but do not contribute to the welfare of consumers, and even though some of them are perfectly legal, these practices should be discouraged as far as possible. The competitive anomaly of marketing exclusivity should at least be effectively transitory and under control. Companies should not be allowed to abuse IPRs and modify or use IP legislation to extend monopoly/exclusivity beyond its originally intended purposes.

Conclusions

The fact that the market fails in allocating resources to innovation in health does not guarantee that regulators, experts and public officials will automatically do better. But the appropriate use of HTA can be a key tool to ensure that public decisions are as efficient as possible, given the limited information and the uncertainties that have to be faced any time a decision is taken along the life cycle of a health technology.

The procedures to measure innovation will always have a high degree of subjectivity and arbitrariness. Most actual procedures and attempts to measure innovation go along similar methodological lines and resemble the aggregate approach of Grabowsky & Wang [11] or Light [12], or the scoring system used by Motola et al. [13], which define innovation as a set of relevant dimensions, each dimension having several discrete levels. The global innovation score is computed by aggregating with a certain procedure or algorithm the values of the individual dimensions.

HTA and more specifically cost-effectiveness analysis (CEA) do indirectly influence innovation in its role as a tool to regulate the price of health products.

Recommendations

Health authorities should first define social health needs and innovation goals and priorities. Then they should identify all the participants involved in the process of health technology innovation and their respective motivations as well as the factors that influence them and all existing or potential policy tools that can be used along the life cycle of a technology, to provide the right incentives to the stakeholders. HTA can play a central role in identifying the most innovative technologies; but just knowing that a new technology is efficient might not lead to its adoption by the health system. Health authorities should use this information when designing and applying policies in the areas of funding and promoting biomedical R&D, IP, licensing, pricing and financing health products, competition policy, and so on.

Innovation should be defined and measured as the contribution of a new technology to the effects that society values in health technologies in relation to the best available therapeutic option. For purposes of adoption, pricing and reimbursement of the added value of a new technology should reflect first of all the additional therapeutic benefit to the patients and consumers; it should also consider economic benefits in the form of savings in global treatment costs, as they free resources that can be reallocated to other health or social uses. It might also consider other benefits to patients and consumers, such as convenience of administration of a treatment, as well as benefits to caregivers and relatives.

There are various mechanisms available in the present life cycle of health products that can be used to promote innovation, and other alternative mechanisms have been proposed. The main message of this essay is that HTA should be systematically incorporated in all these mechanisms, because HTA is the best analytical tool available to assess added value and, hence, steer R&D and innovation of health technology in the appropriate direction. Of course, HTA might not always be as precise as desirable from a scientific or academic perspective, but rather speculative, especially in the early stages of the technology life cycle. But even if the results of HTA are fraught with uncertainty and are less precise and reliable than one would like, they can be of great value to regulators, payors and innovators, which, even at these early phases must take decisions that affect the innovation process. A valid even if imprecise assessment at the time an R&D investment has to be made is more valuable to the policy-maker responsible for promoting innovation, and certainly to the decision-making innovator, than a highly precise HTA available when the investment required to develop the innovation has been partly or fully made and the allocation of resources is largely irreversible.

Innovations embodied in a technology that do not result in immediate benefits for society, but might facilitate them when they are used in future technologies, might also justify some type of reward, as long as they are not appropriated by the innovator by means of property rights and are open for use to all members of society. But it is not clear by whom, when and how this reward should be paid and what would be the right amount. Some form of prize to be paid *a posteriori* from a special fund for promoting innovation would be a more appropriate source of funding than a premium price to be paid by consumers or from public health budgets.

Something that should clearly be enforced in order to ensure the validity and credibility of HTA and allow the identification of the truly innovative technologies is the pre-registration of RCT in public registries, coupled with the obligation of full standardised reporting of the protocols and results of the trials. The reasons are quite obvious: unless these rules are enforced, health professionals, or the scientific community or the drug regulatory authorities (DRAs) cannot be sure if they only have access to a biased sample of the existing evidence, because innovators might not disclose the existence of RCTs that give unfavourable results for the products they promote; or they can disclose the trials, but somehow hide the unfavourable results.

For DRAs it would be quite easy to enforce transparency at the licensing stage: all they have to do is to only accept as part of the submission dossiers RCTs that fulfilled the two conditions mentioned before, i.e. preregistration of the trial and full disclosure of protocol and results. Companies would be forced to comply, because otherwise non-registered trials with favourable results would not be accepted as evidence of efficacy and safety. An additional, more radical proposal to avoid the obvious conflict of interest of innovators designing and carrying out the trials for their products would be for DRA to request that at least some key trials for the licensing procedure should be done by independent organisations selected by random procedures. For instance, Baker [37] states that in order to attain the desirable level of transparency, clinical trials should be planned and financed by the public sector and carried out by entities independent from the industry.

This book was supported by an unrestricted educational grant from Celgene.

REFERENCES

1. Garber AM. To use technology better. Health Aff. (Millwood) 2006;25(2):w51-3. Available from: http://www.ncbi.nlm.nih.gov/pubmed/16464903. Last accessed June, 2014.

2. Schumpeter JA. Capitalism, socialism and democracy (1942). New York: Harper and Roe Publishers, 1942.

3. OECD. Oslo manual. Guidelines for collecting and interpreting innovation data. 3a ed. OECD Publications; 2005. Available from: http://www.keepeek.com/Digital-Asset-Management/oecd/science-and-technology/oslo-manual_9789264013100-en#page5.

4. OECD. The measurement of scientific and technological activities proposed standard practice for surveys on research and experimental development. Frascati Manual 2002; Paris: OECD Publications; 2002. Available from: http://browse.oecdbookshop.org/oecd/pdfs/free/9202081e.pdf.

5. Huot L, Decullier E, Maes-Beny K, Chapuis FR. Medical device assessment: scientific evidence examined by the French national agency for health - a descriptive study. BMC Public Health. 2012;12:585. Available from: http://www.pubmedcentral.nih.gov/articlerender.fcgi?artid=3490794&tool=pmcentrez&rendertype=abstract. Last accessed July, 2014.

6. Feldman MD, Petersen AJ, Karliner LS, Tice JA. Who is responsible for evaluating the safety and effectiveness of medical devices? The role of independent technology assessment. J Gen Intern Med. 2008;23 Suppl 1:57-63. Available from: http://www.pubmedcentral.nih.gov/articlerender.fcgi?artid=2150636&tool=pmcentrez&rendertype=abstract. Last accessed July, 2014.

7. Van Nooten F, Holmstrom S, Green J, Wiklund I, Odeyemi IAO, Wilcox TK. Health economics and outcomes research within drug development: challenges and opportunities for reimbursement and market access within biopharma research. Drug Discov Today. 2012;17(11-12):615-22. Available from: http://www.ncbi.nlm.nih.gov/pubmed/22366662. Last accessed July, 2014.

8. Kennedy I. Appraising the value of innovation and other benefits, A short study for NICE. 2009: p. 52. Available from: http://www.nice.org.uk/proxy/?sourceUrl=http://www.nice.org.uk/media/98F/5C/KennedyStudyFinalReport.pdf.

9. Green C. Considering the value associated with innovation in health technology appraisal decisions (deliberations): a NICE thing to do? Appl Health Econ Health Policy. 2010;8(1):1-5. Available from: http://www.ncbi.nlm.nih.gov/pubmed/20038189. Last accessed July, 2014.

10. European Commission. Working Group on Pricing and Reimbursement C of the V of IM. Enterprise and Industry 2013. Available from: http://ec.europa.eu/enterprise/sectors/healthcare/competitiveness/pharmaceutical-forum/wg_pricing_en.htm. Last accessed June, 2014.

11. Grabowski HG, Wang YR. The quantity and quality of worldwide new drug introductions, 1982-2003. Health Aff (Millwood). 2006;25(2):452-60. Available from: http://www.ncbi.nlm.nih.gov/pubmed/16522586. Last accessed June, 2014.

12. Light DW, Lexchin J. Will lower drug prices jeopardize drug research? A policy fact sheet. Am J Bioeth. 2004;4(1):W1-4. Available from: http://www.ncbi.nlm.nih.gov/pubmed/15035915. Last accessed July, 2014.

13. Motola D, De Ponti F, Rossi P, Martini N, Montanaro N. Therapeutic innovation in the European Union: analysis of the drugs approved by the EMEA between 1995 and 2003. Br J Clin Pharmacol. 2005;59(4):475-8. Available from: http://www.pubmedcentral.nih.gov/articlerender.fcgi?artid=1884813&tool=pmcentrez&rendertype=abstract. Last accessed July, 2014.

14. Motola D, De Ponti F, Poluzzi E, Martini N, Rossi P, Silvani MC, et al. An update on the first decade of the European centralized procedure: how many innovative drugs? Br J Clin Pharmacol. 2006;62(5):610-6. Available from: http://www.pubmedcentral.nih.gov/articlerender.fcgi?artid=1885166&tool=pmcentrez&rendertype=abstract. Last accessed July, 2014.

15. Morgan SG, Bassett KL, Wright JM, Evans RG, Barer ML, Caetano PA, et al. "Breakthrough" drugs and growth in expenditure on prescription drugs in Canada. BMJ. 2005;331(7520):815-6. Available from: http://www.pubmedcentral.nih.gov/articlerender.fcgi?artid=1246080&tool=pmcentrez&rendertype=abstract. Last accessed July, 2014.

16. Lexchin J. How safe are new drugs? Market withdrawal of drugs approved in Canada between 1990 and 2009. Open Med. 2014;8(1):e14-e19. Available from: http://www.openmedicine.ca/article/viewFile/613/535.

17. Toole AA. Does Public Scientific Research Complement Private Investment in Research and Development in the Pharmaceutical Industry? J Law Econ [Internet]. University of Chicago Press. 2007;50(1):81-104. Available from: http://ideas.repec.org/a/ucp/jlawec/y2007v50i1p81-104.html. Last accessed July, 2014.

18. Toole AA. The impact of public basic research on industrial innovation: Evidence from the pharmaceutical industry. Res Policy. 2012;41(1):1-12. Available from: http://www.sciencedirect.com/science/article/pii/S004873331100117X. Last accessed July, 2014.

19. Barton JH, Emanuel EJ. The patents-based pharmaceutical development process: rationale, problems, and potential reforms. JAMA. 2005;294(16):2075-82. Available from: http://www.ncbi.nlm.nih.gov/pubmed/16249422.

20. Gold ER, Kaplan W, Orbinski J, Harland-Logan S, N-Marandi S. Are patents impeding medical care and innovation? PLoS Med. 2010;7(1):e1000208. Available from: http://www.pubmedcentral.nih.gov/articlerender.fcgi?artid=2795161&tool=pmcentrez&rendertype=abstract. Last accessed June 2014.

21. Rai AK. The ends of intellectual property: health as a case study. Law Contemp Probl. 2007;70(2):125-30.

22. Adang EMM. Economic evaluation of innovative technologies in health care should include a short-run perspective. Eur J Health Econ. 2008;9(4):381-4. Available from: http://www.ncbi.nlm.nih.gov/pubmed/18188622. Last accessed July 2014.

23. Nathan C. Aligning pharmaceutical innovation with medical need. Nat Med. 2007;13(3):304-8. Available from: http://www.ncbi.nlm.nih.gov/pubmed/17342145. Last accessed July 2014.

24. Rovira J. Intellectual property rights and pharmaceutical developmen. In: Costa-I-Font J, Courbage C, Mcguire A, editor. The economics of new health technologies – incentives, organisation and financing. Oxford: University Press; 2009. p. 219-40.

25. Mueller-Langer F. Neglected infectious diseases: are push and pull incentive mechanisms suitable for promoting drug development research? Health Econ Policy Law. 2013;8(2):185-208. Available from: http://www.pubmedcentral.nih.gov/articlerender.fcgi?artid=3592259&tool=pmcentrez&rendertype=abstract. Last accessed July 2014.

26. Tunis SR, Turkelson C. Using health technology assessment to identify gaps in evidence and inform study design for comparative effectiveness research. J Clin Oncol. 2012;30(34):4256-61. Available from: http://www.ncbi.nlm.nih.gov/pubmed/23071248. Last accessed July 2014.

27. Ladabaum U, Brill J V, Sonnenberg A, Shaheen NJ, Inadomi J, Wilcox CM, et al. How to value technological innovation: a proposal for determining relative clinical value. Gastroenterology. 2013;144(1):5-8. Available from: http://www.ncbi.nlm.nih.gov/pubmed/23153872. Last accessed July, 2014.

28. Warren BC. Flexible drug patent terms: a Proposed mechanism to stimulate global innovation and health 2013 Feb 28; Available from: http://papers.ssrn.com/abstract=2229715. Last accessed July 2014.

29. Del Llano J. Discussion point: should governments buy drug patents? Eur J Health Econ. 2007;8(2):173-7. Available from: http://www.ncbi.nlm.nih.gov/pubmed/17225128. Last accessed July 2014.

30. Weisbrod B. Solving the Drug Dilemma. Washington Post. New York; 2003; Available from: http://www.globalaging.org/pension/us/socialsec/dilemma.htm.

31. Stiglitz J. Innovation: A better way than patents. New Sci. 2006;(2569):20. Available from: http://www.newscientist.com/article/mg19125695.700-innovation-a-better-way-than-patents.html.

32.   Love J, Hubbard T. The big idea: prizes to stimulate R&D for new medicines. KEI Research Paper. 2007 p. 37. Available from: http://www.keionline.org/misc-docs/bigidea-prizes.pdf.

33.   Hollis A. An efficient reward system for pharmaceutical innovation. Calgary; 2004 p. 29. Available from: http://www.who.int/intellectualproperty/news/Submission-Hollis6-Oct.pdf.

34.   Goldacre B. The drugs don't work: a modern medical scandal. The Guardian 2012;20. Available from: http://therefusers.com/refusers-newsroom/the-drugs-dont-work-a-modern-medical-scandal-uk-guardian/#.U7Wn7fl_s1Z. Last accessed June 2014.

35.   Longworth L, Youn J, Bojke L, Palmer S, Griffin S, Spackman E, et al. When does NICE recommend the use of health technologies within a programme of evidence development? a systematic review of NICE guidance. Pharmacoeconomics. 2013;31(2):137-49. Available from: http://www.pubmedcentral.nih.gov/articlerender.fcgi?artid=3561612&tool=pmcentrez&rendertype=abstract. Last accessed July 2014.

36.   Persson U, Svensson J, Pettersson B. A new reimbursement system for innovative pharmaceuticals combining value-based and free market pricing. Appl Health Econ Health Policy. 2012;10(4):217-25. Available from: http://www.ncbi.nlm.nih.gov/pubmed/22676213.

37.   Baker D. Financing drug research: what are the issues? Washington, DC; 2004 p. 27. Available from: http://www.cepr.net/documents/publications/intellectual_property_2004_09.pdf.

CHAPTER 3

The Wisdom Tooth of Health Technology Assessment

Ricard Meneu

The first published guidance from the National Institute for Clinical Excellence (NICE) started with the words "*the practice of prophylactic removal of pathology-free impacted third molars should be discontinued in the NHS*" [1]. Since then, NICE has produced almost 300 more technological appraisals of medical devices, tests, surgical procedures and, mainly, drugs. Maybe it is time to assess whether health technology assessment (HTA) has reached its coming of age or is merely an impacted molar in the decision-making process.

The overall objective of HTA is to help obtain the greatest health gains within financial constraints, informing decision makers on how to balance the pressures of demand and supply for new technologies within a health-system budget by grounding decisions in a clear, transparent and coordinated process [2]. This paper will point out some of the complexities observed in the development of HTA – in its different conceptions and applications, its fuzzy and discrepant results, the disparity of views on its usefulness and meaning – with the aim of helping to produce more explicit guidance towards achieving the goals originally set. That guidance should inevitably pass through a comprehensive, significant, and rigorous **evaluation of the cumulative experience, and should be oriented to improving its role as a technical tool in "health policy".**

A New Old Science?

Despite its success and paramount position in HTA literature, NICE was not the first organisational attempt to provide scientific input to the decision-making process. As any reader of this book already knows, the organisational beginnings of "technology assessment" started with the establishment of the Office of Technology Assessment (OTA) as an office of the US Congress from 1972 to 1995, to provide Congressional members and committees with objective and authoritative analysis of complex scientific and technical issues [3]. In 1995, during Newt Gingrich's "Contract with America" period, Congress withdrew funding for the OTA, calling it an "unnecessary agency" that duplicated govern-

© Springer International Publishing Switzerland 2015
J.E. del Llano-Señarís and C. Campillo-Artero (eds.), *Health Technology Assessment and Health Policy Today: A Multifaceted View of their Unstable Crossroads*,
DOI 10.1007/978-3-319-15004-8_3

ment work, and it was abolished. At that time, some specific HTA agencies were already operating in some European countries.

Fortunately, the OTA Legacy website (https://www.princeton.edu/~ota/ns20/pubs_f.html) preserves in electronic form the complete collection of OTA publications, from the seminal *Drug Bioequivalence* (1974) [4] to the posthumous *Hospital Financing in Seven Countries* (1995) [5], including the classics *Development of Medical Technology: Opportunities for Assessment* (1976) [6], *Assessing the Efficacy and Safety of Medical Technologies* (1978) [7], *The Implications of Cost-Effectiveness Analysis of Medical Technology: Methodological Issues and Literature Review* (1980) [8], or even the *Variations in Hospital Length of Stay: Their Relationship to Health Outcomes* (1983) [9] .

All this work had already been done when NICE began its activities reviewing such classic and widespread practices as the extraction of wisdom teeth. This attention to current practices was abandoned shortly after, focusing only on new technologies. HTA is a science-based process, but also a flourishing health technology. Hence HTA is a technology that is old but without having been properly evaluated. However, HTA deserves a thorough evaluation to assess its effectiveness and to identify the uses, methods, configurations and settings where its effectiveness is greatest. This is especially important considering the very different focus and tasks of these agencies, ranging from a priority focus on drugs (UK) to an almost complete abstention from evaluating these products (the Spanish agencies).

For a process of such critical importance to all stakeholders – governments, patients, providers, payers, and medical technology firms alike – one would expect a large and growing body of research on its structure, its process, and especially, its outcomes. However, a review of the existing literature on HTA reveals a startling lack of depth and scope, particularly on the impact HTA has had on healthcare budgets, efficiency, and on societal health outcomes [10].

More than three decades after setting the conceptual, methodological and organisational basis of HTA, our ability to evaluate it *qua* technology should be beyond any doubt. This does not seem to be the case. We are eager to assess any healthcare innovation with only a handful of papers, fuelled by the promoters of the technology, published in carefully chosen journals. But we are hesitant about the pros and cons of the appropriate way to assess the functioning of the multiple HTA experiences accumulated over the years. **Overall, the available knowledge to assess the effectiveness of HTA is just a bunch of "case series" and "case reports", with little external validity and usually surrogate outcomes.**

Assessing the Assessments

As with any interventions in healthcare, a demonstration of their own cost effectiveness may be expected of HTA programmes, i.e., that the health and/or economic benefits resulting from an HTA programme outweigh the cost of the programme itself. But the task of measuring the impact of HTA seems to range from the elementary to the infeasible. Even if a recommended decision is adopted, it may be difficult or impossible to attribute this policy to the HTA. Furthermore, systematic attempts to document the dissemination, processes and impacts of HTA programmes are infrequent. **A partial explanation of the limited (to say the least) assessment of HTA is its very heterogeneous configuration among jurisdictions.**

Differences in culture, history, politics, healthcare financing, and the underlying ratio-nale for undertaking HTA in general, have all had important effects on the makeup and function of HTA in each country. On this point, a review conducted by the UK's Office of Health Economics revealed few systematic within-country patterns in HTA configuration and behaviour across any of six dimensions measured [11]. Such heterogeneity among HTA systems could confound an unstructured approach to eliciting common "lessons learned." HTA activities may vary, and in fact they do, according to the degree of linkage with decision making. They can range from simply providing information to the decision makers to a more comprehensive process that engages with clinicians, patients, health-system budget holders or research funders [2].

Those different configurations have been reviewed by a "pan-European think tank and market-oriented network" [12], with its focus on the politics, not on the science. The scope of this analysis considers: the process of HTA-related policies; the transparency of HTA bodies and of HTA decisions; the governance of HTA bodies; the mandate of HTA bodies, the independence of HTA bodies, the relationships with key stakeholders (indus-try, physicians, patients); the political dependency on the state; and the degree of competi-tion between HTA bodies in a given country. The conclusion crudely stated is: "*A far from perfect or even standardised system*". In terms of the political economy of HTA, the main findings, mostly already known, are:

- In funding, some countries dedicate considerable resources to HTA, while others do not.
- In scope, some HTA bodies appraise only selected new drugs, while others ap-praise most new and some old drugs.
- In relevance, some countries implement most HTA recommendations, while oth-ers hardly use them at all.
- In transparency, some HTA bodies adhere to international appraisal standards, while others construct their own methods.
- In stakeholders' involvement, some HTA bodies involve patients and expert groups, while others do not.

Given that all HTA programmes stem from a common source, this is more surprising. One might expect the programmes to be more homogeneous, differing only in details dictated by local conditions. But the differences we see are considerably deeper, and they affect such things as the types of decisions to which technology assessment (TA) is ap-plied, their nature and content, the mandates given to those applying them, the types of outcomes they should consider, the criteria for drawing conclusions and the extent to which the conclusions are binding [13].

The remit and governance of HTA bodies and associated decision makers and stake-holders differ between countries according to their general mission and overall policy objectives. As one component of the broader healthcare decision-making process, the role of HTA programmes typically reflects a health system's history, ethos and values as well as key policy objectives. Consequently, assessments often coincide with decisions on the reimbursement, pricing and utilisation of drugs or other current policy measures, and sometimes not [14]. The majority of HTA organisations limit their role to assessments only. NICE, however, is involved in both phases: during assessment, issues of efficacy, safety, effectiveness and cost are addressed while broader impacts on the National Health Service (NHS), patients and society may be attended to in the appraisal. Thus, the National Institute for Health and Clinical Excellence produces mandatory government guidelines [15], so that its HTA recommendations are likely to have a different level of impact to those issued by organisations that are not directly integrated into the decision-making process. Notwithstanding the constraints faced by NICE, it is considered to be by far the most advanced example of an attempt to utilise a consistent framework for the adoption of technology in a government-funded healthcare system.

The different perspectives about what the measurable product of HTA should be (reports, dissemination, the decisions adopted on the technologies evaluated, etc.) complicates having a shared view on its effects. This is so especially when from the varied functions and organisational designs of HTA agencies it cannot be expected that the impact of their assessments will be similar. Consequently, the impacts of different HTAs are variable and inconsistently understood. Whereas some reports are translated directly into policies with clear and quantifiable impacts, the findings of some "definitive" HTAs with authoritative, well-documented assessment reports go unheeded or are not readily adopted into general practice [16].

It may be useful to employ a recent characterisation showing HTA as having three distinct components or phases [17]:

- The first component is a "science" phase, where research and analysis are carried out. At this stage technologies are assessed using discipline-specific appropriate scientific methods and judgements.
- A second phase in HTA is a "policy" one, where societal values and judgements are brought to bear on scientific evidence to arrive at a policy decision.
- The proposed third phase in HTA has been called a "population" phase, where evidence-informed recommendations are implemented and the decisions derived from these recommendations can be assessed.

Most of the documents produced by HTA organisations fall into the "science phase" domain. The information provided by HTA is reasonably standardised and shared among its different producers and users. It is a legitimate source of pride, and enough – even too much – (biblio)metrics is dedicated to that information. An upcoming analysis of the production of documents by Spanish agencies' reviews a total of 570 documents [18]. Of these, 301 (52.8%) were the agencies' own documents, while 269 (47.2%) were articles published in scientific or technical journals. Analysing the citations of these documents (own documents and journal articles), a total of 1,790 citations were generated by the 570 documents from the agencies, a citation ratio close to "pi (π) per paper". Those citations were distributed in 1,579 (88.2%) journal articles and 211 (11.8%) monographs and other publications. Of the 1,790 citations, a mere 17% (n = 304) were self-citations.

However **this bibliometric interest becomes worrying when trying to pass it off as a surrogate measure of the results of the HTA. This is worrying since the purpose of HTA is to inform decisions, not merely produce more information.** An expression of this "citationphilia" or "bibliobsession" can be seen when considering "bibliometric and citation analysis as methods identifying the impact of research, generating evidence of international use" [19].

It is easy to agree that "Health Technology Assessment" is both a scientific process and a health technology. As a scientific process it involves systematic literature searches; critical reviews of scientific and other studies; evidence syntheses and the formulation of conclusions; and recommendations on the information assessed and the context of decision making. **However, the ultimate value of HTA in a health system depends on its contribution to improving health status or increasing efficiency rather than increasing knowledge. In this respect, HTA does not differ much from other health technologies and must be subject to the same rigorous standards of evaluation"** [20].

From Peer Review to Ceteris Paribus

Away from the academic comfort of citations, bibliometric analysis and the "Impact Factor", there is the real harsh world of decisions, especially relevant when such broadly shared information is translated into very different choices. The frequency and magnitude of such "losses in translation" should not be surprising, although it often seems to be so.

From the founding texts of HTA, emphasis has consistently been given that information is just an input in to decision-making process. Let us remember: HTA is "aimed mainly at informing decision making regarding health technologies" [21]. Its main purpose is to inform technology-related policy making in healthcare [22], or "its aim is to inform the formulation of safe, effective, health policies that are patient focused and seek to achieve best value" [23]. Even more explicitly, "technology assessment is a form of policy research that examines the short- and long-term social consequences (e.g., societal, economic, ethical, legal) of the application of technology. The goal of technology assessment, is to provide policy-makers with information on policy alternatives" [24]. In this same sense, "technology assessment (TA) is a category of policy studies, intended to provide decision makers with information about the possible impacts, costs and consequences of a new technology or a significant change in an old technology. (…) TA provides decision makers with an ordered set of analysed policy options and an understanding of their implications for the economy, the environment, and the social, political and legal processes and institutions of society" [25].

As HTA is a mere "ordered set of analysed policy options, and an understanding of their implications", when social values and judgements and scientific evidence are taken into account to make a policy decision, it is likely that the adopted choices will differ from those which are preferred technically.

The kind of values and judgements considered, their weighting and legitimacy (opportunism, electoralism) can vary greatly among decisions. Yet we can simplify the analysis by considering just two groups of observable differences between decisions.

- Among jurisdictions, resulting in different decisions for the same technologies in non-identical contexts.
- Among technologies with similar efficacy, cost-effectiveness ratio, incremental cost-effectiveness ratio (ICER), and so on, varying the authorisation criteria or the threshold cost applied.

For the first case, a study that compared the NICE recommendations with those of the Canadian and Australian agencies [26] showed that NICE recommended 87.4% (174/199) of submissions for listing compared with the Canadian rate of 49.6% (60/121) and 54.3% (153/282) shown by the Australian Pharmaceutical Benefits Advisory Committee. Recommendations varied considerably between countries, possibly because of differences in the technologies reviewed, but also because of different agency processes, including the capability to negotiate on price. The data suggest that the three agencies all make recommendations that are consistent with evidence on effectiveness and cost effectiveness but that other factors are often important, as will be seen below.

An important issue is the transferability of evidence between different countries and healthcare systems. Clinical and epidemiological evidence is usually considered transferable, while resource utilisation, costs and cost effectiveness are more context-specific. But several methodological issues, particularly measuring health benefit, choice of comparator and comparability of treatment patterns and populations, affect the transferability of cost-effectiveness estimates [2].

For the second kind of discrepancies, a recent research paper from the Health Economics Research Centre [27] about the influence of factors other than cost effectiveness on NICE decisions shows that cost effectiveness alone correctly predicted 82% of decisions. According to this, NICE considers other decision-making criteria as well as cost effectiveness. These include the severity of underlying illness; stakeholder persuasion; end-of-life treatments; disadvantaged populations; and technologies affecting children. Nonetheless, the weights attached to these additional criteria are rarely quantified and their importance and impact are therefore even more uncertain than cost effectiveness.

Beside cost effectiveness, the single factor that emerged from the analysis as exerting a significant effect on decisions is the type of disease that the technology is intended to prevent, diagnose or treat. The NICE rejections were significantly less likely for cancer and musculoskeletal disease, but significantly more likely for respiratory disease. But other than certain diseases, no variables other than cost effectiveness significantly predicted NICE decisions

Also, recent research to identify the cost effectiveness of healthcare services in the Scottish NHS [28] shows that the estimated cost per quality-adjusted life-year (QALY) of services at the margin varies widely both between services and among different estimates of cost per QALY for the same service.

On the basis of studies of this kind, it is not possible to give evidence-based recommendations on the way to increase the impact of HTA on decision making. A wider concept for evaluation should be developed [29]. Although limited in its magnitude and space, these discrepancies represent a major challenge to the claims of measuring HTA results based on decisions finally taken.

Some authors challenge the validity of such an approach by considering decision making to be a very complex process, insufficiently understood if the perspective concentrates only on the final decision. Therefore, it can be misleading to judge the impact of HTA reports only by comparing their recommendations and the corresponding policy decisions, because this runs the risk of ascribing an impact even in cases where the HTA report (or its content) is not even known to the decision maker [20].

This is even more so considering, as other recent research concludes, that "services may be displaced as part of a response to the cumulative impact of all types of cost pressures, including cost-increasing health technologies newly recommended by NICE, but such displacements were not direct responses to the publication of individual NICE technology appraisal (TA) decisions" [30].

Ultimately, the impact of economic evaluation on the allocation of healthcare resources is hard to ascertain because of the difficulties in specifying the counterfactual. But **the difficulties common to any health policy assessment cannot excuse the need for a greater evaluative effort.**

The Lurker at the Threshold

Among the criteria used by HTA agencies, insurers or payers when assessing whether to reimburse or pay for particular treatments, one standard approach involves evaluating the price of a treatment against the extra QALY it offers. Threshold values are used as a general strategy. Rather than use HTA as a tool to say "yes" or "no" at a given price, it will be used to set the maximum acceptable price, based on the evidence of how many additional QALYs are created in comparison with the best available alternative [2].

The consistency of this criterion – and we must remember it is the main predictor of final decisions – implies setting a threshold above which no technology will be included, approved or financed. Some agencies then apply a straightforward threshold of, for example, EUR 30,000 per added QALY (usually calculated as ICER), only funding drugs whose prices put them below that threshold (or mainly at the closer lower figure). Some HTA agencies, therefore, also require information on the potential budgetary impact of each drug. Others, such as Sweden, incorporate an estimate of a drug's social impact in terms of productivity gains for the patients and, consequently, the overall economy.

In most countries, including the UK, a cost-effectiveness threshold for healthcare reimbursement decisions has never been formally evaluated. In some countries, such as the existing system in the UK, a standard cost-effectiveness threshold is applied to all new products, with some flexibility to take account of additional relevant factors, including societal preferences. However, the mechanism for taking wider factors into account is not completely transparent and may lead to perceptions that important factors are not adequately reflected in the assessment process [31]. Discussing probabilistic ranges rather than a single threshold enables to have considerable discretion over decision, but also minimises debate about the legitimacy of the approach employed and disputes about the precise value that such a 'threshold' should take. However, it results in uncertainty [27].

Some of these uncertainties have led some analysts [32] to **argue that the explicit or implicit decision-making threshold of acceptable cost effectiveness has been set higher than that which would have been used by decision makers operating under a budget constraint. They also argue that as a result of this use of economic evaluation, manufacturers have just priced up to the threshold, whereas otherwise prices would have been lower.**

The objection to the setting of an explicit or implicit threshold is the likely "excessive" appropriation of "consumer surplus". In a non-competitive market, given the temporary monopoly provided by the patent system, this capture is absolutely unrelated to the technology, but dependent on the threshold. Given the inexistence of counterfactual, there is no straightforward rebuttal to these arguments [33].

Moreover, the setting of cost-effectiveness thresholds in healthcare resource allocation decisions in some jurisdictions is controversial, as estimates are not based on empirical evidence, and using them for decisions may not lead to optimal resource allocation decisions [34].

Besides, with explicit or implicit thresholds, the pivotal consideration of cost effectiveness can promote some undesirable "commercial strategies". Such strategies can sometimes be perceived even in the most prestigious journals. So, in a recent white paper from The Economist Intelligence Unit Healthcare [35], in the chapter "Overcoming the barriers: Preventing HTA rejections" , we can read: *"The easiest way of getting past the HTA barrier would seem to be by offering a rebate on the price, thereby increasing the cost-effectiveness of the product. Many pharmaceutical companies have done just that, although examples are rarely publicly disclosed"*.

There is nothing to object to a reduction of the intended price, even if it remains too high, at exactly the limit of the threshold. But what about other strategies suggested to avoid rejections? The first one is *"Offer true innovation"*. This would be excellent, but it is already stated that *"this is the hardest requirement to match"*. The next one is *"improve targeting: the burden that a drug places on healthcare budgets, and its cost-effectiveness, can be vastly improved by better targeting. An increasing number of regulatory approvals, particularly in oncology, rely on companion diagnostics, which can also help with HTA"*. The central and unresolved problem of how to assign value to each component is pointed out elsewhere. And, finally, if none of this works, *"offer a risk-sharing deal. Many companies at risk of a rejection offer a deal that explicitly links the price or budget paid for a particular drug with patient outcomes"*. That means postponing the decision on the cost to future discussion, case by case, of the effectiveness achieved.

Therefore, a foreseeable strategy given these considerations would include: 1) getting the approval for the indication/target group with greater (maximum) efficacy; 2) obtaining the highest price allowed for this efficacy given the level where the threshold is set; and 3) trying to extend usage through expansion of the indication, or by means of "professional diffusion" after bombarding with claims about the health benefits lost imposed by the restricted usage.

If the producers manage to expand that niche after authorisation, that is something which today goes far beyond the general practice of HTA agencies. **But in the absence of reliable re-assessments and evaluations of the impact of the decision on utilisation, we risk falling into an undesirable scenario: one in which we will be trapped by the clamp of the unduly high prices and inappropriate overuse.**

From assessment to health policy

Reasonable concern about technical matters sometimes hides the central aim of HTA, which is none other than the contribution to an improvement in health policy decisions. Ideally, all the work developed during the last 40 years is intended to bridge the world of research with the world of decision making [36]. From this research, HTA attempts to project and estimate relevant outcomes associated with health technology policy choices to inform healthcare decisions [37,38]. Such projections and estimates should help decision makers to foresee the consequences of the various possible "courses of action", but rarely provide a straightforward choice about the (best) alternative to adopt. However, it is becoming more usual to encounter **criticism of the final decisions taken because they differ from the "technical" advice or recommendations provided. These recommenda-**

tions are usually formulated from an ideal point of view: efficiency = effectiveness; absence of real world overuse or inappropriate underutilisation, and so on.

The issue related to the misuse of information by decision makers deserves some closer attention. That widespread concern seems much greater than that shown by researching and understanding the variables and elements that make up the differences in the decisions observed. It is not uncommon to read that policy makers do not understand the basic facts of healthcare: that much useless technology finds its way into the healthcare system; that much technology is overused and misused; that industry consciously promotes the overuse of technology for financial reasons; that doctors are not trained to make rational choices in healthcare; and that results in much harm, waste and misuse of scarce healthcare resources.

The need for more research on the complexity of decisions is a tediously recurring claim. But what is actually needed is a greater understanding of the real context in which they occur. This context seems to be much better known about than accepted, but even less internalised or integrated into global analysis.

HTA itself must take part of the blame for the presumed ignorance of the policy makers. At least its actors agree, stating that HTA staff members have generally not been actively involved in "dissemination". Unfortunately, better "dissemination" is not the solution, but just one part of the problem. The dissemination of information alone will not achieve significant changes in an environment such as that generally described. In as much as the concern about dissemination continues to be focused on the length and language of the documents issued, few changes can be expected.

HTA must try to deploy other kinds of rhetorical strategies [39], different from confidence in the superiority of "technical purity". This is just the opposite of the temptation to supplant the policy decision by the supposedly uncontaminated technical recommendation. It seems to forget that, as noted above, after the "scientific phase" there is a second distinct phase in HTA, the "policy" phase, where social values and judgements read the evidence to arrive at a policy decision. The scientific work supplements, but does not replace, the final decision. As Culyer recently contends, "It is an important value that the social value judgements of scientists, clinicians, social workers and 'experts' in general, are no more worthy of special weight than those of ordinary citizens" [40].

Furthermore, many organisations conducting HTA today use formal expert committees that include healthcare providers, researchers and members of the public to examine and deliberate on the scientific evidence available from assessments, with the goal of creating recommendations for policy makers. These "deliberative" approaches, particularly when they bring together decision makers and researchers, could be a much more effective approach to ensuring that knowledge from HTA (evidence) is correctly interpreted and applied, particularly compared to simply producing scientific reports in the hope that this will be translated into policy by others [41,42].

Over the past decade, public distrust in unavoidable value-laden decisions on the allocation of resources to new health technologies has grown. In response, some healthcare organisations have made considerable efforts to improve their acceptability by increasing transparency in the decision-making processes. However, the social value judgements (distributive preferences of the public) embedded in them, are yet to be defined. While the need to explain such judgements has become widely recognised, the most appropriate approach to accomplishing this remains unclear [43].

As recently noted by Michael Rawlins [44], those undertaking a health technology assessment (HTA) also have to exercise judgements. The judgements necessary for HTA to make are twofold: scientific judgements relate to the interpretation of the science; social value judgements are concerned with the ethical principles, preferences, culture and aspirations of society. Although competent HTA bodies should be able to exercise scientific judgements, they have no legitimacy to impose their own social values. These must ultimately be provided by the general public.

Finally, for the improvement of health policy decisions, what seems to be most often forgotten – by the actors of both phase I and II – is the relevance of phase III. The third phase in HTA, called the "population" phase, is when the consequences of decisions from the recommendations can be evaluated. That might involve **re-assessing the decision and the impact of the decision. It may also involve supporting policymakers or providers in their attempts to use HTA recommendations, or promoting the use of HTA-driven policies through the use of specific tools or other interventions. Good evaluations in this phase can feed back to future assessments of technology, which in turn can feed back to policy changes** [31]. That seems the most relevant and necessary effort in enhancing the assessment of HTA, and it is still mostly pending.

Putting it all together

Nowadays, HTA is a growing field internationally, fostered by the need to support clinical, managerial and policy decisions, and fuelled by advances in methods of evaluation in the applied and social sciences, including clinical epidemiology and health economics [31]. HTA is becoming an increasingly important policy tool to help policy makers define and measure (i.e. capture) value from the use of health technology [3].

While there is general consensus that HTA is needed and provides value, the ways in which assessments are produced and employed vary considerably, raising issues around its most effective use in policy making. There are still many questions – both on a theoretical and an empirical basis – about most of the main desirable features of HTA, whatever this acronym means in each jurisdiction.

The main achievements of HTA cannot be overlooked. Certainly, HTA effort has contributed to an improvement (even a qualitative change) in the process of decision making by:

- Establishing a generalised set of criteria to decide on the incorporation of new technology (and less commonly to validate others that have already been widely implemented).
- Increasing awareness of opportunity costs and cost effectiveness, at least in some partial frameworks of OC, CE, etc.
- Promoting greater attention to relevance of outcomes research.
- Generally speaking, increasing methodological rigour and openness.
- Providing great doses of transparency – though varying a lot among jurisdictions – in a previously very dark domain.
- And, in some ways, providing some externalities in knowledge, both on the technologies assessed and the relations between the actors in the healthcare market.

Even though it is not a "public good", the spread of information inherent to HTA has a social value attached.

As a practical consequence of this achievement, a number of beneficial changes in reimbursement processes have been observed, such as a trend towards requiring the measurement of more meaningful clinical endpoints. Also, the consideration of cost effectiveness has thrown into sharper relief the fact that a given healthcare technology could deliver high value for money in one patient sub-group, but offer almost no added value (compared to the alternatives) in another patient sub-group [33].

Furthermore, **on the debit side a lot of unsolved issues, already pointed out elsewhere [45], remain active. These include the methods of topic selection and priority setting, the proper fit between social values and QALYs, the dynamic consequences of cost-effectiveness thresholds, and last but not least, the appropriate implementation, monitoring and review of the guidelines issued.**

Other unresolved issues are related to the recurrent complaint about the misuse of information by decision makers and to the fact that HTA focuses almost exclusively on new and emerging technologies, where the collated scientific evidence can be very sparse, too new and more likely biased

From a European standpoint, the EU states – not merely the agencies – would do well to devote more attention to HTA processes that are clear, coordinated and incorporate economic evaluation on some common basis. This could facilitate meaningful collaborative deliberations on the basis of the available scientific evidence, especially the evidence that is easily applied in different local contexts. HTA has become increasingly institutionalised, focusing on the cost effectiveness of health technologies. But there is a growing perception of "local flavours" in measuring cost effectiveness, apart from the increasing incorporation of other considerations, which are not always sufficiently explicit. In this way it may be that this model will become increasingly and visibly dysfunctional.

The wide spread presence of a still emerging, evidence-based policy tool called Health Technology Assessment (HTA) can be considered to have been established, to say the least. The assessment of this not-so-new technology is still pending. **But, like all technologies, Kranzberg's First Law applies: "Technology is neither good nor bad; nor is it neutral" [46]. Perhaps HTA must abandon certain claims to having impossible neutrality and set the focus on a better demonstration of its own profitability.**

This book was supported by an unrestricted educational grant from Celgene.

REFERENCES

1. NICE. National Institute for Clinical Excellence. Guidance on the extraction of wisdom teeth. Technology Appraisal Guidance No. 1. March 2000. Available at: http://www.nice.org.uk/nicemedia/live/11385/31993/31993.pdf.

2. Blomqvist A, Busby C, Husereau D. Capturing value from health technologies in lean times. C.D. HOWE Institute. Commentary No. 396. Toronto. 2013.

3. Banta D. What is technology assessment? Int J Technol Assess Health Care. 2009;25 Suppl 1:7-9. doi: 10.1017/S0266462309090333.

4. (https://www.princeton.edu/~ota/disk3/1974/7401_n.html).

5. (https://www.princeton.edu/~ota/disk1/1995/9525_n.html).

6. (https://www.princeton.edu/~ota/disk3/1976/7617_n.html).

7. (https://www.princeton.edu/~ota/disk3/1978/7805_n.html).

8. (https://www.princeton.edu/~ota/disk3/1980/8013_n.html).

9. (https://www.princeton.edu/~ota/disk3/1983/8329_n.html).

10. O'Donnell JC, Pham SV, Pashos CL, Miller DW, Smith MD. Health technology assessment in evidence-based health care reimbursement decisions around the world: an overview. Value Health. 2009;12(Suppl. 2):S1-5.

11. Towse A, Buxton M. Three challenges to achieving better analysis for better decisions: generalisability, complexity and thresholds. OHE briefing no 42, October 2006.

12. Healy P. Pugatch MP. Theory versus Practice: discussing the governance of health technology assessment systems, Stockholm Network. London 2009.

13. Eddy D. Health technology assessment and evidence-based medicine: what are we talking about? Value Health. 2009;12(Suppl. 2):S6-7.

14. Sorenson C, Drummond M, Kristensen B, Busse R. How can the impact of health technology assessments be enhanced? European Observatory on Health Systems and Policies, World Health Organization 2008.

15. www.nice.org.uk/guidance/index.jsp?action=byType.

16. Goodman C. HTA 101. Introduction to Health Technology Assessment. Bethesda, MD: National Library of Medicine, National Information Center on Health Services Research and Health Care Technology, 2004. Available from: http://www.nlm.nih.gov/nichsr/hta101/hta101.pdf .

17. Schwarzer R, Siebert U. Methods, procedures, and contextual characteristics of health technology assessment and health policy decision making: comparison of health technology assessment agencies in Germany, United Kingdom, France, and Sweden. Int J Technol Assess Health Care. 2009; 25(3):305-14.

18. Parada A, Gutiérrez-Ibarluzea I, grupo AUnETS. Evaluación del impacto bibliográfico de las agencias y unidades españolas de evaluación de tecnologías sanitarias. MInisterio de Sanidad, Servicios Sociales e Igualdad. Madrid 2014.

19. Wright D, Milne R, Price A, Tose N. Assessing the international use of health technology assessments: exploring the merits of different methods when applied to the National Institute of Health Research Health Technology Assessment (NIHR HTA) programme. Int J Technol Assess Health Care. 2013;29(2):192-7.

20. Gerhardus A, Dorendorf E, Røttingen JA, Sarriá Santamera A. What are the effects of HTA reports on the health system? Ch. 6. In: Velasco Garrido M, Kristensen FB, Palmhøj Nielsen C, Busse R (eds). Health technology assessment and health policymaking in Europe. Current status, challenges and potential. Copenhagen (Denmark): World Health Organization, on behalf of the European Observatory on Health Systems and Policies; 2008. Available in: www.euro.who.int/Document/E91922.pdf.

21. HTA Glossary. HTAi (Health Technology Assessment International). Oct 8, 2013. (http://htaglossary.net/health+technology+assessment+%28HTA%29).

22. WHO. Health technology assessment. http://www.who.int/medical_devices/assessment/en/.

23. EUnetHTA (European network for Health Technology Assessment) http://www.eunethta.eu/about-us/faq.   24.   Banta HD, Luce BR. Health care technology and its assessment: an international perspective. New York, NY: Oxford University Press; 1993.

25. Coates & Jarratt, Inc. Course workbook: technology assessment. Anticipating the consequences of technological choices. Washington, DC. 1992.

26. Clement FM1, Harris A, Li JJ, Yong K, Lee KM, Manns BJ. Using effectiveness and cost-effectiveness to make drug coverage decisions: a comparison of Britain, Australia, and Canada. JAMA. 2009 Oct 7;302(13):1437-43.

27. Dakin H, Devlin N, Feng Y, Rice N, O'Neill P, Parkin D. The influence of cost-effectiveness and other factors on NICE decisions. HERC research paper 05/14. Oxford: Health Economics Research Centre. 2014.

28. Schaffer SK, Sussex J, Devlin N, Walker A. Searching for Cost-effectiveness Thresholds in NHS Scotland. Office of Health Economics. Research paper 13/07. London 2013.

29. Gerhardus A, Dintsios CM. The impact of HTA reports on health policy: a systematic review. GMS Health Technol Assess. 2005 Nov 2;1:Doc02. Available at: http://www.ncbi.nlm.nih.gov/pmc/articles/PMC3011311/pdf/HTA-01-02.pdf.

30. Schaffer SK, Sussex J, Hughes D, Devlin N. Opportunity Costs of Implementing NICE Decisions in NHS Wales. Office of Health Economics. Research paper 14/02. London 2014.

31. Husereau D, Cameron CG. Value-based pricing of pharmaceuticals in Canada: Opportunities to expand the role of health technology assessment? Canadian Health Services Research Foundation. Paper 5. Ottawa 2011 (http://www.cfhi-fcass.ca/sf-docs/default-source/commissioned-research-reports/Husereau-Dec2011-EN.pdf?sfvrsn=0).

32. Birch S, Gafni A. Economists' dream or nightmare? Maximizing health gains from available resources using the NICE guidelines. Health Economics Policy and Law. 2007;2:193-202.

33. Drummond M. Twenty years of using economic evaluations for reimbursement decisions. What have we achieved? CHE Research paper 75, University of York, 2012.

34. Gafni A, Birch S. Inclusion of drugs in provincial drug benefit programs: should "reasonable decisions" lead to uncontrolled growth in expenditures? CMAJ. 2003;168(7):849-51.

35. The Economist Intelligence Unit Healthcare. Value-based healthcare. The implications for pharma strategy, London, 2014.

36. Peckham M. Scientific basis of health services. London: BMJ Pub. Group; 1996.

37. Lavis JN, Wilson MG, Oxman AD, Lewin S, Fretheim A. SUPPORT Tools for evidence-informed health policymaking (STP) 4: using research evidence to clarify a problem. Health Res Policy Syst. 2009;7 Suppl 1:S4.

38. Lehoux P, Denis J-L, Tailliez S, Hivon M. Dissemination of health technology assessments: identifying the visions guiding an evolving policy innovation in Canada. J Health Polit Policy Law. 2005;30(4):603-41.

39. McCloskey D. Knowledge and persuasion in economics. Cambridge University Press, 1994.

40. Culyer AJ. Social values in health and social care. London: Commission on the Future of Health and Social Care in England – The King's Fund. 2014. Available: http://www.kingsfund.org.uk/sites/files/kf/media/commission-background-paper-social-values-health-social-care.pdf.

41. Innvaer S, Vist G, Trommald M, Oxman A. Health policy-makers' perceptions of their use of evidence: a systematic review. J Health Serv Res Policy. 2002;7(4):239-44.

42. Mitton C, Adair CE, McKenzie E, Patten SB, Waye Perry B. Knowledge transfer and exchange: review and synthesis of the literature. Milbank Q. 2007;85(4):729-68.

43. Stafinski T, Menon D, Marshall D, Caulfield T. Societal values in the allocation of healthcare resources: is it all about the health gain? Patient. 2011;4(4):207-25.

44. Rawlins MD. Evidence, values, and decision making. Int J Technol Assess Health Care. 2014; 30(2):233-8.

45. Drummond M, Sorenson C. Nasty or nice? A perspective on the use of health technology assessment in the United Kingdom. Value Health. 2009;12 Suppl 2:S8-13.

46. Kranzberg's M. Technology and history: "Kranzberg's Laws" Bulletin of Science, Technology Society. 1995;15:5-13.

CHAPTER 4

Regaining Health Technology Assessment from Oblivion: Improving and Integrating Regulation of Drugs, Medical Devices, Diagnostic Tests and Surgical Innovations

Carlos Campillo-Artero

Introduction

Is there a broad, all-encompassing structure that meets the regulatory needs of medical innovations? This chapter will try to make the case that the answer is indisputably no, and provide some groundwork for improving and integrating regulation of drugs, devices, diagnostics and surgical innovations.

The spectrum of innovation in medicine is far-flung, but not unmanageable. At one end there are minor changes that go virtually unheeded and are inherent in individual practice, while at the other end lie innovations that are permitted into general practice use only after their efficacy and safety have been adequately proven in randomised controlled trials. Between these polar opposites there are innovations that are permitted into ordinary use after a more limited evaluation has been carried out, or even after no evaluation at all. It is felt – accurately or not – that they do not require the same level of evidence of efficacy and safety before being approved for clinical use.

When it comes to drugs, medical devices, diagnostic tests and surgery, in this order, a downwards gradient of regulation emerges. The purview of drugs continues to eclipse that of devices, diagnostic tests and surgery. In contrast to devices, diagnostics and surgery, the assessment of drugs is based on much more stringent criteria and consequently it provides a reasonable evidence base of their efficacy and safety. Over the past few years, there has been an unacceptably high incidence of adverse events caused by some medical devices. These adverse events have triggered alarm bells and laid bare some long-standing weaknesses in the regulatory process. The assessment and licensing of diagnostic tests are chiefly based upon their accuracy with almost a total disregard to their contribution to health outcomes. Most surgical procedures are adopted and diffused into clinical practice with little or no scientific evidence. Despite the existence of schemes for their accurate and timely assessment, surprisingly, demand for their regulation is scanty.

With regard to devices, tests and surgery regulations have not kept pace with the dynamics and intricacies of their innovation as it has done with drugs. As it stands, regulation

© Springer International Publishing Switzerland 2015
J.E. del Llano-Señarís and C. Campillo-Artero (eds.), *Health Technology Assessment and Health Policy Today: A Multifaceted View of their Unstable Crossroads*,
DOI 10.1007/978-3-319-15004-8_4

does not even hold sway over the minimal efficacy and safety standards for diagnostics and surgical innovations. Some proposals – still unsuccessful – suggest bringing their regulatory processes into line with evidentiary standards of efficacy, safety and quality. Furthermore, evidence-based regulatory methods and schemes for their assessment, licensing, pricing, reimbursement, and evaluation need to be tailored to their special features and implemented without further delay. There is also a need for recredentialing of physicians before they can be allowed to use a new device, order a new test and perform a new procedure.

There is a need to further improve information on efficacy and safety for drug approval, coverage and reimbursement, and to make their postmarket use efficient, together with the interests running counter it. Budgetary and spending pressures call for generating pre-approval evidence of their relative (not absolute) efficacy, safety and incremental cost effectiveness, and postmarket evidence of relative effectiveness, safety and incremental cost effectiveness over standard technologies. It has been recently emphasised that pre-approval assessment of their safety needs to be largely improved owing to regulatory errors: type I, II and III (their opportunity costs) [1–4].

Different regulatory authorities and stakeholder's demands seem to be slowly starting to make headway towards strengthening the generation of evidence on relative efficacy and safety, along with that resulting from comparative effectiveness research for drugs [5]. Value-based assessment and value-based pricing should be consistently applied in tandem, and take into consideration recently developed and expanded assessment criteria such as, inner fairings, prospective health, proportional (weighted quality-adjusted life-years [QALYs]) shortfall and wider societal benefits [6,7]. This also should apply to devices, diagnostics and surgery.

Innovation in this area is mostly incremental. As with drugs, real device, diagnostics and surgical innovations should be separated from refinements, line-extensions, "me-too devices" and, by and large, commercial novelties. The chances of increasing the market share of "me too" devices, tests and procedures, along with the ensuing losses in social efficiency, are far from slim [8].

The reluctance of regulatory officials to undertake a comprehensive overhaul, especially of the more unregulated medical technologies, fights shy of stifling innovation by the industry with heavy regulation and incurring extra costs contingent on the ensuing increase in bureaucratic overload [9,10]. These arguments are untenable.

Several countries with established HTA programmes do not have national programmes for regulating and providing guidance on tests and interventional procedures. Among those with HTA systems in place, there is substantial variability in the methods, processes, extent and comprehensiveness, and in the nature (binding, expected or voluntary) of implementation guidance. Organisations responsible for it are also heterogeneous. They all use efficacy and safety in the assessments, but only few include economic evaluation. Patient inconvenience and societal costs are seldom considered. Dissemination and adoption of HTA agencies' recommendations still face serious difficulties in being translated into policy [11-13].

It has long been known that regulation is not strongly associated with the existence of market failures. In light of the theories of regulation (normative analysis as a positive theory, capture theory, economic theory, and Stiglerian/Peltzman and Becker models), we may be currently witnessing the cumulative and interacting effects of severe regulation failures and the reluctance to undertake the needed regulatory overhaul such as the negative (health) externalities, shortage of information, long-standing inconsistencies in regulatory agencies' information, regulatory agencies captured by industries, conflict of interests and changes in professional self-regulation [14].

This chapter tries to make the case that, (i) there is enough knowledge and regulatory commonalities among drugs, devices, diagnostics and surgical procedures that a consistent and common regulatory framework can be lay down and implemented for them; (ii) expenditure on harmful, ineffective and unproven technologies should be stopped; (iii) resourcing, systemic, environmental, institutional, organisational, implementation and managerial factors are important, along with postmarket surveillance; (iv) disinvestment is also important; (v) to achieve improvement, incentives should be brought in line with the objectives that the pursuit of a better regulation embraces; (vi) prevention of bad health and inefficiency does not depend on increased regulation, but on better regulation.

Given that the wealth of research and information in this realm has been largely devoted to drugs, this chapter will exclusively focus on the regulation of devices, diagnostics and surgical innovation. In the last section, several common measures for improving and integrating the regulation of these four types of medical technologies are proposed. Finally, since the contents of this chapter embody social value judgements – those about society – another held premise is that social efficiency is at issue too.

Medical Devices

Over the last years a number of institutional reports on medical device (MD) regulation have been issued in several countries. These concern the unacceptably high incidence of clinical adverse events caused by MDs and their high recall rates. Moreover, the frequent phasing out of some devices that pose a greater risk to health has triggered alarm concerning the long-standing weaknesses and deleterious effects of many regulatory processes [15–17].

These reports show that in the US a considerable number of high-risk MDs have obtained approval via mechanisms intended for medium- and low-risk MDs, which do not require such a comprehensive clinical evaluation. Further, only 27% of such devices have been tested in clinical trials before marketing. These events are similar in scale to those observed in other countries and the European Union (EU), even though they are less known owing to the worrisome shortage of data and lack of transparency existing in Europe with respect to these regulatory matters. Several authors have portrayed the EU regulatory system as one getting out of whack, "fragmented, privatised and largely opaque, due to a history of the collective and systematic failure of the regulatory-industrial complex" [8,9,18,19]. Conflict of interest, regulatory capture and revolving doors stand out as some of the root causes of the problem.

The regulation of devices

In the US, the US Food and Drug Administration (FDA) is invested with the authority to obtain "reasonable assurance of safety and effectiveness" before marketing MDs [9,18,20]. MDs are classified into class I (e.g. stethoscopes, tongue depressors), which are regarded as posing very little risk to health and are only subjected to "general controls," such as sterility tests. Class II MDs, which pose a moderate risk (e.g. wheelchairs, earphones, ultrasound machines, computed tomography scanners) have to pass general and "special controls" as part of a review process known as 510(k). If the device is shown to be "substantially equivalent" to a similar, marketed device, no further data are required, but performance and postmarket surveillance requirements may have to be fulfilled. The US Supreme Court acknowledges that substantial equivalence is no guarantee that an MD is safe and effective [17,21–24].

Class III devices keep patients alive, but they can pose a high risk to health (implantable cardioverter defibrillators, hip prostheses, pacemakers). Clearance can be obtained only subject to presentation of clinical trials showing "reasonable assurance of effectiveness and safety" under the so-called premarket application (PMA) [15–17,20]. However, new class III devices developed by modification of other devices already on the market can be approved without the need to present new clinical trials, and some can get clearance through process 510(k). The FDA can conduct investigations, compel the manufacturer to perform postmarket studies on class III devices and initiate recalls [3–5,15–17,20].

In the EU, MD regulation is the responsibility of each of the 27 member states. No single agency is in charge, which is contrary to what happens with pharmaceuticals. In the EU, MDs are classified similarly with the exception of class II, which is split into IIa (i.e. blood-pressure cuffs, ultrasound machines, magnetic resonance imaging [MRI] machines, positron emission tomography [PET] scanners), and IIb (i.e. X-ray machines), and class III [20,22,25].

Class I MDs are approved after being presented to the regulatory authority and the device manufacturer has issued the mark of Comformité Européenne (CE mark). The class II and III devices are reviewed by one of the approximately 80 Notified Bodies (NBs) accredited by each country's competent authority. These are independent, for-profit private firms whose work, which is fee-based, is paid for in part by the manufacturer, who is free to choose the NB. If the NB of a particular country deems it satisfactory, it grants the CE mark and the manufacturer can then market the device throughout the EU. To be approved, MDs must satisfy certain "essential requirements" and are subject to performance and reliability testing in accordance with the risks inherent to their intended use (which is decided by the manufacturer) [8,14,18,20,22,26]. Since 2011, the EU has made it mandatory for manufacturers to notify all severe adverse events to the competent authorities of the member states, directly to the European Databank on Medical Devices (EUDAMED), and for the NBs to participate in postmarket surveillance.

Magnitude and main characteristics of the problem

One of the most troublesome criticisms of the adequacy of this review process appears in several reports issued by the US Government Accountability Office (GAO), the FDA and the Institute of Medicine (IOM). One serious problem the reports show is that approval is often granted on the basis of studies that lack rigour, have no control group and are subject to bias. The recall reports for some devices show inconsistencies, and the absence of clear guidelines for recall review, even though PMA "is the most stringent type of device marketing application required by the FDA" [15–17,27].

Two improvement measures are to establish a *de novo* process for rigorous assessment of MD efficacy and safety requiring a revision of class III devices through the postmarket surveillance or reclassification of certain devices as class II, and to set up an integrated process for acquiring, analysing and quickly acting upon information on postmarket use [15–17].

In Europe, transparency is lacking, pre-approval trials and other studies conducted are not publicly accessible, ambiguous standards are applied willy-nilly, and the scientific evidence presented is weak, as is generally true of the review, approval and surveillance systems as a whole, which are no guarantee of safety (the number of recalls of class III devices has risen sharply in the UK without a parallel rise in the number of alerts issued by the competent authorities). These issues have been associated with preventable morbidity and mortality. The FDA has denied its approval for some devices marketed in the EU [17,25,27–29].

The clinical information they must present can take the form of a literature review if the device is equivalent to another that has already been approved and in the market, or it can be a review of randomised controlled trials when lingering doubts regarding safety need to be addressed. For class III devices, the manufacturer must conduct human clinical investigations, but he is not compelled to perform randomised controlled trials or to present head-to-head comparisons showing "similar effectiveness" or proof of the MD's impact on clinical outcomes [20,25].

Although the rules are meant to be applied identically across the EU, each NB has different requirements. Moreover, there is no system in place to prevent a device company from shopping around among the NBs until approval is obtained. When a company's application fails, submission of a new application to another NB is banned. NBs are not compelled to inform the national authority when they issue a CE mark. Since the EU system lacks a central record of applications, there is no current way to ascertain whether companies resubmit applications [9,29].

The regulatory system in the EU has not developed in tandem with technological advances in MD. New devices based on slight technical modifications are constantly emerging, and their safety and effectiveness must be repeatedly put to the test [8].

In the EU, reviews are more focused on device performance than on clinical effectiveness, contrary to what happens in the US. The CE mark certifies that an MD meets manufacturing standards and is safe when used as designed. However, there is no explicit requirement to show benefit of absolute efficacy (needless to say, relative [incremental] efficacy), and safety certification is not required to be based on clinical data. As the current regulatory system stands, the safety of an MD is dealt with in an unsatisfactory way and, strictly speaking, efficacy is not dealt with at all [8,9,20,21,25].

In 2008, the EU took its first step towards deep revision and standardisation (not yet completed) of the large number of documents involved, in an effort to clarify and strengthen the legal framework within a single document. However, prompted by the incidents surrounding the Poly Implant Prosthesis, in February 2012 the European Commission announced a series of immediate corrective measures and issued a reminder that the MD legislation will be approved in the near future [8,20,25].

Some experts foretell that these proposals will fall short and will not go as far as those in place in the US, their flaws notwithstanding, and therefore will not allow the EU to gain a stricter grip on the regulation of MDs. They do not impinge on the root causes of the problem, and will not come into effect until 2014 at the earliest. The regulatory system is badly in need of a broad and systemic overhaul rather than that of patchy changes introduced in a piecemeal fashion [8–10,30].

Postmarket surveillance

The coordination and analysis of postmarket surveillance in the EU varies widely, with many notifications taking place in a handful of countries and not made public. The US has no active requirement that adverse events be notified to the manufacturers, and off-label use is very high (in Medicare it is as high as 69%). The adverse event notification rate is very low, although measures to improve it are under way. The quality and supervision of MD postmarket surveillance is even more deficient than for drugs [17,20,25,27,31,32].

When implanted devices number in the hundreds of thousands or even millions, their surveillance becomes very difficult. The guarantee of device effectiveness and safety offered by postmarket surveillance is greatly hindered by the complex interplay between design, safety during implantation, the learning curve of the physicians implanting the devices, patients' individual and aggregate risk of suffering adverse events and the lack of a comprehensive national surveillance system.

Leaving aside the unfortunate case of breast implants, weaknesses discussed have been set forth in detail elsewhere using as examples hip prostheses and cardiovascular devices. The factors causing these problems are already present from the initial phases of MD development, and the weaknesses observed compromise them all [22,33].

Diagnostic Tests

It has long been put forward that assessing the value of a diagnostic test must not be based upon its accuracy alone, but should go further and encompass the ultimate added value (health benefit) that is derived from its use in clinical practice. In short, the difference in health outcomes between the new and the best current available test [34–36].

It is noteworthy that accuracy parameters are surrogate endpoints. They are tantamount to those surrogates being used when assessing efficacy and safety of drugs in randomised controlled trials. Results obtained in studies carried out in the preliminary and preclinical phases or in those only using surrogates may prove clinical validity (meaning that the test is positive in people with a given disease and negative in those without the disease and that positive results predict disease and negative results predict its absence), but do not demonstrate clinical utility (meaning that the test's ultimate health benefits outweigh the risks) [37–40]. At issue is the decisive need to translate intermediate results into applied, practical clinical knowledge. All studies of diagnostic tests that dodge measures of its real influence on health outcomes fall short as an adequate basis for regulatory decision making and should thus be considered incomplete.

Furthermore, the added (incremental) value of a diagnostic test can be down to its incremental effectiveness and incremental safety in improving both patient management and clinical outcomes, and to do so in a cost-effective manner.

An important fraction of studies on accuracy of diagnostic tests focuses on the test in isolation. One of the most overriding flaws is overestimation (over-interpretation) of clinical applicability of study results. Startling false assertions of their clinical utility are legion. Despite the wealth of published guidelines devoted to improving their quality and reporting, there is still ample room for design, analysis and reporting improvement [36,38,41–48].

Frames for evaluation of tests

Diagnostic tests can and should be evaluated in a phased manner similar to that of new drugs. A number of formal frames to streamline the process of diagnostic test development have been proposed. With a view to finding out if randomised controlled trials are needed before deciding to license a new test or whether observational studies will suffice, all downstream consequences of the test should be captured beforehand. The methodology underlying this decision consists of designing the pathway showing the way in which the new test would be expected to contribute to improving health outcomes from both the incremental and the widest clinical perspectives. *Ex ante* test evaluation, randomised controlled trials, analog flow diagrams, have been described for this purpose. They first consist of depicting the current test-treatment pathways (sorting out the comparator), as well as that for the new test, and identifying if the latter is a substitute, an add-on or a triage test [34–36,38,48–50].

Two paramount dimensions of quality of diagnostics should be considered. On the one hand, factors required to assure the quality of a test: improvement of the diagnostic thinking process, availability, appropriateness (selection of treatment subgroups that would benefit the most), detection of true extra cases, timeliness (reduction of the time lag between diagnosis and treatment), acceptability, compliance patient management, safety (avoidance of side effects, those of the tests itself and those of unnecessary treatments), avoidance of other tests and treatments, changes of treatments, and cost effectiveness. On the other hand, the indispensable and often forgotten systemic and organisational elements that need to be in place in order to assure the quality of the tests supporting system infrastructure: professional staff, organisation, equipment, registries, audits, training, quality management, leadership, incentives [34–36,38,48–50].

When it comes to external validity, caution should be exercised whenever the studies are not carried out in clinically meaningful setting and roles, when differences exist in the adoption and diffusion of the test over time and across health systems, as well as in the positivity of thresholds used and if case mix differs among study populations (spectrum bias).

Rates of inappropriate interventions, including diagnosis tests, have stayed virtually constant or worsened over the last decade. In an attempt to curve the consequences of this problem, a host of initiatives have been launched ("Do Not Do" and "Choosing Wisely" campaigns) [51–55]. Once identified, either an atlas of variation can be created or studies intended to directly identify over- (prescription-indication) and underuse (indication-prescription) can be conducted.

Biomarkers

It has been repeatedly claimed that the current approach to the discovery, development, uptake and regulation of new biomarkers is still slow and socially inefficient to meet the growing needs of the healthcare systems. Numerous attempts to identify biomarkers have been mere fishing expeditions, as shown by the low rate of clinically useful biomarkers in contrast to the initial claims of their potential usefulness [39,40,56].

Scientific underpinnings to biomarker development are imperfect, market pressure is high, patient populations are markedly heterogeneous, and for those biomarkers linked with drug safety or treatment response oftentimes putative predictive biomarkers lack validation in subsequent pivotal studies [56–58]. It all applies to diagnosis (presence or absence of abnormality or disease), prognosis (need for treatment), predictive (response to treatment) and pharmacokinetic (dose that should be administered) biomarkers.

Despite this inadequacy of biomarkers research and development, hundreds of new potential biomarkers pop up in the medical literature every year. However, a large number of studies are devoid of sufficient methodological rigour and suggest new biomarkers on the basis of cherry-picked data.

Validation of biomarkers refers to the assessment of the measurement performance characteristics of the biomarker's assay, and qualification, to the fit-for-purpose process of linking a biomarker with biological processes and clinical outcomes. The use in early drug clinical trials of biomarkers that have not been sufficiently qualified leads to overestimates of efficacy, harm and inefficiency as a result of both false positive and negative results. This could also worsen if the biomarker reaches phase III trials and the market [39,40,59–61].

Improving regulation of biomarkers means that newly qualified biomarkers are implemented safely in trials, directed at high specific fit-for-purpose clinical contexts, their utility is not expanded beyond initial qualification claims until enough evidence is collated, and those that have been recently qualified are used as second-tier tests and harnessed as follow-up tools in specific situations rather than prematurely deployed into routine clinical practice [61].

A trade-off should be established between the need to continue discovering and developing new biomarkers and that of concentrating on those for which some experience and knowledge has been gathered and need to be confirmed. In order to resolve this quandary, some strength-of-evidence criteria have been set forth for the initial selection of biomarkers for further investigation. Qualification frameworks, including recommendations for designing phase II and III trials in which biomarkers are integrated, have also been outlined to establish the minimum stringent evidence needed to support narrowly defined fit-for-purpose and initial qualification claims, and to allow collating more evidence for linking it with clinical outcomes, and subsequently for approval: adjust decision making and change it on the basis of the best available data; integrate biomarker and clinical information on a regular basis; validate its clinical benefit; and maximise utility functions per resource unit expended [39,30,56,57,59].

As current regulation stands, there are high opportunity costs (type III regulatory error) in two angles of regulation. First, the opportunity costs incurred when a proof-of-concept hypothesis regarding a biomarker that may have contributed to some clinical benefit is not tested. Second, those associated with harm resulting from its premature approval: over-diagnosis, unnecessary repetition of tests and the downstream treatment cascade that they can unleash [1,2,56].

Concerning the regulation of biomarkers, the same can be said of drugs and medical devices: stringent scientific criteria should be applied in ascertaining their efficacy and safety by means of clinical trial fundamentals and methodology: analytical validity, clinical validity and clinical utility (the three main criteria for approval and licensing). Relative (incremental) diagnostic value should substitute for absolute value as well, and incremental cost effectiveness should be set as the fourth barrier criterion for coverage and reimbursement. Claims against adopting a value-based pricing approach for diagnostics are groundless.

Omics

As for the genomic-based technologies, despite the high expectations of ground-breaking discoveries of diagnostic, prognostic and response biomarkers and some success in genetic diagnosis, a small fraction of the putative tests have reached full clinical application. The whole genome sequencing still falls short of providing clinical useful guidance and having impact on the risk of common complex diseases. Progress is slower and science has come to be more difficult than expected. The continuous dramatic increase in the availability of these tests (e.g. direct-to-consumer) alongside the continuous fall in the costs of genome sequencing, pose a mounting challenge owing to the lack of regulation of the assessment and market approval of a great majority of them. Moreover, it could worsen the array of potential negative externalities due to lack of regulation [62–66].

Putting aside some well-known examples of somatic mutations and molecular diagnostic technologies that are strong predictors of drug response and adverse reactions, from the whole population of potential markers standpoint, these facts also apply to the realm of pharmacogenetics since a number of approved drugs that contain pharmacogenetic information omit action-oriented information for clinicians and patients. Additionally, as new drugs enter the market and substitute for those in place, semi-developed pharmacogenomics knowledge becomes obsolete even before this knowledge is translated into clinical practice knowledge [65–67]. The abovementioned limitations of methodological validity in connection with diagnostic tests are especially noticeable in the realm of omics.

For the integration of genetic testing into the purview of diagnostic tests to be adequate, a regulatory system that ensures the analytical and clinical validity and clinical utility of genetic tests should be put in place. Further, the need for closing the gap in translational research is particularly important in omics research and calls for the impending need of overcoming fragmentation of knowledge by integrating different disciplines. Qualification of genomic and peptidomic biomarkers is also needed. Poor designs, biases, sample size issues, access to specimens, a large gap between statistically detectable associations and clinically meaningful information, low replicability, the corroborated overestimation of results of published studies (chiefly in cancer and cardiology), economic evaluations carried out for genetic tests with insufficiently proven analytic and clinical validity and other threats to the internal and external validity of omics studies should be foreseen and controlled [38,57,63–71].

Though more is known about the limitations that omics research faces, it is premature to make sound predictions regarding its future. Emerging molecular research methods, system biology, bioinformatics and statistical methods hold promise for gaining insight, and applications of proposals for streamlining research frameworks and reducing the translational gap are underway. One of the challenges for regulatory bodies is to keep pace with these changes and regulate accordingly.

Companion diagnostics

As for companion diagnosis, the main funders of clinical studies that provide information on clinical utility are drug developers (co-development) and public research bodies; diagnostic companies have a limited role. Current regulatory and reimbursement systems are not providing sufficient evidence standards thereof. National and international testing and outcomes databases are needed. It is unclear whether the private companies can undertake the endeavour to produce scientific evidence as to the clinical utility and economic value of diagnostic tests on a regular basis. There is some reluctance to limit market size and increase the complexity of trials despite other designs being available that can accrue useful information if well conducted. Consequently, incentives to produce the type of evidence needed should rise and be aligned.

In this area, value is created by means of adequately selecting subgroups of patients who will benefit the most, accurately predicting and thus increasing the likelihood of treatment response, decreasing that of side effects, improving adherence, and thereby improving health outcomes. Increasing the investment in pre-approval studies without a clear likelihood of achieving these goals and in the absence of aligned incentives does not make too much economic sense [67,68,72,73].

Furthermore, there is room for improving the limitations of economic evaluations of these tests, especially the assumption of high accuracy and the omission or underestimation of the downstream costs, clinical utility and health consequences beyond the test. (In this regard, it is worth perusing the NICE's Diagnostics Assessment Programme [www.nice.org.uk/diagnostics], the Australian and the US regulatory systems) [73,74].

Evidence requirements and reimbursement processes for companion diagnostics are idiosyncratic and variable across countries, as is the perception of their value. Since generating this kind of evidence is costly, public funding may be needed. Fostering evidence generation for companion diagnostic begs for much greater harmonisation, setting adequate accuracy and clinical utility standards and unequivocal and consistent signals to developers as far as prices are concerned on the basis of added value [68].

When a companion diagnosis is marketed along with a drug, what produces value is the combination of both; it is a joint product. Both drug and test developers should be rewarded for due innovation. A thorny and unresolved problem is how to assign value to each component. As for the pricing of the combination, some authors champion flexible and value-based pricing and encourage advancing in such issues from a dynamic efficiency standpoint, especially because of expectations of further innovations and developments of new companion tests [73]. This is an unresolved issue.

Measures presented in the last section of this chapter are intended to provide some groundwork for improving and integrating their regulation.

Surgery

Surgical practice has an intrinsically iterative nature. It advances chiefly through a process of trial and error. While there is a unique culture and deep tradition in surgery, the systematic study of surgical innovation is relatively new. It has been unstructured, subject to high variability, and inconsistently supported by evidence (relatively few observational studies, seldom using control groups, and scattered, scarce and delayed randomised controlled trials). As surgical specialties have evolved since their Flexnerian-spurred inception, innovations have been mostly incremental with only some disruptive exceptions. Surgical research is reportedly not filling the basic research gap nor the minimum standards applied to drugs and medical devices. These facts notwithstanding, there are examples of some successful innovations being framed by means of scientific assessment [75–80]. However, surgical innovation continues to be unregulated.

One of the few studies conducted on the existence of systems aimed at both influencing innovation and regulating the use of surgery in different countries, found substantial variability in the type and funding of organisations in charge, as well as in the criteria used for the selection of procedures, the types, sources and rigour applied for the appraisal of evidence about their efficacy, effectiveness, safety, and cost effectiveness, in the rules and format of assessment recommendations, and in the status of guidance, when it exists [11].

Systematic regulation, evaluation and rational promotion of innovation in surgery are critical from both the effectiveness and safety binomial and the efficiency standpoints [78]. The most comprehensive modelling of the stages of surgical innovation, development, assessment, appraisal and postmarket evaluation is the so-called Innovation, Development, Exploration, Assessment, Long-term follow-up (IDEAL) model [81,82]. Its two centrepieces are that it allows framing the entire process – from the inception of the surgical innovation to its mid- and long-term post-adoption stages – and that it provides a rigorous, relatively parsimonious and useful model for regulation.

According to this model, stage 1 (Innovation) describes the first use of a new procedure, prompted by the need for a new solution to a clinical problem. It is performed by one or a small group of surgeons in one or few patients. Stage 2a (Development) consists of the planned use of the procedure in a small group of patients to refine or modify the technique. Learning curves are of note in this phase. Stage 2b (Exploration) kicks in once the main technical aspects of the procedure have been worked out and outcomes with larger numbers of patients are needed. Learning curves are also important. Stage 3 (Assessment) aims to assess efficacy (effectiveness) by comparing it to current alternatives with larger numbers of patients. The new technique should be sufficiently evolved to warrant full evaluation by means of randomised controlled trials. It is the cornerstone of the learning path. Finally, in stage 4 (Long-term study) the procedure has been fully adopted and its purpose is to assess its long-term effectiveness and safety. It is tantamount to the postmarket surveillance stage for drugs [81].

HTA systems for surgery have also lagged behind those of drugs and medical devices. There is still no agreement as to how they should be introduced into the regulatory apparatus, organised and applied to current innovation, assessed, licensed, priced, reimbursed and subjected to postmarket surveillance. Evidence-based information has not been yet collated in this realm and is still scarce.

Singularities and complexities of the surgical procedures

Some specific and troublesome aspects of surgery are noteworthy and should be considered when laying down the groundwork, the rules and the standards for regulation: the learning curve, the perceived irreversibility of the surgical act, the absence of a systematic approach of using trials for assessment, and the uncertain widespread acceptance of evidence-based information. Moreover, due to the importance of its assessment in pre-adoption studies as well as during its diffusion, the surgeon's performance should be given special attention. Its accurate measurement could be particularly difficult since it is determined, among other factors, by his/her surgical knowledge, prowess, preferences and experience. So too is that of the members of the surgical team, the pre-, intra- and postoperative organisation and management, the type of surgical resources available, and leadership. The facts that surgery is traditionally devoid of systematic training in research, evaluation methods and consolidated models of apprenticeship should also be taken into account [79,82–84].

Methodological difficulties in evaluating surgery

Several well-known reasons explain why randomised controlled trials are more difficult to conduct in surgery than with drugs. These include absence of masking, use of placebo and the application of the principle of intention-to-treat [83]. Difficulties often arise when deciding the most appropriate outcome measures for efficacy, effectiveness and safety, how and when (short- mid- long-term) to measure them, and how to minimise the use of surrogate measures. Moreover, their quality in journals of different surgical specialties has been found to be lower than those published in medical journals [12,85–87].

Further, it is critical to ascertain the effect of learning and to find the best way to ascertain prowess and to account for its impact on health outcomes. The early stages of assessment tend to focus on complications of surgical expertise (i.e. duration of the interventions, blood loss). For complex procedures, learning may have to await a high number of procedures [83]. The intricacies of innovation jargon, terminology and outcomes measurement should be standardised in order to reduce the lack of comparativeness of studies (for surgical complications one solution maybe the adoption of the Clavien-Dindo classification). Special attention should also be paid to quality control and compliance measures on a regular basis, including the post-adoption stage [81,83,88,89].

Randomisation should begin as soon as it is feasible, before the adoption curve of the technology stabilises, to enable monitoring of the learning curve and to evaluate short-term effects, efficacy and costs. Buxton's law summarises the quandary: "it is always too early (for rigorous evaluation) until, unfortunately, it is suddenly too late" [90,91].

Although randomised controlled trials are more difficult to conduct in the field of surgery than with drugs for all these reasons, several design variants have proved to be successful for overcoming some of these methodological obstacles. Nevertheless, extreme caution should also be exercised when using them given that none are free from limitations or immune to biases. Among them, parallel group non-randomised studies, controlled interrupted-time series, stepped wedge designs, expertise-based randomised trials stand out as the more frequently used alternatives to the "canonical" randomised, parallel controlled trial [81,90,92].

Tracker trials deserve a special mention, since they are especially useful when there is rapid technological change, as often occurs in the case of medical devices and surgical techniques. Their main feature is that they permit modifying experimental subgroups as the trial proceeds and new technologies arise. Since data on operator experience are collected, learning curves can be taken into account. They are, however, methodologically more complex than conventional trials [81,82,90].

Other acceptable options to the classical randomised controlled trials are pragmatic trials, which should be used when evidence from randomised controlled trials is lacking. The potential usefulness of comparative effectiveness studies in surgery needs to be highlighted. Finally, even though observational studies tend to provide estimates of larger effects than randomised controlled trials in surgery, and that in surgery between-study heterogeneity is more frequent than among trials, these studies when designed and conducted appropriately could also provide useful information as to the effectiveness and safety of new surgical techniques [5,93–95]. As with the other kinds of technologies described in this chapter, and as opposed to absolute, relative (incremental) efficacy, effectiveness, safety and cost effectiveness are most needed to be ascertained.

Lack of regulation

Despite the broad arsenal of research and evaluation methods currently available, there are no regulatory procedures for licensing surgical treatments on the basis of high-quality scientific evidence [11,81,82,84]. Under the current regulatory ethics paradigm, innovative treatments are regarded as questionable until they are framed in a research protocol with formal mechanisms of informed consent, though it can be very difficult to decide when to move from an early exploratory stage of innovation to a formal investigation [75,82]. According to the Belmont Report, the fact that a therapy is innovative does not mean that it constitutes research. It becomes research when it is formally structured as an investigation by means of a sound research protocol. This Report states that "significant" innovations should be incorporated early on in a research project in order to establish efficacy and safety while preserving its original diagnostic or therapeutic objectives [96,97]. However, this has been never translated into formal regulation.

Lack of major public or private funding for surgical research partly results from the absence of rules and barriers to market entry of surgical innovations [81], and it may persist, *ceteris paribus*, should regulators fail to pursue a broad regulatory overhaul. Surgical research should follow the same scientific, ethical and regulatory principles as drugs, devices and medical tests [82].

Due to its idiosyncratic features, determining which agencies should oversee surgical innovation and approval of new procedures is an extremely tangled issue. In this regard, both the Australian Safety and Efficacy Register of New Interventional Procedures-Surgical (ASERNIP-S) and NICE's Interventional Procedures Programme could be considered as the main references of a regulatory body nowadays [98,99].

Variations in surgery

A host of studies have long shown that the use of surgical procedures varies across regions, within countries and among countries. Many factors are associated with regional rates of surgery in different clinical contexts: differences in disease incidence, diagnostic testing with asymptomatic, subclinical or symptomatic disease, testing-treatment cascade, patient's willingness to undergo surgery. Nonetheless, regional variation of rates linked to disease burden and patient demand tend to be small, and, taken together, these factors fail to fully explain the phenomenon [100].

Differences in the extent to which surgeons factor in their treatment decisions and patient's preferences can also explain variations. The most preference-sensitive diseases are those for which surgical decisions have heterogeneous trade-offs (e.g. early stage prostate cancer-radical prostatectomy). Environmental factors play a role in explaining variations as well. The dynamics of diffusion and adoption of surgical innovations, the extension and substitution effects and how surgical trainees are taught are other key factors associated with regional variations. Financial incentives along with regulatory constraints are associated with international variations, but they are not major determinants of regional variations within countries with common reimbursement and regulatory rules (regions may have high rates for some procedures but not for others – the extent to which specific procedures vary within countries is consistent, and little correlation exists between a region's use of surgical procedures and its overall use of healthcare) [100].

These factors notwithstanding, the main reasons for variation of these rates are physician's beliefs, attitudes, motivations, even enthusiasm, technological fascination, clinical discretion and schools of thought about the indications of surgery, those of physicians who refer patients to surgeons, as well as the style with which physicians practice (the so-called surgical signature). Variations can be high or low without translating necessarily either appropriate or inappropriate use of procedures or surgeons breaking the rules of scientific evidence or infringing upon clinical guidelines. As to the methods intended to reduce unwarranted variations, the scientific evidence collated is scanty, and it only allows the suggestion that some strategies can reduce variation [100–105].

Proposals for improving and integrating regulation

There are no "one-size-fits-all" rules or standards for regulating surgical innovation. The way innovation occurs in surgery cannot be substantially changed due to its idiosyncrasies. The methods for its assessment, appraisal and evaluation have to be adapted to them. Attempting the opposite is far-fetched. However, despite its singularities, the assessment of surgery has many commonalities with other complex, pharmacological and non-pharmacological interventions. Measures presented in the last section of this chapter are intended to provide some groundwork for improving and integrating its regulation.

Indispensable Measures for Improving and Integrating Regulatory Reform of Drugs, Medical Devices, Diagnostic Tests and Surgical Innovations

The untenable notion that reinforcing pre-approval regulatory control mechanisms stifles innovation and delays patients' access to technologies that are potentially beneficial to their health has become platitudinous. Once again, the trade-off should always favour assurance of efficacy, safety, quality and cost effectiveness of health technologies based on an appropriate evidence level and commensurate with the risk profile [1,2]. Delayed access should be weighed against potentially harmful, premature adoption of medical technologies owing to imperfect information.

Table 4-1. Measures for improving and integrating the regulation of drugs, medical devices, diagnostic tests, and surgical innovations.

Area of improvement	Drugs	Medical devices	Diagnostic tests	Surgical innovations
Principles governing regulation	Regulation should be evidence-based, self-improving, timely, and achieve participation of all stakeholders			
Assessment, appraisal, coverage, pricing, reimbursement	Coordinate and harmonise these functions and assign them to public, independent, technically competent agencies, that include expert clinicians and foster cross-fertilisation among all stakeholders			
Governance	Apply relevant governance criteria to regulation: voice and accountability, government effectiveness, regulatory quality, rule of law, control of corruption			
Unequivocal identification of technology	ATC codes	ICD codes	ICD codes	ICD codes
Risk classification	All technologies should be accurately and reliably classified on the basis of the risks they pose to health			
Decision criteria on approval, coverage, reimbursement, disinvestment	Relative efficacy, safety, and effectiveness, and incremental cost effectiveness	Relative efficacy, safety, and effectiveness, and incremental cost effectiveness	Relative efficacy, safety, effectiveness, and incremental cost effectiveness, as well as analytical validity, clinical validity, and clinical utility. Biomarkers should be validated and qualified before approval. Apply a phased evaluation based on principles of randomised controlled trials	Relative efficacy, safety, and effectiveness, and incremental cost effectiveness. Apply a phased evaluation based on recommendations included in the Innovation, Development, Exploration, Assessment, Long-term follow-up (IDEAL) model
Insufficient evidence	Use conditional approval schemes and selective reimbursement, and make them contingent upon notification			
Postmarket surveillance	Strengthen surveillance systems in all steps of development and post-adoption, and foster the study of clinical variations and comparative effectiveness			
Value-based principles	Value-based assessment and pricing models ought to be further developed and gingerly applied in tandem, considering new theoretical developments			
Social efficiency	Minimise social costs and inefficiencies due to externalities, send unequivocal signals regarding innovation, social values and willingness to pay, bring incentives into line and make them consistent with the objectives of regulatory overhaul			

The current regulatory framework is plagued with negative externalities. In some cases it seems that regulation is being introduced more in response to industry demand than to redistribute health and wealth. Putting aside the fact that patents, intellectual rights and other incentives to research and development have been called into question, governments should apply clear rules to the game, comply with governance principles and thus counter the effects of the influence of interest groups. In all likelihood, there are ways to attain this without stifling innovation. The fact that the measures for improvement are well known delegitimises the current standstill, those who pay lip service to them or delay their implementation.

It should not be forgotten that undue incentives and other factors drive clinicians to over-diagnose and over-treat: these can include fee for service, performance measures that encourage volume over value, defensive medicine, technological fascination and a weak regulatory system. Even though large majorities favour reducing unnecessary care, a small fraction support ending fee-for-service. As Upton Sinclair put it, "It is difficult to get a man to understand something, when his salary depends upon his not understanding it" [53,56].

Finally, different proposals and models regarding value-based pricing have been used with drugs. They are currently under development and streamlining. Therefore, they need to be carefully assessed, scrutinised and fully justified before ushering them into practice [6,7,106,107]. The risk of winding up with airy-fairy theory lacking practical application is not negligible as well as its associated opportunity costs. This caveat notwithstanding, the use of full-blown value-based pricing should be fostered with medical devices, diagnostic tests and surgical innovations.

There are no "one-size-fits-all" rules or standards for a comprehensive regulatory overhaul. Contrarily, they should be tailored to the specific technology, area, clinical context and in some instances to the individual patient. Nonetheless, certain measures should be regarded as commonalities and indispensable for regulatory reform (Table 4-1). It should be emphasised that the regulatory overhaul should be multilevel, meaning that it should include government intersectoral actions (health, legislation, economy, commerce), central and local levels of government, public and private sectors, and several stakeholders. There is no reason not to apply the following decalogue of principles and standards to all four types of medical technologies.

1. The regulation (including adoption and diffusion phases as well as disinvestment) of drugs, devices, diagnostics and surgical innovations should be evidence-based, self-improving, timely, accountable, and achieve the participation of all stakeholders.

2. Assessment, appraisal, approval, coverage, reimbursement and pricing of these four groups of technologies are compartmentalised, highly variable, heterogeneous, and their borders are blurred. Medical technology regulatory and assessment agencies and authorities have overlapping and ill-defined functions. Too many regulatory guidelines undergo frequent amendment. Therefore, there is an impending need to coordinate and harmonise their approval and licensing by agencies that are public, independent, highly competent, that include expert clinicians and promote collaboration (cross-fertilisation) among all stakeholders.

3. The application of governance criteria to the regulatory activity should be guaranteed in all key phases of the policy-making process. Patients should be kept informed, their autonomy to make their own choices should be respected, health il-

literacy should be combated vigorously and patient participation in the deliberative and decision-making regulatory processes should be assured. Professionalism in all instances of the regulation at macro, meso and micro levels should be promoted. Accountable, transparent and conflict of interest-free regulatory bodies should be guaranteed. Regulatory capture, revolving doors, conflict of interests and conceal-ment of risks and detrimental side effects require special oversight. The reporting of competitive performance and benchmarking should be made mandatory.

4.   A unique identifier and an International Classification of Diseases (ICD) code should be assigned on a timely basis to every medical device, diagnostic and new surgical procedure. Comprehensive, reliable, internationally harmonised and permanently updated registries of real innovations are of paramount importance.

5.   Clear and reliable algorithms should be used to classify these technologies in ac-cordance with their health risk profiles, and appropriate mechanisms should be instated for rapid detection of hidden risks.

6.   Decisions on approval, coverage, reimbursement and disinvestment for these technologies should be based on stringent criteria of relative (not absolute) effica-cy, safety, quality and incremental cost effectiveness. As for diagnostics, including biomarkers, omics and diagnostic companions, decisions should not be limited to their accuracy, but should also specifically embrace their analytical validity, clinical validity and clinical utility. Due validation and qualification of biomark-ers should be assured. The efficacy and safety of certain technologies, such as informatics programmes that support medical decision making or clinical algo-rithms, should also come under scrutiny, together with that of devices consisting of a combination of mechanical, biological and pharmacological components, given their rising emergence onto the market. Reducing heterogeneity in these evaluation methods is a key issue. High-quality randomised controlled trials should be required for all drugs and class III devices, for diagnostics (includ-ing biomarkers and companion diagnostics) and surgical procedures whenever it is deemed necessary. The use of composite and surrogate variables as primary endpoints should be minimised, and fuzzy terms and jargon such as "reasonable assurance," "substantially equivalent", "probable benefits", and "significant surgi-cal innovation" should be abolished.

7.   When evidence on efficacy, effectiveness, safety and quality is scarce or insuffi-cient, value of information analysis should be used to ascertain opportunity costs of both premature and delayed introduction of innovations, as well as to estimate if the value of information that would be obtained is worth its costs. Conditional approval schemes of the sort employed for drugs should be used (i.e. only in research, coverage with evidence development). All resources necessary to make them cogent and to overcome known barriers for their deployment and compli-ance should be provided, and transferring their inherent risks to patients and tax payers should to be avoided. Notification of all the information needed for both conditional approval schemes and postmarket surveillance should be encour-aged, and reimbursement under such schemes should be made contingent upon notification.

8.   Post-surveillance for all these technologies should be strengthened, and surveil-lance systems at all steps of development and post-adoption of complex and high-

risk diagnostics and surgical procedures need to be in place. Regular surgical audits to take account of mortality, morbidity, quality standards and monitoring health outcomes should be performed. Homogeneous and consistent national or international evidenced-based surgical quality improvement programmes and guidelines should be applied in order to reassure quality, reduce unwarranted variations, inform effectiveness and cost-effectiveness evaluations, and estimate over- and underuse on a regular basis. Incentives to promote their appropriate use and avoid overuse should be created. Clinical variations and comparative effectiveness research should be promoted to gather evidence in the postmarket phase.

9. As for insurance, co-insurance and copayment, rigorous value-based pricing schemes should be established. Value-based assessment and value-based pricing principles and models should be further developed, and gingerly and consistently applied in tandem, taking into consideration recent expanded assessment criteria such as proportional shortfall and wider societal benefits.

10. The social costs and inefficiencies owing to the negative externalities of undue regulation must be minimised. Responsible value-based (not commercial) innovation should be encouraged and rewarded. Clarification of the blurred signals payers send out with respect to social values and willingness to pay for drugs, devices, diagnostics and surgical innovations is required. Incentives need to be brought into line, and made consistent with the objectives of regulatory overhaul.

Acknowledgements

I would like to thank Vicente Ortún, Juan del Llano, Juan Carlos Valdovinos and Juan José Artells for their useful comments on an earlier version of this chapter.

This book was supported by an unrestricted educational grant from Celgene.

REFERENCES

1. Eichler HG, Bloechl-Daum B, Brasseur D, Breckendridge H, Leufkers H, Raine J, et al. The risks of risk aversion in drug regulation. Nature Revs Drug Discover. 2013;12:907-15.
2. Bauer P, Köning F. The risks of methodology aversion in drug regulation. Nature Revs Drug Discover. 2014;13:317-8.
3. Guo JJ, Pandey S, Doyle J, Bian B, Lis Y, Raisch DW. A review of quantitative benefit-risk methodology project for assessing drug safety and efficacy-report of the ISPOR risk-benefit management working group. Value Health. 2010;13:657-66.
4. European Medicines Agency (EMA). Benefit-risk methodology project. Work package 5 report: field tests. 2001. Available at: http://www.ema.europa.eu/docs/enGB/documentlibrary/Report/2011/09/WC500112088.pdf.

5. Mestre-Ferrándiz J, Deverka P, Pistollato M, Rosenberg E. The current drug development paradigm: Responding to US and European demands for evidence of comparative effectiveness and relative effectiveness. London: Office of Health Economics; 2014.

6. National Institute for Health and Care Excellence, Centre for Health Technology Evaluation. Value based assessment of health technologies. London: NICE; 2014.

7. Van de Watering EJ, Stolk EA, van Exel NJA, Brouwer WBF. Balancing equity and efficiency in the Dutch basic benefits package using the principle of proportional shortfall. Eur J Health Econ. 2013;14:107-15.

8. Cohen D, Billingsley M. Europeans are left to their own devices. Br Med J. 2011;342:d2748 Available at: http://www.bmj.com/content/342/bmj.d2748.pdf%2Bhtml.

9. McCulloch P. The EU's system for regulating medical devices. Br Med J. 2012;345:e7126 Available at: http://www.bmj.com/content/345/bmj.e7126.pdf%2Bhtml.

10. Coombes R. Europe's plan to tighten regulation of devices will not reach US standards. Br Med J. 2012;345:e6303. Available at: http://www.bmj.com/content/345/bmj.e6303.pdf%2Bhtml.

11. Plum J, Campbell B, Lyratzopoulos G. How guidance on the use of interventional procedures is produced in different countries: An international survey. Int J Technol Assess Health Care. 2009;25:124-33.

12. Barkun JS, Aronson JK, Feldman LS, Maddern GJ, Strasberg SM, for the Balliol Collaboration. Surgical innovation and evaluation 1. Lancet. 2009;374:1089-96.

13. Banta D. Dissemination of Health Technology Assessment. In: del Llano-Senarís J. Campillo-Artero C, dir. Health technology assessment and health policy today: a multifaceted view of their unstable crossroads. Barcelona: Springer Healthcare; 2014:147-56.

14. Viscusi WK, Vernon JM, Harrington JE. Economics of regulation and antitrust. Boston: MIT Press; 1995.

15. Institute of Medicine. Public health effectiveness of the FDA 510(k) clearance process: measuring postmarket performance and other selected topics: workshop report. Washington, DC: National Academies Press; 2010.

16. Institute of Medicine. Public health effectiveness of the FDA 510(k) clearance process: balancing patient safety and innovation: workshop report. Washington, DC: National Academies Press; 2010.

17. Institute of Medicine. Medical devices and the public's health. The FDA 510(k) clearance process at 35 years. Washington, DC: National Academies Press; 2011.

18. Kmietowocz Z, Cohen D. Device licensing bodies sometimes put business before safety, and investigation finds. Br Med J. 2012;345:e7138.

19. Challoner DR, Vodra WW. Medical devices and health—creating a new regulatory framework for moderate-risk devices. New Engl J Med. 2011;365:977-9.

20. Kramer DB, Xu S, Kesselheim AS. Regulation of medical devices in the United States and European Union. New Engl J Med. 2012;366:848-55.

21. Curfman GD, Redberg EF. Medical devices—balancing regulation and innovation. New Engl J Med. 2011;365:975-7.

22. Campillo-Artero C. A full-fledged overhaul is needed for a risk and value-based regulation of medical devices in Europe. Health Pol. 2013;113:38-44.

23. Fox DM, Zuckerman DM. Regulatory reticence and medical devices. The Milbank Quarterly. 2014;92:151-9.

24. Sorenson C, Drummond M. Improving medical device regulation: The United States and Europe in perspective. The Milbank Quarterly. 2014;92:114-50.

25. The Commission of the European communities. Council Directive 93/42/EEC of 14 June 1993 concerning medical devices. Available at: http://eur-lex.europa.eu/LexUriServ/site/en/consleg/1993/L/01993L0042-20031120-en.pdf; 2012.

26. Wilmshurst P. The regulation of medical devices. Unsatisfactory, unscientific, and in need of a major overhaul. Br Med J. 2011;342:d2822. Available at: http://www.bmj.com/content/342/bmj.d2822.

27. US Government Accountability Office. Testimony before the special committee on aging, U.S. Senate. Medical devices. FDAs premarket review and postmarket safety efforts. Washington, DC: GAO; 2011.

28. Fraser AG, Krucoff MW, Brindis RG, Komajda M, Smith Jr SC. Commentary: International collaboration needed on device clinical standards. Br Med J. 2011;342:d2952.

29. Cohen D. EU approval system leaves door open for dangerous devices. Br Med J. 2012;345:e7173.

30. European Commission. Communication from the Commission to the European Parliament, the Council, the European Economic and Social Committee and the Committee of the Regions. Safe, effective and innovative medical devices and in vitro diagnostic medical devices for the benefit of patients, consumers and healthcare professionals. COM(2012) 540 final; 2012.

31. Resnic FS, Normad SL. Postmarketing surveillance of medical devices – filling in the gaps. New Engl J Med. 2012;365:875-7.

32. Henegan C, Thompson M, Billingsley M, Cohen D. Medical device recalls in the UK and the device-regulation process: retrospective review of safety notices and alerts. Br Med J Open. 2011;1:e000155.

33. Horton R. Offline: a serious regulatory failure, with urgent implications. Lancet. 2012;379:106.

34. Helfand M. Web exclusive White paper series on diagnostic test evaluation. Med Dec Making. 2009;29:634-5.

35. Lord SJ, Irwig L, Bossuyt PMM. Using the principles of randomized controlled trial design to guide test evaluation. Med Dec Making. 2009;29:E1-E12.

36. Lijmer JG, Leeflang M, Bossuyt PMM. Proposals for a phased evaluation of medical tests. Med Dec Making. 2009;29:E13-E21.

37. Annes JP, Giovanni MA, Murray MF. Risks of presymptomatic Direct-to-consumer genetic testing. N Engl J Med. 2011;363:1100-1.

38. Lumbreras B, Parker LA, Porta M, Pollán M, Ioannidis JPA, Hernández-Aguado I. Overinterpretation of clinical applicability in molecular diagnostic research. Clin Chem. 2009;55:786-94.

39. Korf BR, Rehm HL. New approaches to molecular diagnosis. JAMA. 2013;309:1511-21.

40. Institute of Medicine. Genome-based diagnostics: Clarifying pathways to clinical use: Workshop Report. Washington, DC: The National Academies Press; 2012.

41. Bossuyt PM, Reitsma JB, Bruns DE, Gatsonis CA, Glasziou PP, Irwig LM, et al. The STARD Statement for reporting studies of diagnostic accuracy: Explanation and elaboration. Clin Chem. 2003;49:7-18.

42. Whiting P, Rutjes AWS, Reitsma JB, Bossuyt PM, Kleijnen J. The development of QUADAS: a tool for the quality assessment of studies of accuracy included in systematic reviews. BMC Med Res Methodol. 2003;3:25.

43. Lumbreras B, Porta M, Márquez S, Pollán M, Parker LA, Hernández-Aguado I. QUADOMICS; An adaptation of the quality assessment (QUADAS) for the evaluation of the methodological quality of studies on the diagnostic accuracy of "-omics"-based technologies. Clin Biochem. 2008;41;1316-25.

44. Lumbreras B, Porta M, Márquez S, Pollán M, Parker LA, Hernández-Aguado I. Sources of error and its control in studies on the diagnostic accuracy of "-omics" technologies. Proteomics Clin Appl. 2009;3:173-84.

45. Lumbreras B, Porta M, Márquez S, Pollán M, Parker LA, Hernández-Aguado I. QUADOMICS; An adaptation of the quality assessment (QUADAS) for the evaluation of the methodological quality of studies on the diagnostic accuracy of "-omics"-based technologies. Clin Biochem. 2008;41;1316-25.

46. Parker LA, Gómez N, Lumbreras B, Porta M, Hernández-Aguado I. Methodological déficits in diagnostic research using "-omics" technologies: Evaluation of QUADOMICS tool and quality of recently published studies. PloS ONE. 2010;5(7): e11419. Doi:10.1371/journal.pone.0011419.

47. Ransohoff DF. How to improve reliability and efficiency of research about molecular markers: roles of phases, guidelines, and study design. J Clin Epidemiol. 2007;60:2205-19.

48. Beastall GH. Adding value to laboratory medicine: a professional responsibility. Clin Chem Lab Med. 2013;51:221-7.

49. Bossuyt PMM, McCaffery K. Additional patient outcomes and pathways in evaluations of testing. Med Dec Making. 2009;29:E30-E38.

50. Trikalinos TA, Siebert U, Lau J. Decision-analytic modelling to evaluate benefits and harms of medical tests: uses and limitations. Med Dec Making. 2009;29:E22-E29.

51. Laine C. High-value testing begins with a few simple questions. Ann Intern Med. 2012;156:162-3.

52. Siwek J, Lin KW. Choosing wisely: more good clinical recommendations to improve health care quality and reduce harm. Am Fam Phys. 2013;88:164-8.

53. Dyer O. The challenge of doing less. Br Med J. 2013;347:f5904 doi: 10.1136/bmj.f5904.

54. Elshaug AG, McWilliams JM, Landon BE. The value of low value lists. JAMA. 2013;309:775-6.

55. Qaseem A, Alguire P, Dallas P, Feinberg LE, Fitzgerald FT, Horwitch C, et at. Appropriate use of screeing and diagnostic tests to foster high-value, cost-conscious care. Ann Intern Med. 2012;156:147-9.

56. Beckman RA, Clark J, Chen C. Integrating predictive biomarkers and classifiers into oncology clinical development programmes. Nature Revs Drug Disc. 2011;10:735-48.

57. Lumbreras B, Ibern P. La regulación de los biomarcadores y su papel en la medicina estratificada. Gest Clín Sanit. 2010;12:122-5.

58. Zolg JW, Langen H. How industry is approaching the search for new diagnostic markers and bio-markers. Mol Cell Proteomics. 2004;3:345-54.

59. Mattes W, Gribble Walker E, Abadie E, Sistare FD, Vonderscher J, Woodcock J, et al. Research at the interface of industry, academia and regulatory science. Nature Biotechnol. 2010;28:432-3.

60. Editorial. Biomarkers on a roll. Nature Biotechnol. 2010;28:431.

61. Sistare FD, Dieterle F, Troth S, Holder DJ, Gerhold D, Andrews-Cleavenger D, et al. Towards consensus practices to qualify safety biomarkers for use in early drug development. Nature Biotechnol. 2010;28:446-54.

62. Hutson S. To save lives, initiative pushes for standardized diagnostic tools. Nature Med. 2010;16:11.

63. Mayor S. Whole genome sequencing fails to predict risk of most common diseases. Br Med J. 2012;344:e2535.

64. Howard HC, Borry P. Direct-to-consumer pharmacogenomics testing. Pharmacogenomics. 2011;12:1367-70.

65. Kitsios GD, Kent DM. Personalized medicine: not just in our genes. Br Med J. 2012;344:e2161.

66. Hudson KL. Genomics, health care, and society. N Engl J Med. 2011;365:1033-41.

67. Towse A, Ossa D, Veenstra D, Carlson J, Garrison L. Understanding the economic value of melecular diagnostic tests: Case studies and lessons learned. J Pers Med. 2013;3:288-305.

68. Towse A, Garrison L. Economic incentives for evidence generation: Promoting an efficient path to personalized medicine. Value Health. 2013;16:539-43.

69. Begley CG, Ellis LM. Drug development: raise standards for preclinical cancer research. Nature. 2012;483:531-3.

70. O´Donnell CJ, Nabel EG. Genomics of cardiovascular disease. N Engl J Med. 2011;365:2098-109.

71. Porta M, Hernández-Aguado I, Lumbreras B, Crous-Bou M. "Omics" research, monetization of intelectual property and fragmentation of knowledge: can clinical epidemiology strengthen integrative research? J Clin Epidemiol. 2007;60:1220-5.

72. Institute of Medicine. Refining processes for the co-development of genome-based therapeutics and companion diagnostic tests. Workshop Summary. Washington, DC: The National Academies Press; 2014.

73. Garau M, Towse A, Garrison L, Housman L, Ossa D. Can and should value based pricing be applied to molecular diagnostics? London: Office of Health Economics; 2012.

74. Fang C, Otero HJ, Greenberg D, Neumann PJ. Cost-utility analyses of diagnostic laboratory tests: A systematic review. Value Health. 2011;14:1010-18.

75. McKneally MF, Daar AS. Introducing new technologies: Protecting subjects of surgical innovation and research. World J Surg. 2003;27:930-5.

76. Biffl WL, Spain DA, Reistma AM, Minster RM, Upperman J, Wilson M, et al. Responsible development and application of surgical innovations: a position statement of the Society of University Surgeons. J Am Coll Surg. 2008;206:1204-9.

77. Chang DC, Matsen SL, Simpkins CE. Why should surgeons care about clinical research methodology? J Am Coll Surg. 2006;203:827-30.

78. Roskin DJ, Longaker MT, Gertner M, Krummel TM. Innovation in surgery. A historical perspective. Ann Surg. 2006;244:686-92.

79. Meakins JL. Surgical research: act 3, answers. Lancet. 2009;374:1039-40.

80. Ellis H. The Cambridge Illustrated history of surgery. Cambridge: Cambridge University Press; 2009.

81. McCulloch P, Altman DG, Campbell WB, Flum DR, Glasziou P, Marchall JC, et al. No surgical innovation without evaluation: the IDEAL recommendations. Lancet. 2009;374:1105-12.

82. Ergina PL, Cook JA, Blazeby JM, Boutron I, Vlacien PA, Reeves BC, et al. Challenges in evaluating surgical innovation. Lancet. 2009;374:1097-104.

83. Wahr JA, Prager RL, Abernathy JH, Martinez EA, Salas E, Seifert PC, et al. Patient safety in the cardiac operating room: Human factors and teamwork. A scientific statement from the American Heart Association. Circulation. 2013;128 doi:10.1161/CIR.0b03e3182a383fa.

84. Sitges-Serra A. Technology or technolatry: where are surgeons going? Cir Esp. 2012;90:156-61.

85. Wente MN, Seiler CM, Uhl W, Buchler MW. Perspectives of evidence-based surgery. Dig Surg. 2003;20:263-9.

86. Solomon MJ, LcLeod RS. Clinical studies in surgical journals—have we improved? Dis Colon Rectum. 1993;36:43-8.

87. Balasubramanian SP, Wiener M, Alshameeri Z, Tiruvoipati R, Elbourne D, Reed MW. Standards of reporting of randomized controlled trials in general surgery. Can do we better? Ann Surg. 2006;244:663-7.

88. Dindo D, Demartines N, Clavien PA. Classification of surgical complications: a new proposal with evaluation in a cohort of 6336 patients and results of a survey. Ann Surg. 2004;240:205-13.

89. Clavien PA, Barkun J, De Oliveira ML, Vauthey JN, Dindo D, Schulick RD, et al. The Clavien-Dindo classification of surgical complications. Five-year experience. Ann Surg. 2009;250:187-96.

90. Lilford RJ, Braunholtz DA, Greenhalgh R, Edwards SJL. Trials and fast changing technologies: the case for tracker trials. Br Med J. 2000;320:43-6.

91. Buxton MJ. Problems in the economic appraisal of new health technology: the evaluation of heart transplants in the UK. In: Drummond MF, ed. Economic appraisal of health technology in the European Community. Oxford: Oxford University Press; 1987.

92. Cornu C, Kassai B, Fisch R, Chiron C, Alberti C, Guerrini R, et al. Experimental designs for small randomized clinical trials: an algorithm for choice. Orphanet J Rare Dis. 2013;8:48. Available at: http://www.ojrd.com/content/8/1/48.

93. Shikata S, Nakayama T, Noguchi Y, Taji Y, Yamagishi H. Comparison of effects in randomized controlled trials with observational studies in digestive surgery. Ann Surg. 2006;244:668-76.

94. Ioannidis P, Haidich AB, Pappa M, Pantazis N, Kokori SI, Tektonidou MG, et al. Comparison of evidence of treatment effects in randomized and nonrandomized studies. JAMA. 2001;286:1887-92.

95. Russell I. Evaluating new surgical procedures. Br Med J. 1995;311:1243.

96. Strasberg SM, Ludbrook PA. Who oversees innovative practice: Is there a structure that meets the monitoring needs of new techniques? J Am Coll Surg. 2003;196:938-48.

97. US Department of Health and Human Services. The Belmont Report. Ethical principles and guidelines for the protection of human subjects of research. Washington, DC: DHHS; 1979. Available at: http://www.hhs.gov/ohrp/humansubjects/guidance/belmont.html.

98. Maddern G, Boult M, Ahern E, Babidge W. ASERNIP-S: International trend setting. ANZ J Surg. 2008;78:853-8.

99. National Institute for Health and Clinical Excelence. Interventional procedures programme. Methods guide. London: NICE; 2007.

100. Birkmeyer JD, Reames BN, McCulloch P, Carr AJ, Campbell WB, Wennberg JE. Understanding of regional variation in the use of surgery. Lancet. 2013;382:1121-9.

101. McCulloch P, Nagendran M, Campbell WB, Price A, Jani A, Birkmeyer JD, et al. Strategies to reduce variation in the use of surgery. Lancet. 2013;382:1130-9.

102. Birkmeyer JD. Progress and challenges in improving surgical outcomes. Br J Surg. 2012;99:1467-9.

103. Birkmeyer JD, Sharp SM, Finlayson SRG, Fisher ES, Wennberg JE. Variation profile of common surgical procedures. Surgery. 1998;124:917-23.

104. Wright JG, Hawker GA, Bombardier C, Croxford R, Dittus RS, Freund DA, et al. Physician enthusiasm as an explanation for area variation in the utilization of knee replacement surgery. Med Care. 1999;37:946-56.

105. Editorial. Variation in surgery and surgical research. Lancet. 2013;382:1071.

106. Claxton K, Longo R, Longworth L, McCabe C, Wailoo A. The value of innovation. York: Centre for Health Economics, University of York, Leeds University, School of Health and Related Research, University of Sheffield; 2009.

107. Paris V, Belloni A. Value in Pharmaceutical pricing, OECD Health Working Papers, No. 63. Paris: OECD Publishing; 2013.

PART II: ISSUES

Four Issues in Cost-Effectiveness Analysis and Health Technology Assessment: a View from the Touch-line

Anthony J. Culyer

Introduction

Like many fathers and grandfathers, I have spent long hours in bad weather on touch-lines urging on bunches of muddy little – and not so little – knots of boys and girls in amateur soccer league matches (in my case it has been almost exclusively soccer – a game I never played myself). That is how I feel these days about CEA, or economic evaluation. The field may not be exactly muddy and the players not so little, and this is a game I once tried myself to play, but I am essentially an onlooker these days. If there are sides to support, I'm not sure which side I'm on, but there are things to notice and often it's easier to see them from the touch-line than it is in the thick of play.

I shall discuss four matters that I have noticed from the touch-line: the uncertain nature of cost-effectiveness analysis, the specificity and generalisability of CEA results, QALYs vs DALYs, and the perspective from which CEAs ought to be done.

Issue 1: Cost-Effectiveness Analysis – What Is It?

Definitions

If you look up 'cost-effectiveness analysis', 'cost-utility analysis' and 'health technology assessment' in the Health Technology Assessment international (HTAi) Glossary [1], this is what you find:

Cost-Effectiveness Analysis (CEA)

An economic evaluation consisting of comparing various options, in which costs are measured in monetary units, then aggregated, and outcomes are expressed in natural (non-monetary) units.

J.E. del Llano-Señarís and C. Campillo-Artero (eds.), *Health Technology Assessment and Health Policy Today: A Multifaceted View of their Unstable Crossroads*, DOI 10.1007/978-3-319-15004-8_5

Cost-Utility Analysis (CUA)

*An economic evaluation consisting of comparing various options, in which costs are measured in monetary units and outcomes are measured in utility units, usually in terms of utility to the patient (using quality-adjusted life years, for example). **Note:** This is a form of cost-effectiveness analysis in which the effectiveness of an option is adjusted on the basis of quality of life.*

Health Technology Assessment (HTA)

*The systematic evaluation of the properties and effects of a health technology, addressing the direct and intended effects of this technology, as well as its indirect and unintended consequences, and aimed mainly at informing decision making regarding health technologies. **Note:** HTA is conducted by interdisciplinary groups that use explicit analytical frameworks drawing on a variety of methods.*

I dare say each of us could quibble about these definitions – let alone those of the profusion of other related approaches of analysis: benefit-cost analysis (BCA), budget-impact analysis (BIA), comparative effectiveness research (CER), cost-benefit analysis (CBA), cost-consequences analysis (CCA), cost-efficiency analysis (CEA), cost-minimisation analysis (CMA), cost-per-QALY analysis (CQA), cost-value analysis (CVA), distributional cost-effectiveness analysis (DCEA), extended cost-effectiveness analysis (ECEA), generalised cost-effectiveness analysis (GCEA), health intervention technology assessment (HITA), health technology assessment (HTA), intervention cost-effectiveness analysis (ICEA), relative effectiveness assessment (REA), sectoral cost-effectiveness analysis (SCEA), all of which are near synonyms for one another.

Health and utility

I find the distinction made between two in particular (CEA and CUA) both unnecessary and misleading. HTAi distinguishes 'natural' outcomes and outcomes adjusted for 'quality of life', which in turn is identified with the index of strength of preference that economists have traditionally called 'utility'. My distinction would be between CEA using health-adjusted life-years as an outcome and CEA using utility-adjusted life-years as an outcome. This distinction can seen in terms of an outcome Q, defined as the change in health status ΔH,

$Q = \Delta H$,
and another measure of outcome, Q' such that
$Q' = U(\Delta H)$:
the utility of a change in health status.

Q and Q' are plainly not the same thing, conceptually speaking, since one is a function of the other, which would not matter much if one were a simple multiple of the other, or a linear transformation, both of which seem improbable on any reasonable interpretation of 'utility'. An apparent confusion between the two seems to have arisen because the methods used to reveal the ranking of alternative health states, H_1 and H_2, resemble the methods for measuring $U(H_1)$ and $U(H_2)$ and thus give rise to a failure to perceive the difference between statements like $H_1 > H_2$, and statements like $U(H_1) > U(H_2)$. The usual methods (standard gamble, time trade-off and person trade-off) all utilise a notion of 'equivalence' or 'indifference' when comparing states of health described in terms of people's capabilities (such as ability to tie shoelaces) and feelings (such as pain or lassitude), which suggests that the methods might be used to create indifference or 'iso-utility' curves. Analysts slide all too easily between the proposition that H_1 and H_2 are equally healthy or unhealthy, which is a relatively objective observation, though one nonetheless embodying value judgements[1], and a supposition that they have equal utility, which is a subjective evaluation of strength of preference over the states. If the subject of the experiment is being asked to express a prefer-ence for one over the other, then it is appropriate to interpret the revealed numbers as $U(H_1)$ and $U(H_2)$ but if, instead, the subject is asked to rank states in terms of *more or less health*, which is what our ministers of health commonly ask us to do (amongst other things), then an entirely different type of judgement is being required. In that case it is a matter of (rela-tive) construct validity or, perhaps better, 'construct plausibility', and it does not necessarily follow that states judged to be equal in terms of health are also states between which one is 'indifferent', having no ordered preference.

By 1987 Drummond et al. [2] had established a usage that has dominated the litera-ture ever since. In 2002 Gold et al. [3] could write "When the denominator of the CE ratio is computed using QALYs, the cost-effectiveness analysis is referred to as cost-utility analysis" (p. 117). It remains nonetheless an unfortunate convention. I do not believe that most of us truly believe that the CE ratios we commonly play with can be represented as $\Delta C/\Delta U(H)$. We think of them more naturally as $\Delta C/\Delta H$. In all likelihood, the econo-mist's expectation is that the marginal (private or social) utility of H falls as H increases $(\partial^2 U/\partial Q)/\partial Q^2 < 0)$. Unless it does not and is constant, it is hard to see how readily $\Delta U(H)$ maps on to ΔH. The same applies if we think in terms of marginal rates of substitution rather than marginal utilities. If we think of health maximisation at all, we think we are maximising H [4] rather than $U(H)$. It would be good to discover whether, and under what circumstances, the distinction matters empirically. I would judge that it would not matter with respect to mere measurement if the health measure and the utility measure were related by a constant ratio but the distinction would still matter conceptually and for policy purposes because the utilitarian interpretation immediately causes the norma-tive element – the social value judgements – to be interpreted as a matter of *preference*. Indeed, many of our official agencies recommend in their Reference Cases that the out-come measure *ought* usually to be founded on preferences – presumably those of patients or patients-to-be but this is plainly a political choice and one to which such agencies are

---

1   By 'relatively objective' I mean that descriptive vignettes of the sort commonly used in the usual measures are usually observable (like someone's ability to fasten shoelaces) and scalable (can do it faster or more competently than another person, or than they were last week by the same person) while the value judgements come in when applying weights to the various 'dimensions' of the vignettes in order to make an overall judgement of their 'state of health' and in assigning numbers to those overall states that indicate how much more or less health one state represents compared with another. Using values is inescapable but they do not have to be preferences. I imagine them to be social value judgements made by accountable decision makers concerned to reflect a view of the social good in their decisions.

entitled, I presume, to make. The textbooks, however, ought to leave the question open: maybe preferences are an appropriate basis, and maybe potential patients are the appropriate judges, especially if the process of CEA is conceived essentially by decision makers as one that mimics that of a well-functioning market; or maybe not, as when the basic value judgements of decision makers relate to people's ability (or capability) to live as full lives as health permits, achieve life's goals and, in general, to flourish as human beings. The main purpose of health care is to enable them to do that whether or not it also makes them as satisfied as can be, or have the maximum utility possible, or be deliriously happy.

To flourish as a human being is not the same thing as to maximise one's utility (preferences, happiness, etc.). One may flourish by doing things or having things (though flourishing can hardly only be about 'doing' or 'having') that one would *prefer* not to do or have but that one thinks (or someone thinks) one *ought* to do or have. Moreover, judgements about the contribution that better health may make to flourishing are not only not a matter of subjective preference; they may also be matters on which it is better that the judgement be an accountable external one and maybe even an expert one, partly on the ground that most individuals are poorly informed about the complex links between health care, health and flourishing and partly on the ground that the context for the contribution of economic evaluation is typically one of public policy, in which publicly accountable agencies are required to make the required judgements about what is best for society. They may or they may not wish to base these judgements on the preferences of the people. The matter is for decision makers to decide and for analysts to elicit the choice from them.

Thus, it is abundantly clear that removing preference-based value judgements from the measured comparison of health states would not remove the need for judgement to be exercised, nor does it mean that values are not being expressed, nor does it remove the need to choose whom it is appropriate to do the judging and valuing. What is different is that the choices are sequenced differently: first value judgements have to be made about the characterisation of states of health (identifying the various dimensions), second value judgements have to be made as to whether the states compared can be ranked or judged to be equivalent as 'health states' using values that are not necessarily preferences (whether they are is a matter for decision makers); third, numbers entailing values are attached to states deemed equivalent, or not as the case may be. Fourth, social values (weights) may attach to these numbers according to who is in the various states ('children', 'mothers', 'bread-winners', those 'near death' ...) which effectively amount to judgements about fair interpersonal discrimination. In an easy case the comparison may be made between states defined entirely in terms of changes in mortality or life expectancy, with each cause accorded an equal weight, and the valuation by weighting such changes according to specific characteristics (like 'child', 'mother', etc.). The more sophisticated case includes physical and mental functioning (often called 'health-related quality of life'). With quantitative scores attaching to descriptive states of health multiplied by the change in time expected to be spent in such states, and then again applying social values in the form of weights ($w > 1$ in the case of those in whose favour it is wished to discriminate and $w < 1$ in cases when one wishes to discriminate against). Again, these are political judgements about which it seems better for general textbooks, context-free Reference Cases and other 'how to do it' methodological guidance to *require that the choice be made* (and even offer assistance to help decision makers make it) but *not to prescribe the answer*. Only when the Reference Case is context specific - specifically one required by a legitimate authority, such as the board of an insurance agency responsible to its owners or its members, or a government setting standards for decisions about technologies included in the 'benefits bundle', or (possibly) a donor wanting to ensure that its aid funding is spent according to its criteria rather than the clients' criteria - does it seem appropriate for the political values to be explicit, specific and laid down in advance.

Cost-effectiveness analysis what's in and what's out

The needless proliferation of terms alluded to earlier for which we already have perfectly satisfactory labels like 'cost effectiveness' or 'economic evaluation' is a modern irritant [5]. I presume it must have some usefulness, if no more than to create reputations for inventors of neologisms. But definitions like HTAi's have a more interesting light to shed than semantics and etymology. If you look at them closely, you see that they are graduated, moving from the specific to the general. Thus, CEA is *economic* and deals in outcomes expressed in *natural units*, CUA is also economic but deals in *adjusted* outcome measures (I would call them 'measures of health or health gain' rather than 'utility' or 'quality of life'). HTA is silent on 'economic', though the word 'systematic' may include the 'economic', whatever that may be; it also includes indirect and unintended consequences, implying that neither CEA nor CUA is interested in them (surely not true); and it is explicitly located in a decision making context, suggesting that CEA and CUA are context-free procedures (surely not!). Just for good measure, our lexicographers throw in the feature that HTA procedures are 'multi-disciplinary', implying that CEA and CUA are not or, at any rate, are somewhat less 'multi-disciplinary' (dubious).

Making definitions is not an easy thing to do[2] so I do not want to take the authors of the HTAi definitions too much to task. I can see what they are getting at. HTA is broader in scope than CUA which in turn is broader than CEA. There are questions to pose about this broadening of scope, which is important for the future of any of these methods, whatever the label attaching to them. But before addressing them, let us note that the HTAi graduation can be taken a good deal further. For example, HTA is not only essentially multi-disciplinary, it is – or ought to be – multi-professional and, even more broadly, multi-stakeholder. (I shall not define 'stakeholder' here, nor, indeed, shall I define 'profession'). Moreover, it is plain that, from the beginning, the CEA of health technologies has required inputs from clinicians, epidemiologists and biostatisticians and so has never been considered a single-disciplinary activity. It is also the case that CEA (and CUA) have for long been considered – at least by their more reputable practitioners – to be *aids to* rather than *substitutes for* thought, where the thinking is ultimately that of decision makers in public and private health insurance agencies. At one level they are charged with determining formularies and the insured bundle of services and, hence, technologies. At a higher level they determine the characteristics of systems (such as universal healthcare) and the use of other technologies (a term now being used in a very broad sense) that may not be conventionally seen as a part of 'healthcare' but which are nonetheless determinants of health that can be adjusted and compared for their impact on the health of populations, technologies such as supporting effective early parenting, improving workplace

---

2   My own lexicographic efforts are in [6].

health and safety, improving the housing stock, enhancing immigrants' language skills, and reducing child poverty.

So it must be decided what is in the scope and what is out. What is not necessary is for every gradation of inclusion or exclusion to require a relabelling of the analysis. 'Economic evaluation' or 'cost-effectiveness analysis' will do.

Now to my questions: what *are* the important extensions to the most basic sort of CEA that we ought to be developing? Regarding the study of indirect and unintended consequences, we have early starts in the form of impacts on people's financial circumstances, such as the avoidance of future major private healthcare expenditures [7,8] a significant part of which is concerned with assessing the value of risk reduction. There is behavioural cost-effectiveness analysis [9,10] that addresses issues to do with the behaviour of professionals, patients and other players as determinants of cost effectiveness. There is the work of NICE and other agencies on facilitating implementation of guidance and recommendations [11]. There is also a burgeoning literature on what is variously called 'distributional cost-effectiveness analysis' [12] or 'extended cost-effectiveness analysis' [13], which aims to provide relevant information for decision makers about the consequences in terms of fairness of an investment or disinvestment for the distribution of health cost burdens or health itself.

Cutting across these substantive additions to the costs and benefits considered to be within the scope of CEA is the question of how best they might be combined or 'added up' in the presence of evidence of widely variable precision, relevance and completeness, some of which is quantitative and some qualitative, some agreed and some disputed, and some of which entails directly conflicting values, as when successful anti-smoking campaigns prove to be cost-effective ways of reducing exposure to cancerous agents but also widen health disparities by being more effective with better educated population groups. To help us here, we have algorithmic mathematical programming approaches [14], Multi-criteria Decision Analysis [15], or Multi-criteria Optimisation [16]. Finally, there is the literature on the design of the decision-making processes which give effect to all of the foregoing [17].

Of the various questions these trends raise, five are of particular interest:

- Is there a limit to the addition of 'extensions', at which point considerations that may be of relevance to those making policy judgements are additional to, and separate from, CEA?
- Where do these various 'extensions' within CEA come from and do they really address the concerns of policy decision makers in the developed world and the low and middle income countries (LMICs)?
- What mechanisms are used, or are being developed, to ensure that the scoping of CEAs (with whatever 'extensions') is fit for purpose?
- How best may we combine the various elements through a decision rule or set of rules?
- Independently of the answers to the foregoing (or maybe not independently of them) what set of general principles are best for designing the decision-making context: the participants in the process and the design of the process itself?

Answering these questions will answer the existentialist question "what is CEA?" Of course, *there may be more than one answer* because inclusion or exclusion will depend, in part, on specific contexts of culture, history and political aspiration. In such cases case are we back again into the morass of labelling? I would hope not for it may be that there is only one answer, which is that CEA is a flexible concept, like extra-welfarism, capable of adaptation to a variety of contexts and derived from a variety of health-related social welfare functions. If that really is the answer, then the most important thing is not to find a label different from 'CEA' or 'economic evaluation' but simply to be explicit about the large variety of scopes and procedures that are available, all of which are 'in the family' of CEA, and to make a selection from the variety the first task of analysis in any given analytical situation.

Issue 2: How Specific, How General?

The foregoing idea of CEA permits great variation from study to study according to context: local budgets, system characteristics, social value judgements and constraints; but is nonetheless grounded in context-specific appraisals of technologies to support decision makers in specific jurisdictions. More general is what Murray and colleagues [18] call 'sectoral CEA' and 'generalised CEA'. These are not identical but each addresses similar problems, like sub-optimisation through the exclusion of some comparator technologies (such as unrelated cost-ineffective interventions) and the difficulty of generalising from one context (say a middling wealthy country) to another (say a poor sub-Saharan country). The first problem is akin to the famous parable of Jesus Christ: "why beholdest thou the mote that is in thy brother's eye, but considerest not the beam that is in thine own eye? Or how wilt thou say to thy brother, Let me pull out the mote out of thine eye; and, behold, a beam *is* in thine own eye? Thou hypocrite, first cast out the beam out of thine own eye; and then shalt thou see clearly to cast out the mote out of thy brother's eye" (St Matthew's gospel, 7: 1-5). Giving attention only to motes when beams abound is not normally the best way to focus one's attention. The second is akin to focusing all one's attention on the features that makes each person an individual to the neglect of the many features that they share through their common humanity and which may therefore form the basis for relevant inter-jurisdictional comparisons.

Sectoral CEA proceeds (a) by conscious removal of the more common *differentiating* features of jurisdictions so as to make the result of any CEA more or less context-free and (b) through the *grouping* of interventions so that the results for each group are representative of each member, such as the use of antibiotics in general for a particular disease, or the use of general platforms for the delivery of immunisation programmes. This need not mean reducing the epidemiological evidential database to include only interventions that are efficacious but it would mean reducing it to indicators of 'representative' effectiveness. Similarly, it does not mean ignoring all costs, whether internal or external, but it does mean including only such cost categories as are commonly met in jurisdictions across which decision makers may want to be able to generalise. Its application in a specific context plainly requires qualitative judgements about the adjustments that might need subsequently to be made in order for local decision makers to have reasonable confidence that their decisions will on balance improve local health care efficiency or the fairness in the distribution of financial burdens and health outcomes. It is easy to imagine that having to make such adjustments would cause the approach to lose most if not all of its claimed cost-saving features. The presumption is, of course, that this way of doing CEA will be a less resource-intensive method in terms of research and analytical skills than bespoke CEA and that it will not seriously prejudice the quality of the process and its outcome. My guess is that the sectoral approach is likely to be most applicable when it is least needed – in very poor countries where the technologies in question are relatively simple clinical interventions whose cost effectiveness is well-known and the outcome is appropriately measured in terms of life-years (unadjusted) – and least applicable when it is most needed – when the technologies are complex, costly, involve several interventions together or sequentially, and which may not be clinical in nature, as when modes of delivery or patterns of finance are at issue, or that are matters for disinvestment rather than investment. Its use in complex technologies in poor countries (technologies such as delivery platforms for multiple vaccination programmes, training and support programmes for surgical assistants, or the trade-off between a universal programme of benefits without copays and a universal programme with a wider range of benefits and copays) may mean that the context-dependency becomes too great for sectoral CEA to help much.

Generalised CEA proceeds in similar fashion but with the additional twist that the decontextualisation is extended by having a standardised comparator, which is not 'usual practice' or 'another intervention' but 'natural history without intervention'. Again, we do not know how frequently decision makers in specific countries will want comparators that are specific to their practice patterns rather than placebo or no intervention at all.

Both sectoral and generalised CEA address real issues. The key question is whether they are the best way of addressing them. There are, after all, alternatives, including the use of generalised epidemiological/social models of the determinants of health, expert opinion to identify likely interventions for disinvestment, and the creation of regional 'clubs' for jurisdictions which judge themselves to be sufficiently similar to permit a shared common context and possibly even a shared analytical advisory resource platform. It remains to be demonstrated that sectoral and generalised CEA actually are less resource-intensive than more bespoke methods. The ultimate test must surely be the judgement of the end users: the jurisdictional decision makers and their advisers. The null hypothesis that sectoral and generalised CEA are relatively ineffective is doubtless difficult to refute. Putting the burden of 'proof' the other way round is no less daunting. However, these are not good reasons for failing to put them to the empirical test.

Issue 3: Quality-adjusted Life-years *Versus* Disability-adjusted Life-years – Can There Be a Winner?

It is surprising that there is no really satisfactory critical comparison of QALYs and DALYs that can account for the asymmetry of their use (the former mostly in the developed world, the latter mainly in the LMICs) and assign to either an appropriate role in the measurement of population health (or disability) or in the economic evaluation of interventions that are expected to increase health (decrease disability). It is a nice question as to whether the matter can be settled only by a "new paradigm" [19] or whether the differences are matters of convenience that are interchangeable without changing the basic character of either, or whether, setting these differences aside, one is no more than the reciprocal of the other [20].

DALYs (that is, measures using that label) were originally constructed for the purpose of quantifying disease burden, while the primary intention of QALYs was to measure intervention effects. However, as far as intervention effects in LMICs are concerned, use of DALYs easily dominates that of QALYs, while the reverse is true of applications in the wealthy countries. This merely locates a motivation on the one hand and a customary practice on the other and is hardly a substantive distinction, though one that surely calls for an account. The fact, moreover, that there is little dialogue between the DALY users and the QALY users must be regarded as unfortunate and again calls for explanation. Both are topics, perhaps, in the sociology of health economics, a better grasp of which might enable the generation of more permeable membranes between the QALY silo and the DALY silo.

The DALY was introduced in Box 1.3 of the 1993 World Health report by the World Bank and the World Health Organization and later by Murray [21]. It made only passing (and incorrect) reference to the QALY and provided no account of its necessity on account of deficiencies of the QALY (see the critique by Williams [22] and the side-stepping response [23]). This was the account given in 1993: the number of years of life lost was defined as the difference between the actual age at death and the expectation of life at that age in a low-mortality population. For disability, the incidence of cases by age, sex, and demographic region was estimated on the basis of community surveys or, failing that, expert opinion. The number of years of healthy life lost was then obtained by multiplying the expected duration of the condition (to remission or death) by a weight that indicated the severity of the disability. The death and disability losses were then combined, and future years of healthy life were valued at progressively lower levels by discounting and by age weights reached by consensus, so that years of life lost at different ages were given different relative values. The value for each year of life lost rises steeply from zero at birth to a peak at age 25 mainly due to parental responsibilities, and then declines gradually with increasing age. Since then it seems that the DALY has come somewhat closer to the QALY, for example, by using the results of experiments in which lay people rather than 'experts' made pairwise comparisons between states.

As far as QALYs are concerned, an early quality adjustment to life-years was made in 1968 [24] though the term 'quality-adjusted life-years' was not used. A full statement of the standard gamble methodology for deriving 'health values' of days was by Torrance [25], though he did not use the term 'quality-adjusted life-year' either. A precursor of the EuroQol version was Culyer et al. [4] where an economic 'state-of-health indicator' was propounded and which was not necessarily preference-based. At this stage of development of outcome measures, no one was in any doubt that what was being measured was H (health) not U(H). The first use of 'quality-adjusted life-year' (QALY) was by Zeckhauser & Shepard [26], who certainly wrote as neologists and advocated use of the standard gamble. The various experimental alternatives for the QALY calibration (visual analogue scaling, standard gamble, time trade-off and person trade-off) have been well-explored over many years with much attention being given to the nature and proper source of the values embodied in the measure itself, in the making of interpersonal comparisons of H [or U(H)], and to assumptions like constant proportional time trade-off and constant marginal rates of substitution.

QALYs and DALYs plainly have much in common. Trivially, both go beyond the mere consideration of changes in mortality as a measure of benefit. Trivially again, the DALY focuses on bad things to be averted (though two life-years are to be preferred to one of equal disability) and the QALY on good things to be gained. This may be no more than a convention about signage. It seems to be an intrinsic characteristic of the DALY that it commonly (though not invariably) attributed different weights to life-years lived at different ages whereas it is an open question for QALYs whether externalities, such as the better care of dependents, should be accounted for by weighting the measure according to age or by taking explicit account of the externality as a differentiable benefit. The DALY does seem to be intrinsically limited to disability viewed as a "reduction in human function" [21] whereas all versions of the QALY have a more comprehensive set of attributes, loosely described by some as 'health-related quality of life' or 'dimensions'. However, as Linus Jönsson has pointed out to me, both DALYs and QALYs assign a weight to account for morbidity and assume additivity between weighted morbidity and mortality. Both claim that weights incorporate an element of 'social preference'. The only difference may now be how the weights for health states (and age groups) are constructed – but the specific method for estimation of weights is not intrinsic to the QALY concept. So, if the same health state weights and age weights are used, ΔH would be identical irrespective of whether QALYs or DALYs were used to compute it.

The idea that the one is no more than the reciprocal of the other is easily seen by means of a simple figure (Figure 5-1). The vertical axis on the left measures increasing health and that on the right measures decreasing disability. The horizontal axis measures time spent in various states of health or disability. Suppose that an individual's health profile is initially that indicated by P_1, indicating total health up to death at t_4 as area A (I set aside any need for discounting). With this profile, an individual spends $0t_1$ in state h_2, $t_1–t_2$ in state h_3, etc. Suppose also that the expected impact of an intervention is to change P_1 to P_2 with death occurring at t_5. Taking the QALY approach, the life-time health gain is the difference between the areas under the two profiles, i.e. the shaded area C. In an economic evaluation comparing this intervention with another, the differential health benefit (ΔH) would be the difference between the benefits (areas like C) predicted from each intervention and this provides the denominator of the ICER. Now view the matter from the DALY approach. The profiles are again P_1 and P_2. We now add a distinctive feature of DALYs: a "target" life expectation (which has been the subject of much discussion in the literature) shown as T in the figure. The "burden" of the condition is the sum of the areas B and C: the difference between a lifetime (0T) of full health and the health actually experienced (area A). The introduction of the intervention again generates the profile P_2 and the burden falls to area B: the difference between a lifetime of full health and the health actually experienced with the intervention (A+C). The net gain is thus again area C in terms of reduced disability years, exactly equivalent to the net gain viewed from the QALY side. The DALY is thus the reciprocal of the QALY. Note that this result does not depend on the choice of T for T > t_5, arbitrary though this is.

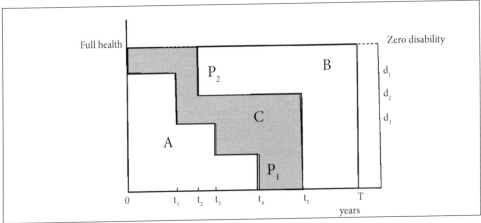

Figure 5-1. Symmetry of health outcome under QALYs and DALYs.

We are driven, I think, to the conclusion that any differences between QALYs and DALYs that may be of consequence for health policy lie, at the individual level, in the scope of the terms "quality of life" and "disability" (both of which are somewhat variable within the literature of each), the experimental means used to elicit trade-offs between the elements defined in the scope (again variable within each tradition and indeed substitutable between them), and the weights used (and the method of their derivation) to score the combinations. At the population level, again differences may arise as to how individual QALYs and DALYs are added up, with what weights (e.g. according to social role) but none of these characteristics seem to be *intrinsic* to either QALYs or DALYs. Airoldi and Morton demonstrate that having T dependent on the expectation of life at the time of death (t_4 or t_5) makes the predicted benefit under DALYs different from that under QALYs and even that a paradox can occur by which the DALY method predicts an increase in DALYs (i.e. a bad outcome) for a health increasing intervention. This seems to be a good ground for scepticism about the value of the DALY approach that uses a death-dependent target life expectation but does not destroy the legitimacy of a DALY that avoids it.

My conclusion – as an outside observer – is that the differences between QALYs and DALYs are, with the exception of the death-dependent DALY approach, of little more significance than those between alternative ways of calculating QALYs or of the various versions of DALYs. The historical question remains – what was the point of introducing DALYs as an alternative to QALYs in the first place and the sociological question also remains – why the silos? The policy question also remains – are DALYs more suited to research and policy in LMICs and QALYs to research and policy in rich countries? I personally can't see it.

Much commentary seems to me to have been misplaced. For example, it is not true, as asserted by Murray [21], that the DALY is to be preferred on account of the fact that the value judgements embodied in it are more explicit, for they are neither more nor less explicit than those embodied in the QALY. Nor is it a fair criticism of DALYs, as claimed by Anand & Hanson [27], that use of a standardised maximum life expectancy in excess of those commonly met in LMICs implicitly assumes that healthcare interventions are the only means through which the existing expectations of life can be lengthened. The DALY assumes no such thing. It is no advantage, contrary to Robberstad [20], of the QALY (standard gamble style) that its measurement takes account of risk aversion. The gamble merely introduces a bias in the measure against the uncertain experimental prospects compared with the 'sure thing', which has nothing whatsoever to do with any real world uncertainty about treatment outcomes or any other attribute of an intervention or its comparator.

QALYs and DALYs are both vulnerable to unfair criticisms. For example, the interpersonal value judgement that in summing health over individuals a set of non-unity weights ought to be applied according to their future life expectation is a value judgement that either (or neither) concept, DALY or QALY, can in principle embody. It is unfair to castigate either for embodying a value that is not one's own: a disagreement about policy rather than about the rival merits of QALYs and DALYs. But some criticisms apply equally. For example, some complain that DALYs reduce 'death' merely to zero functioning, while the QALY hardly scores strongly by allowing in principle that there can be 'states worse than death'. There are also a number of issues concerning both QALYs and DALYs when used as measures of disease burden as distinct from health benefits of health-affecting interventions. Particularly that they – and other measures – do not rank states of health consistently [27].

Attention is sometimes drawn to the difference in the estimation methods used in QALYs and DALYs [28]. Thus, the DALY was based on a universal set of standard weights based on expert opinions whereas QALYs are commonly derived from experimentally elicited preferences. But this difference was again not intrinsic and in any case has not applied since 2010. One could equally have DALYs constructed from experiments and QALYs from expert judgements. Moreover, it is not evident that the one method is superior to the other. One might reasonable ask, as I did above, why the QALY (or DALY) should be based on people's *preferences* for health states as distinct from their judgement, or experts' judgements, or socially accountable people's judgements about the construct validity of alternative states ('has one more or less *health* than the other' rather than 'is one more or less *preferred* than the other'). Dan Hausman [29] believes that the first of these questions is a nonsense if 'health' is taken to be a value-free concept. In this he is surely right. The questions then become 'what kind of values?' and 'is there a role for individual preferences?' The answers are likely to be context-dependent, hanging on history and culture, the authority and accountability of the decision maker, whether the analysis is done at the behest of an aid donor or an aid recipient, the prevalence of notions of 'solidarity' & 'communitarianism' within the jurisdiction of application, as well as convenience and practicality. What ought to be clear, however, is that the answers are not for analysts or textbook writers. Their proper tasks are to get the questions right and to help decisions makers to find the answers that are right for them.

I think we need some impartial guidance. Are there circumstances when the DALY is to be preferred to the QALY? Are there issues of practicability and ease of use that should be our concern? Are there issues of communication and the effectiveness of Knowledge Transfer and Exchange that favour one over the other? We have come a long way since the nuanced judgement of Gold & Muennig [30] that: "DALYs were primarily intended to document information about the comparative health of populations. Accuracy and responsiveness to more nuanced changes in health status at the individual level were less important than accumulating a database that could provide reliable data with respect to the descriptive epidemiology of fatal and nonfatal health outcomes. At their start, QALYs focused on the evaluation of medical intervention… [and] placed a greater emphasis on issues such as measure responsiveness, sensitivity and reliability" (p. 129-300). The passage of time has blurred these differences but we now still have two more or less independent streams of analysis that rarely intersect. The principal benefit that I anticipate is, therefore, that we might be able to derive a set of principles that suggest the circumstances under which one is likely to be more useful than the other so that they will each turn out to be complementary: each will have a role for which it is particularly suited and we will have a clear understanding of why that is so. My historical and sociological questions remain to be answered. Answering them may indicate ways of making permeable the thick membranes that currently seem to clothe our solos.

Issue 4: Societal Perspective – Is There No Alternative?

It is commonly asserted that the appropriate perspective from which a CEA ought to be conducted is the societal perspective. That view is expounded in well-known texts [2,31–33].

There seems to be one good argument for the societal view and it is this: only if the societal approach is adopted will decision makers be confronted with a full information set of the costs and consequences of alternative actions; anything less comprehensive will necessarily be subject to omitted variable bias, probably of unknown sign and size, causing either over- or under-investment in new technologies (as well as in old ones) as judged by the potential Pareto criterion. But there are some persuasive counter arguments.

(1)   *To insist upon the societal perspective is to ignore the information costs of CEA*

Conscientiously to search out the most precise estimates of *all conceivable* costs and consequences of a decision, which is what the societal perspective requires, is to presume that the value of the expected improvement in the quality of the decision in question (somehow measured) is always and everywhere greater than the cost of acquiring the additional information that turns a 'narrow' perspective into a societal one. This point seems so evident that it scarcely needs further elaboration: what economist could conscientiously so disown the marginal balancing of cost and benefit as applied to the practice of CEA itself? Nor does the argument depend on any specific *source of valuation* of the additional information, which may or may not be 'societal' in the special sense of being rooted in patient preferences. Either way, in turning a 'narrow' perspective into a societal one, it is preposterous to assume that the value of the expected improvement of a decision is always and everywhere greater than the cost of acquiring the additional information that motivated the turning. But any compromise on the comprehensiveness of the dataset necessarily makes the analysis, to a greater or lesser extent, less than fully 'societal'. I therefore argue that a less than 'societal' approach is the rational approach.

The objection will be raised: this is a caricature of the argument for the societal perspective. The societal perspective requires only that analysis ought to embrace all conceivable costs and consequences *that are materially affected* by the use of the technology being evaluated and only those *whose exclusion would change the outcome* of the economic evaluation. This defence seems wanting in several respects. First, the societal approach would have to be supplemented by guidance as to how the judgement about material consequences was to be reached in advance of the data collection and analysis; second, it is hard to see how the judgement concerning the impact on outcome, which seems to require a kind of sensitivity analysis, can again be done until the data have been collected and the analysis done; third, it assumes that these judgements ought to be exercised independently of the rights and obligations of the decision makers, for example by implicitly requiring them to take account of consequences that are outside their legal or constitutional limits. This third point is taken up later. These difficulties, however, can be avoided by a simple expedient: the guidance should require decision makers to consider their position regarding each, exercising their judgement as required (some of which will be value judgements concerning the 'good society') so that the scoping of an economic evaluation be laid out as an explicit task requiring judgement and decision rather than a settled matter about which the judgement of textbook writers and eminent economists is to count for more than that of responsible decision makers. The questions must be *posed* by people like us but *answered by others*.

(2)   In any case, what is it that economists mean when they speak of a 'societal' perspective?

What is generally in their minds is, I conjecture, a specific philosophical view; one that is *consequentialist*, that is based upon *preferences*, and that is *individualistic*: one that as a matter of principle seeks to combine the preferences of consumers over all the possible consequences of the decision in question in order to make a preference ranking. Merely to state this is to call it into question as even an incomplete basis for public decision making in health policy (or, indeed, any other). This is not an argument against having regard to consequences and individuals' preferences, but one for their careful *weighing*: are ill-informed preferences to count the same as well-informed ones? Are selfish preferences to count the same as generous ones? Are preferences about processes to count the same as preferences about outcomes? Are preferences about very minor matters to be dug out as assiduously as those concerning major matters? Is experienced utility to count the same as remembered utility or decision utility? And they may also need *supplementing* as well: we may want (or decision makers may want) to be satisfied that consequences, like the greater social integration of the lonely elderly or arranging for them to have a more supportive community, which are not states of being, like 'health', are also given appropriate consideration. These consequences are *contexts* of being rather than states of being. They are often capabilities, or things necessary for people to lead satisfactory lives. And the same goes for *transformations* and *changes between states* which can themselves be causes of great good or ill aside from the states to which or from which a person is transitioning (being obliged to quit and re-apply for one's old job is hardly a consequence to be ignored, even though the starting state and the final state may be exactly the same in all respects). The same might be true of changes in the location of care or the pathway through which it is delivered; outcome may remain the same but one is unlikely to be indifferent to the manner in which the change is managed or to the kind of help (if any) one gets towards adapting to change. As healthcare shades into social care the emphasis on subtle outcomes, like being better parents, having a more cohesive and supportive community, reducing loneliness and isolation, becomes more significant. Care is often about *relationships* where what matters is the contribution that enhancements to outcomes, processes and relationships make to the social good not (yet again) as judged by economists but as judged by decision makers.

(3)   Economists do not make better social value judgements than other people

A perspective for economic evaluation is a statement of the costs and consequences, together with their distribution across people and places, which are to be taken into account. For economists to seize authority to stipulate perspectives is presumptuous in the extreme. Stipulating perspectives is not a task for which economists are equipped by technical training, by their ethical rectitude or by political authority granted through due process. Economists are often quite good at *eliciting* the implicit perspectives and values of decision makers and other stakeholders, which is a useful – indeed highly desirable – early step in any economic evaluation, but this is not at all the same as *stipulating* them. In eliciting them they may also encourage decision makers to reconsider their own presumptions and even to weigh the case for adopting a 'societal' perspective. But the process is not, or ought not to be, one of *persuading* decision makers to accept the value judgements that happen to be those preferred by the economist (or, indeed any other analyst) unless they have (very unusually) been granted that authority by a due process.

Economists frequently speak as though "efficiency" were a value-free idea. The question "Is efficiency a good thing?" invariably gets overwhelming support by shows of hands when put to classes of economics students (second undergraduate year and above). I know this, having frequently asked it. It is only after the next question: "And what about super-efficient Nazi death camps?" that hands waver and the realisation dawns that whether being efficient is a good thing depends on what one is being efficient *at*. In economic evaluations of healthcare two common presumptions are that the objective is either some generalised social welfare function or that 'health' is the (or 'a') maximand. The temptation is to treat other significant consequences that are desired outcomes (by decision makers) as constraints on efficiency. In one sense they are but they are also statements, implicit or explicit, about policy objectives. It is important that the delivery of other (costly) desirables be recognised as normally entailing an opportunity cost in terms of health but it is also equally clear that such sacrifices may also be judged to be worthwhile – or, in other words, 'efficient'!

A statement about efficiency is thus, inescapably, an assertion about what is good for society. The job of economic evaluators is not to make this judgement but to help decision makers to make it. Putting probing questions, pointing out potential conflicts and the need therefore for trade-offs, eliciting fundamental social values – all these are tasks for economic evaluation. Our job is to challenge, receive the answers, and then to do the empirical arithmetic. The middle step of these three is not to be usurped. Above all, we should not make the social value judgements. This is directly against the opinion of a notable public sector economist years ago, Ralph Turvey [33]: "...the value judgements made by economists are, by and large, better than those made by non-economists." (p. 96).

(4)   The political and constitutional context of health policy can be ignored

In virtually all jurisdictions, and for reasons well-rehearsed by health economists over many years, arrangements have been adopted to combat the anti-social consequences of unregulated healthcare finance and provision: manifest inequity of financial burdens falling disproportionately on those least able to bear them, externalities, publicness, imperfect agency, monopoly, transaction costs of insurance, arbitrary management of moral hazard and adverse selection, etc. In most jurisdictions, one consequence is the creation of ministries of health with ministers appointed by a due process and accountable, at least in democracies, to a parliament or generally elected assembly of 'society's' representatives. Governments characteristically set budgets across broad categories of economic activity (health, education, the environment, etc.) and also set the rules determining how those budgets are to be spent, the consequences to be taken into account in allocating expenditures, and the processes of accountability for decisions taken. One conspicuous consequence of these processes is that decision makers in such ministries nearly always adopt a 'narrow' perspective (or, worse, *more than one* such narrow perspective!) and even persist in it despite the arguments of economists. Two questions therefore demand an answer: how does one account for this obtuseness (if that is what it is), and by what moral argument do non-elected, unaccountable, economists set themselves above elected and accountable public officers? Those who commission CEAs usually have some form of formal accountability, for example, to senior managers in an organisation, to shareholders, to political masters, or an electorate. In such cases, their governance may require them to take a *particular* perspective of the scope of a CEA and to commission accordingly. It seems presumptuous for economists and decision analysts to offer advice that conflicts with legitimate governance arrangements.

Sometimes it is useful to adopt alternative perspectives to the societal as a kind of sensitivity analysis: would the extension to costs and effects for all society make a difference that matters? Sometimes, it may be of policy usefulness to conduct a study from the perspective of a specific stakeholder, if only to reveal possible pushback or other behaviours that, once anticipated, might be prepared for. There is an implicit in-built assumption in the advocacy for the societal perspective that a *singular* perspective is generally appropriate. However, it is easy to imagine cases where this is not the case. This is particularly so when costs and consequences are distributed across different segments of the population. For example, workplace interventions for health and safety are characterised by benefits that tend to accrue to workers and costs that tend to fall on management and owners or, after allowing for final incidence, upon consumers of the products and in part on workers themselves. In such cases it will often be useful to conduct *two analyses*: one from the perspective of management and one from that of workers. Not only may this enable decision makers better to evaluate distributional impacts but also it enables them again to anticipate pushback behaviours and again to take appropriate pre-emptive steps.

My tentative conclusion is that the emphasis on the societal perspective is misplaced. Reference cases ought to require analysts to adopt instead an *explicit* perspective and encourage them to explore with clients what that perspective ought usefully to be. A handbook of guidance on the most likely possibilities, their advantages and disadvantages, would be a most useful asset.

Conclusions

CEA suffers from an excess of zealous classifiers and typologists which has given rise to a large and unhelpful set of 'types' of CEA and to an equally unnecessary set of limitations on the use of CEA as an aid for thinking decision makers and their advisers. Some have sought to lock it into the conventional economic theory of cost-benefit analysis and the potential Pareto improvement, which has led to an unnecessary insistence on the use of preferences as the only value base for health measurement and consequently of a bastardised form of 'utility' as the maximand of CEA studies. This also leads to advocacy for a particular notion of the social good that may be at odds with the objective of supporting decision makers to achieve *their* objectives. These tendencies have generated rivalries between concepts (like HYs – healthy years, QALYs and DALYs), methods differing by their scope (like CEA, CUA, CCA) and dogmatic rigidity in insisting on particular principles rather than ones that are general and independent of the context of decision making. The alternative approach I suggest is to use an acceptable and reasonable measure of health that confronts the many layers of value that are inherent in it, so that informed choices can be made about each. Many of the developments in CEA have proceeded with little, if any, contribution from the intended users and with too little regard being given to the context of decisions and the suitability of the various processes of decision making that may be feasible and preferred in many different jurisdictions throughout the range of poor, middle-income and rich countries.

I have tried to present some reasons why so much of this is both unsatisfactory and unnecessary. Economic evaluation is commonly (and rightly) presented as *an aid* to decision making and decision makers. It is to inform and help decision makers realise *their* objectives in ways that are consistent and that use resources well. I have tried to show that economists actually manage in lots of ways to insert their own values about what is good for society. This can be done by insisting on a particular perspective (one that appears innocuous but in fact is constitutionally irresponsible), a particular approach to efficiency (one that appears again to be innocuous but that again embodies many implicit contentious social value judgements) and a particular approach to outcomes (which seems humane but that in practice imports judgements that are not for analysts to make). Economic evaluation is, or ought to be, about interrogation – interrogation of decision makers, of evidence, of experts (and indeed all stakeholders), of ideas and models – so that decision makers can form their own judgements as to the steps they will take and be more confident that those steps will deliver their objectives in ways that are manifestly well-informed, credible and defensible.

Acknowledgments

My thanks for their comments on earlier drafts to Dan Hausman, Bengt Jönsson, Linus Jönsson, Magnus Johannesson, Gisela Kobelt and Juan del Llano Señarís. They do not all agree with me, so they cannot in any way be held responsible for the eccentricity or the wrongness of my own views.

This book was supported by an unrestricted educational grant from Celgene.

REFERENCES

1. http://htaglossary.net/HomePage, accessed 19 May 2014.
2. Drummond MF, Sculpher MJ, Torrance GW, O'Brien BJ. Methods for the Economic Evaluation of Health Care Programmes. Oxford: Oxford University Press. 1987.
3. Gold MR, Stevenson D, Fryback DG. HALYs and QALYs and DALYs, oh my: similarities and differences in summary measures of population health. Ann Rev Pub Health. 2002;23:115-34.
4. Culyer AJ, Lavers RJ, Williams AH. Social indicators: health. Soc Trends. 1971;2:31-42.
5. Luce BR, Drummond M, Jonsson B, Neumann PJ, Schwartz JS, Siebert U, Sullivan SD. EBM, HTA, and CER: Clearing the Confusion. Milbank Quarterly. 2010; 88:256-76.
6. Culyer AJ. The Dictionary of Health Economics. Cheltenham: Edward Elgar. 2014.
7. Wagstaff A, Pradhan M. Health insurance impacts on health and nonmedical consumption in a developing country. ICFAI J Risk and Ins. 2005;2:44-68.

8. van Doorslaer E, O'Donnell O, Rannan-Eliya RP, Somanathan A, Adhikari SR, Garg CC, et al. Effect of payments for health care on poverty estimates in 11 countries in Asia: an analysis of household survey data. Lancet. 2006;368:1357-64.

9. Smith DL, Levin SA, Laxminarayan R. Strategic interactions in multi-institutional epidemics of antibiotic resistance. Proc Nat Acad Sci of the USA. 2004;102:3153-8.

10. Megiddo I, Nandi A, Ashok A, Prabhakaran D, Laxminarayan R. IndiaSim: An Agent-based Model for Extended Cost-Effectiveness Analysis of Secondary Prevention of Coronary Heart Diseases in India, CDDEP working paper, Washington DC: CDDEP. 2014.

11. National Institute for Clinical Excellence. Supporting the Implementation of NICE Guidance, London: NICE. 2004.

12. Asaria M, Griffin S, Cookson R, Whyte S, Tappenden P. Distributional Cost-Effectiveness Analysis of Health Care Programmes, CHE Research Paper 91, York: Centre for Health Economics. 2013.

13. Verguet S, Laxminarayan R, Jamison DT. Universal public finance of tuberculosis treatment in India: an extended cost-effectiveness analysis. Health Econ. 2014. doi: 10.1002/hec.3019. 2014.

14. Anand P. The integration of claims to health-care: a programming approach. J Health Econ. 2003;22:731-45.

15. Devlin NJ. Sussex J. (eds.) Incorporating Multiple Criteria in HTA: Methods and Processes. London: Office of Health Economics. 2011.

16. Morton A. Aversion to health inequalities in healthcare prioritisation: a multicriteria optimisation perspective. J Health Econ. (forthcoming 2014).

17. Culyer AJ, Lomas J. Deliberative processes and evidence-informed decision-making in health care – do they work and how might we know? Evidence and Policy. 2006;2:357-71.

18. Murray CJ, Evans DB, Acharya A, Baltussen RM. Development of WHO guidelines on generalized cost-effectiveness analysis. Health Econ. 2000;9:235-51.

19. Bevan G, Hollingshurst S. Cost per quality adjusted life year and disability adjusted life years: the need for a new paradigm. Expert Rev Pharma and Outcomes Res. 2003;3:469-77.

20. Robberstad B. QALYs vs DALYs vs LYs gained: what are the differences, and what difference do they make for health care priority setting? Norsk Epid. 2005;15:193-91.

21. Murray CJ. Quantifying the burden of disease: the technical basis for disability-adjusted life years. Bull World Health Organ. 1994;12:429-45.

22. Williams A. Calculating the global burden of disease: time for a strategic reappraisal? Health Econ. 1999;8:1-8.

23. Murray CJL, Lopez AD. Progress and directions in refining the Global Burden of Disease approach: a response to Williams. Health Econ. 2000;9:69-82.

24. Klarman H, Francis J, Rosenthal G. Cost-effectiveness analysis applied to the treatment of chronic renal disease. Med Care. 1968;6:48-64.

25. Torrance GW. A Generalized Cost-Effectiveness Model for the Evaluation of Health Programs: A Research Report. Hamilton: McMaster University. 1970.

26. Zeckhauser R, Shepard DS. Where now for saving lives? Law and Contemp Probs. 1976;40:5-45.

27. Anand S, Hanson K. Disability-adjusted life years: a critical review. J Health Econ. 1997;16:685-702.

28. Sassi F. Calculating QALYs, comparing QALY and DALY calculation. Health Pol Plan. 2008;21:402-8.

29. Hausman D. Valuing health. Phil Pub Affairs. 2006;34:246-74.

30. Gold MR, Muennig P. Measure-dependent variation in burden of disease estimates: implications for policy. Med Care. 2002;40:260-6.

31. Johannesson M, Jönsson B, Jönsson L, Kobelt G, Zethreaus N. Why Should Economic Evaluations of Medical Technologies have a Societal Perspective? London: Office of Health Economics. 2009.

32. Jönsson B. Ten arguments for a societal perspective in the economic evaluation of medical innovations. Eur J Health Econ. 2009;10:357-9.

33. Turvey R. Present value versus internal rate of return: an essay in the theory of third best. Econ J. 1963;73:93-8.

Measuring QALYs for HTA and Health Policy Decision Making: Bridging the Gap Between Power and Act

José-María Abellán-Perpiñán

Introduction

'Dynamic' and 'energy' are two modern words coming from the Ancient Greek words 'dunamis' and 'energeia', respectively. In times of Aristotle these terms described the tension between potency and actuality. Something can exist potentially in the sense that there is the capability that allows it to become real. In contrast, actuality denotes the fulfilment of that potentiality. Therefore, the dichotomy power-act finishes when, thanks to an activity, something merely possible becomes fully actual.

Although at first sight the previous paragraph can seem misplaced in a chapter about the measurement of quality-adjusted life-years (QALYs), it is actually meaningful since, as reported in different studies [1–3] current methods – visual analogue scale (VAS), time trade-off (TTO) and standard gamble (SG) – used to elicit quality weights, are biased. This means that health state utilities, such as they are usually elicited with these techniques, deviate in some respect from "true" individual preferences. Therefore, such valuations reflect errors and mistakes, and not only random, but also systematic.

The implication for health technology assessment (HTA) from using biased quality weights is that QALY gains are also biased, leading to wrong incremental cost-effectiveness ratios (ICERs). As shown throughout this chapter, here and elsewhere [4], methods and procedures applied to the same health states often result in values that are inconsistent with respect to each other. Inconsistencies mean that more than one utility can be assigned to any particular health state. However, the valid application of cost-utility analysis (CUA) requires that just one utility be attached to the same health state. There may be a large difference in terms of cost per QALY between using one value or another. Just as an indication of the relevance of this problem, bearing in mind the frequency with which instruments like VAS, TTO and SG are used to measure quality of life. According to Garratt et al. [5], out of 409 reports including utility instruments identified between 1990 and 1999, around 88% used, directly or indirectly, these type of methods.

© Springer International Publishing Switzerland 2015
J.E. del Llano-Señarís and C. Campillo-Artero (eds.), *Health Technology Assessment and Health Policy Today: A Multifaceted View of their Unstable Crossroads*,
DOI 10.1007/978-3-319-15004-8_6

Notwithstanding, there are studies [6–9] that have suggested feasible approaches to remove or avoid measurement biases, revealing a gap between the way health state utilities could potentially be estimated and how they are actually elicited, a gap between potency and act. The objective of this chapter is to explain how this gap can be bridged.

One possibility is to use the same measurement methods and to debias "raw" valuations ex-post, by applying corrective formulae provided by different theories. This is the case of prospect theory (PT), probably the most influential non-expected utility theory [10]. Empirical evidence [8,11] supports PT corrections, which suggests that, for example, practitioners should not use uncorrected SG utilities.

The other way is to use less biased techniques like, for example, lottery equivalent methods [9]. The so-called probability lottery equivalent (PLE) method was used by Abellán-Perpiñán et al. [9] to estimate the SF-6D scoring algorithm for Spain, which seems to be more consistent that other algorithms based on SG assessments.

The two approaches will be described in detail, being QALY interpreted throughout the chapter as a utility or preference-based measure. The view adopted in this chapter is, therefore, welfarist, though the distinction between QALYs as measures of health (the extra-welfarist view) and measures of utility is not very decisive on practical grounds.

After all, as Pinto et al. [12], state, "*All that matters is to decide whether or not the maximization of QALYs reflects the way that society wants resources to be allocated in the health sector*". The opinion of the author is that there exists some that can be called "true" preferences, which can be discovered behind individual judgements [13], and that those preferences can be represented by means of QALYs.

The chapter is structured as follows. First, the QALY concept and one of the main health state utility elicitation techniques (the SG) are described. Next, the idea of debiasing is introduced and explained how it can be applied to remove biases. Finally, an alternative (less biased) method of measuring health state utilities is presented. Discussion closes the chapter.

Quality-adjusted Life-years and Health State Utility Measurement

A QALY is the utility of living one year in full health. Hence, the whole utility corresponding to the sequence of different health states (which can be named a lifetime health profile) that people experience throughout their lives can be expressed as a number of QALYs. In this way, a typical health profile can be described as $(q_1 t_1; q_2 t_2; ...; q_n, t_n)$, where q_i stands for the health state or health-related quality of life (HRQoL) someone enjoys for t_i years. The number of QALYs attached to that profile (the utility of the profile) is computed according to this equation:

$$U(q_1, t_1; q_2, t_2; ... ; q_n, t_n) = u(q_1) \, t_1 + u(q_2) \, t_2 + ... + u(q_n) \, t_n, \tag{1}$$

where $u(q_i)$ represents the utility of health state i.

If the health status does not vary across the lifetime, then the profile is reduced to a pair (q, t), and its utility is calculated simply as:

$$U(q,t) = u(q)t \tag{2}$$

Individual preferences have to fulfil some conditions in order to be validly represented under any of the two previous equations. These conditions are of two types. On the one hand, it is assumed that the individual preference relation satisfies the axioms of some utility theory. That is to say, it is assumed that people behave according to the predictions of some model or theory.

For example, it is usually claimed [14] that the SG method is rooted in expected utility (EU) axioms. In fact, all we need to obtain the utility of a health state with the SG is to assume that respondents are EU maximisers [12]. In the SG, a permanent profile (q_1, t_1) is compared to a lottery or gamble (a risky medical treatment) yielding full health for t_1 with probability p and immediate death with probability $(1-p)$. Full health and death can be denoted as q^* and q^0, respectively. If EU is descriptively valid then we know immediately that $U(q_1, t_1)$ equals p. It is not necessary to impose any additional condition to derive the utility of the pair (q_1, t_1).

However, unless we assume that $U(q_1, t_1)$ can be decomposed in a multiplicative way (like equation 2 suggests), a new SG measurement should be performed if a different time horizon was fixed throughout the assessment. For example, imagine that to elicit the utility for health state 'fibrillation auriculaire' t_1 is set in 10 years. Unless preferences for quality and quantity of life are mutually independent, $U(fibrillation\ auriculaire, 10)$ may diverge from the utility elicited for a different duration, say, 5 years. This discrepancy would lead to a dilemma: which utility should we use in CUA?

So, an additional set of conditions is needed to (in principle) avoid that dilemma. Those conditions define the QALY model such as it is described in equations 1 and 2. Conditions for the case in which health status varies over time (equation 1) have been provided by Bleichrodt & Quiggin [15] and Abellán-Perpiñán & Pinto [16]. Assumptions to ensure the validity of equation 2 have been proposed by Pliskin et al. [17] and Bleichrodt & Quiggin [15], among others.

The key question is what happens if some of the assumptions behind QALY calculations are flawed. The QALY model described above is the so-called linear QALY model [18]. This is because the utility for life-years is assumed linear (i.e. all the years receive the same weight). This property is named under EU risk neutrality over life-years. If utility for life duration is not linear (as reported by some researchers), we can still elicit SG utilities, because the SG only requires that a multiplicative QALY model holds, i.e., $U(q, t) = u(q)$ (t). The multiplicative QALY model is still a tractable model as different empirical studies have shown [8,19].

Thus, the potential bias induced by assuming that utility for life-years is linear can be avoided by simply relaxing one of the assumptions that underlie the QALY model. Relaxing linearity makes QALY calculations a little more difficult, but they remain feasible. Nevertheless, there are other more critical biases, since they are caused by the way preferences are elicited. This means that, for example, the utility of 'back pain' can change with the way SG questions are asked. To see this, suppose that a respondent is indifferent between living 38 years in health state q and the gamble that yields 38 years in full health with probability 0.59 and immediate death with probability 0.41. Imagine now that the same individual was asked to set the number of years in state q for which would be indifferent to the previous lottery. According to EU the answer should be 38 years. In other words, preferences should be invariant to the elicitation procedure used. However, Bleichrodt et al. [11] found that, on average, the number of years stated was higher, 44 years.

This answer leads to a utility of 0.51, and a difference in terms of QALYs gained per year with respect to the first way of asking SG questions of 20%.[1] This means that spending 20% more money could be justified depending on which method of asking is used. As Pinto & Abellán-Perpiñán [4] say, this violation of procedure invariance directly affects multi-attribute utility measures based on SG measurements, such as the Health Utilities Index [20] and the SF-6D [21]. It is indeed a serious problem for QALY calculations. Next, we describe two possible solutions to this problem.

First Solution: Debiasing

There is extensive evidence [3,11,22,23] that SG measurements are upwards biased [24]. The SG typically gives higher utility scores than other methods, suggesting very extreme risk aversion. However, these values are elicited under the assumption that EU is able to describe individual preferences. If this assumption were not true then SG scores would not be descriptively valid. Unfortunately, this seems to be the case: EU does not explain reality very well [10].

A first reaction before this fact is to move to a different utility theory, a model able to explain deviations from EU. There is no utility model with greater descriptive power than prospect theory [25,26]. In this context, debiasing means that the bias (too high utilities) caused when SG responses are evaluated under EU can be removed (or at least mitigated) by assuming prospect theory (PT) instead. The following is an example to explain what is meant.

Suppose that an individual is indifferent between the certainty of living 10 years with a colorectal disease and a gamble yielding 10 years in full health with probability 0.9 and death with probability 0.1. Under EU u(colorectal disease) = 0.9. However, PT predicts that high probabilities tend to be undervalued, whereas small probabilities (probabilities typically below 0.3) tend to be overvalued. This means that 0.9 is perceived by the respondent as a lower probability, in such a way that, for example, it is processed as 0.7. In consequence, the deviation with respect to EU is 0.9 minus 0.7 = 0.2. In other words, if 0.2 is subtracted from 0.9, the result (0.7) is the utility as it was elicited free of bias. The true preference is encapsulated in this 0.7, whilst the other 0.2 represents the bias.

In fact, probability distortion, also called probability weighting, is not the only bias affecting SG measurements. Another psychological factor explained by PT is loss aversion. This phenomenon occurs because: (1) people evaluate outcomes as gains or losses relative to a reference point; and (2) losses loom larger than gains. In assessments such as those of our example, respondents usually take the outcome given in advance, i.e., (colorectal disease, 10 years), as the reference point, evaluating the best outcome of the gamble, (full health, 10 years), as a gain, and the worst outcome, death, as a loss. As losses are more heavily weighted than gains, the subjective weight given to live for 10 years with probability 0.5 is lower than that attached to dying with the same probability. The implication of this is that respondents will need a larger probability of the best lottery outcome in order to offset loss aversion. The milder the health state, the greater is the loss aversion.

---

1   If the utility is 0.59 then the benefit of a treatment that restores people to full health is 0.41 QALYs a year. On the contrary, if the utility is 0.51, the benefit is 0.49 QALYs a year.

Accepting that PT can explain these biases (probability weighting and loss aversion) the question is how we can remove them? Bleichrodt et al. [3] and Bleichrodt et al. [11] provide tractable formulae that allow analysts and practitioners to debias SG measurements. For example, and abstracting from loss aversion, according to PT the weight given to 0.9 is, as noted above, around 0.7. This value comes from assuming that probabilities are weighted, $w(p)$, according to the following equation estimated by Tversky & Kahneman [26]:

$$w(p) = \frac{p^{0.61}}{\left(p^{0.61} + (1-p)^{0.61} \right)^{1/0.61}}, \tag{3}$$

The idea of debiasing is not necessarily restricted to the SG. The same approach can be applied to other techniques, such as the VAS, for example. One serious problem with VAS measurements is that ratings are biased by contextual effects [1]. This means that the scores located onto the VAS greatly depend on the set of health states to be rated. A health state may seem milder if it is evaluated within a set that include severe states. On the contrary, it may seem more serious if it is valued next to very mild states. In a similar way that PT formulae can be used to debias SG assessments, the so-called Parducci's Range-Frequency theory [27] provides us with quantitative tools to estimate context-free values with the VAS.

With the VAS method, respondents assign categories (numbers) to health state stimuli such that succeeding categories represent equal steps in value. However, according to the range-frequency theory, characteristics of a VAS response depend on the range and frequency of other health states being rated. Therefore, the valuation of the same state may change if the stimulus range changes (e.g. 0–1 vs 0.3–0.7) or if the frequencies of the stimuli do (e.g. most of stimuli are of similar/dissimilar value to the state being rated).

Schwartz [28] applied range-frequency theory to explain contextual bias in VAS scores reported by Bleichrodt & Johannesson [1]. Robinson et al. [6] confirmed this finding in a later experiment. Both groups applied the following formula:

$$v(q_i) = w \cdot \left(\frac{c(q_i) - c(q_{min})}{c(q_{max}) - c(q_{min})} \right) + (1-w) \cdot \left(1 - \frac{rank(c(q_i)) - 1}{N - 1} \right), \tag{4}$$

where $v(q_i)$ stands for the observed VAS rating of state (q_i) with underlying context-free value $c(q_i)$ in a set of N health states, and $rank(c(q_i))$ denotes the ordinal ranking of health sate q_i within the set of stimuli, with $rank(c(q_{max})) = 1$ and $rank(c(q_{min})) = N$.

The first component on the right side of equation (4) represents the effect of the value of the stimulus (relative to the range of stimulus range), while the second component represents the effect of the rank of the stimulus (relative to the range of ranks). Parameters w and $(1-w)$ denote the weighting given to the value and rank components, respectively.

Robinson et al. [6] found significant differences between the observed (or raw) VAS scores given to the same states valued in two different contexts. For example, state S was rated significantly better when it was valued in a set with other more severe injuries than when it was valued in a set of other less severe injuries (0.574 vs 0.346). Transformed valuations according to equation (4), assuming $w = 0.5$, were, in contrast, quite similar (0.550 vs 0.441), which suggests that range-frequency theory can neutralise or at least diminish context bias.

Second Solution: Using Less Biased Methods

The framing used in SG assessments is based in the comparison of a sure or riskless outcome and a risky alternative (a lottery or gamble). As Kahneman & Tversky [25] noticed, this framing makes that people overvalue the riskless outcome in comparison to the gamble. That is to say, that one of the alternatives confronted is riskless provokes that the probability of the best outcome lottery is inflated in order to make equivalent both options.

Such "certainty effect" is substantially reduced when assessments are made by lottery equivalent (LE) methods in which no riskless outcome is involved [22,23,29]. In fact, this seems to be the main reason why violations of expected utility are less pronounced when both alternatives are risky [30].

Therefore, a way to avoid or reduce SG biases could be to use LE methods. This technique compares two risky alternatives instead of a sure outcome and a gamble. In consequence, the tendency to overvalue the riskless outcome vanishes. A fruitful application of LE methods is provided by Abellán-Perpiñán et al. [9] who estimate the SF-6D scoring algorithm for Spain from a set of direct measurements performed with a PLE method. This method asks for the probability p that makes respondents indifferent between the gamble denoted by (full health, p; death), yielding full health with probability p and death with probability $1-p$, and the gamble denoted by (full health, 0.5; q), yielding full health and the health state q with the same probability.

This framing allows us to elicit preferences for both better-than-death (BTD) and worse-than-death states (WTD). If the respondent prefers the second gamble to the first in the opening question, that is, for $p = 0.5$, it means that q is regarded as BTD. In consequence, the final probability of indifference p^* is elicited between 0.5 and 1. On the contrary, if the first gamble is preferred to the second for $p = 0.5$, then q is considered as WTD, and p^* is elicited between 0 and 0.5. Under EU, assuming the convention that the utility of full health is 1 and the utility of death is 0, the utility of the health state q is calculated as $u(q) = 2p^*-1$.

Authors such as Abellán-Perpiñán et al. [9] show PLE utilities are significantly lower than SG utilities. Five SF-6D health states were elicited in two different groups of people by means of the SG and the PLE, PLE utilities being significantly lower than SG utilities. Using the same example as before, according to this procedure, p would be 0.7 (the same value obtained above by debiasing a 0.9 probability).

A critical implication of using the PLE method is that the 'floor' (the minimum value) of the SF-6D social tariff is significantly lower than that provided by the SG. Spanish SF-6D tariff has around one-fourth of the utility distribution below 0.354, the minimum threshold of the algorithm by Brazier & Roberts [31], and the score assigned to the worst SF-6D health state is far below zero, −0.357. Hence, the new range is much more similar to that predicted by the EQ-5D model [32,33], which suggests the possibility that cost-effectiveness ratios computed by both instruments, SF-6D and EQ-5D, are closer to each other.

Another implication derived from the application of the PLE technique, is that the usual transformation of negative valuations [34] performed to ensure that utilities are bounded between −1 and +1 is unnecessary. As noted before, by construction of the framing, PLE utilities range between −1 and +1, so rescaling is not needed. This is not the case for the SG, which incorporates the possibility of eliciting utilities for health states WTD by using a different framing that that used for BTD.

If state q is regarded as WTD, the SG, in order to estimate $u(q)$, compares immediate death as a sure outcome with the lottery ((full health, q), p; (1-p) (q, t)), in which with probability p the subject recovers full health, and with probability (1−p) she suffers from health state q. If the subject is indifferent between immediate death and the gamble for $p = p^*$, then, $u(q) = -p^*/(1-p^*)$. Valuations computed in this way are not bounded from below, which can give place to skewed distributions for those health states with very large negative valuations. For example, if $p^* = 0.5$, then $u(q) = -1$, whereas if $p^* = 0.9$, then $u(q) = -9$, and if $p^* = 0.99$, then $u(q) = -99^2$.

To avoid the asymmetry between positive (bounded) utilities and negative (unbounded) utilities, the SF-6D value set adjusts raw negative utilities between 0 and −1. The problem with this transformation is that adjusted utilities are no longer "true" utilities [34], that is, they do not represent in a meaningful way the preference that was originally elicited by means of the SG. For example, the change from a condition with a raw utility of −0.5 to another with utility 0.5 means a gain of 1 QALY, but the same gain being the same starting negative value the result of a transformation would correspond to a larger improvement according to the original respondent's preferences. In effect, if −0.5 is the value obtained from the transformation proposed by Patrick et al. [34], $u(q) = -p^*$, then the raw utility equals −1. Therefore, if the health improvement is calculated with respect to the raw valuation, a QALY gain of 1.5 is obtained. All these problems are apparently solved if the framing used to ask for the indifference is the same for both better and worse health states.

Another relatively unbiased method could be the TTO. As is well-known, the TTO asks for the number of life-years x that makes the respondent indifferent living t years in health state q and living x years in full health. Apart from loss aversion, a bias that has occurred with the SG also inflates TTO valuations, there are another two potential TTO biases. Scale compatibility predicts that people give too much weight to the attribute used as response scale to establish the indifference. This means that respondents will tend to focus on life-years rather than in quality of life, in such a way that they will not be willing to trade off many years to improve quality of life. So, both loss aversion and scale compatibility have an upward effect on TTO scores. Notwithstanding, there is a third bias that has the opposite effect: it is a downward bias. This bias is produced because utility for life duration is not linear. If people actually give a lower weight to future years in comparison to near years, then TTO valuations will be underestimating the true utility. In sum, this means that QALYs should be computed as $u(q)s(t)$ and not simply as $u(q)t$, with $s(t) > t$, denoting "impatience".

As loss aversion and scale compatibility lead to an upward bias in TTO valuations, whereas utility curvature leads to a downward bias, it could be hypothesised that these competing biases may cancel out because they go in different directions. This is the conjecture of

---

2   Another problem with the computation of negative utilities is that how extreme they are depends on the unit (e.g. months, semesters, years) used by the analyst to set the indifference [35]. In the examples provided above, the units used were years.

Bleichrodt [24] and Wakker [36]. However, we do not actually know whether this happens. Van Osch et al. [37] found that TTO scores were biased upward rather than having balanced bias. They also reported that TTO values were higher than SG utilities corrected according to PT. On the contrary, Doctor et al. [38] found some evidence supporting the idea that biases in the TTO tend to cancel. Since context effects are not systematic biases because error induced by them changes with context, VAS ratings could be unbiased when contextual factors were varied iteratively over many experiments. Doctor et al. [38] compared VAS and TTO scores over many within-subject studies, finding that measurements become consistent and TTO and VAS values agree. They interpret this finding as an indication that TTO scores may be relatively unbiased within a study.

However, the TTO suffers from the same problem as the SG to measure negative utilities. A different framing is used to elicit preferences for WTD, which leads to valuations that are not bounded from below. This asymmetry between the framings used with the TTO to assess BTD and WTD states was the motivation that lead Robinson & Spencer [39] to develop the 'lead' TTO, whose feasibility was studied by Devlin et al. [35]. This procedure uses a common framing to elicit preferences for BTD and WTD states. The common framing is ensured by adding to the two alternatives posed by the traditional TTO (for BTD states) a lead time in full health. Specifically, if the two alternatives compared in the conventional TTO are:

$$\text{(full health, } x; \text{ death) vs } (q, t; \text{ death)}, \tag{5}$$

where t is the life duration used as stimulus, x is the duration that is varied until the respondent is indifferent between the two options, and death indicates that (full health, x) and (q, t) are both followed by death.

The lead TTO simply adds a common period of time in full health (the lead time) preceding each of the alternatives:

$$\text{(full health, } L_A; \text{ full health, } x; \text{ death) vs (full health, } L_B; q, t; \text{ death)}, \tag{6}$$

where L_A and L_B denotes the lead time of alternatives A and B, respectively.

Initially the lead time is the same in the two alternatives (i.e. $L_A = L_B$). Let $z = L_A + x$, so z is varied until the respondent is indifferent between alternative A and B. If at the point of indifference, $z > L_B$ then state q will be valued positively. On the contrary, if $z < L_B$ then state q will have a negative utility.

Let $w = L_B + t$, then according to Devlin et al. [35] the utility of any health state is calculated as the ratio:

$$u(q) = (z - L_B)/(w - L_B) \tag{7}$$

As Pinto & Rodríguez [40] argue, such a quotient is equivalent to assume that the linear QALY model holds for the case of non-chronic health profiles. Assuming that, we obtain:

$$u(q) = (z - L_B)/t \tag{8}$$

Which is equivalent to the expression shown in equation 7.

Discussion

It has been almost thirty years since GW Torrance published an extensive revision entitled *"Measurement of health state utilities for economic appraisal"* [14]. In this paper three measurement techniques for health state utilities are described in detail: visual analogue scale (VAS), standard gamble (SG) and time trade-off (TTO). Since then, our knowledge about errors, systematic and context-dependent, that may distort utility measurements performed with those techniques has grown largely. And this knowledge is not merely theoretical, but some quantitative tools that can be applied to neutralise or avoid biases are available. However, health state utility measurement is still mostly done by using VAS, SG and TTO methods in the same way that was described by Torrance [14]. This reveals a gap between the way that the 'U' of cost-utility analysis (CUA) could be potentially estimated and how it is actually elicited; a gap between potency and act, such as this chapter remarks in its title.

In this context, there are two ways to bridge this gap. One possibility is to use the same methods, although "raw" valuations should be corrected ex-post, by applying corrective formulae provided by different theories. This is the case of prospect theory (PT), probably the most influential non-expected utility theory. First Bleichrodt et al. [3], then later Bleichrodt et al. [11], used tractable PT formulae to debias SG measurements. There is robust evidence [8] supporting these corrections, suggesting that practitioners should not use uncorrected SG utilities.

A theory applicable to debias VAS assessments is Parducci's Range-Frequency theory [27]. There are different studies [6,28] that have shown how VAS biases vanish when observed scores are fitted according to Parducci's formula. This is a relevant finding because the VAS method has been traditionally considered in Health Economics as a "second-order" technique. Some authors [41] dispute this observation arguing precisely that context effects found in VAS valuation data can be corrected by using range-frequency theory.

An alternative course of action is to search for unbiased methods. In this vein, a promising technique is the probability lottery equivalent (PLE) method used by Abellán-Perpiñán et al. [9] to estimate the SF-6D scoring algorithm for Spain. This technique avoids the overvaluation of the certainty (the extreme dislike of gambling) that yields too high SG utilities. Although further research to explore the validity of this method is needed, it seems able to produce less biased utilities than the SG.

Both TTO and SG have an additional problem besides the biases they can produce, and this problem is how preferences for health states regarded as worse than death are elicited. Firstly, the two techniques use a different framing to assess WTD states and BTD states [14]. This asymmetry, apart from the practical problems that it may cause throughout the interviewing process, might introduce contextual effects (e.g. varying reference point) derived from the change of the framework used to elicit preferences. The framing employed to measure negative utilities leads to 'extreme' values (e.g. −39), since there is not a predefined lower bound. Moreover, how extreme the negative utilities are depends on the unit (e.g. months, semesters, years) used by the analyst to set the indifference [35]. In this way, just a few extreme values can have a great influence on mean utilities. To avoid this asymmetry, both the EQ-5D and the SF-6D value sets adjust raw negative utilities between 0 and −1. The problem with this transformation is that adjusted utilities are no longer 'true' utilities [34], that is, they do not represent in a meaningful way the preference that was originally elicited by means of the TTO and the SG. For example, the change from a condition with a raw utility of −0.5 to another with utility 0.5 means a gain of 1 QALY, but the same gain, being the same starting negative value, the result of a transformation would correspond to a larger improvement according to the original respondent's preferences.

This serious problem may be avoided if alternative methods are used. One of them is the PLE. This is a solution for decision contexts framed in terms of risk and uncertainty. Another option, for decision making in contexts of certainty, is to use the lead TTO developed by Robinson & Spencer [39]. This procedure uses a common framing to elicit preferences for BTD and WTD states. The common framing is ensured by adding to the two alternatives posed by the traditional TTO (for BTD states) a lead time in full health. Valuations elicited in this way are bounded between −1 and +1.

All the previous discussion is relevant for CUA. If QALYs are used as outcome measure in CUA then utility assessment has to be carried out so that quality weights can be assigned to health states in the analysis. As shown here and elsewhere, methods and procedures applied to the same health state often result in values that are inconsistent with respect to each other. Inconsistencies mean that more than one utility can be assigned to any particular health state. However, the valid application of CUA requires that just one utility be attached to the same health state. If not, agents would choose that ICER more convenient for their interests.

Take the case of the SF-6D, for example, in order to illustrate how biases may impact on ICERs. Given the difference in scope of the utility range provided by Brazier & Roberts' [31] tariff and that estimated by Abellán-Perpiñán et al. [9], recovering full health for the most severe health states in the latter tariff can become double the utility gain obtained in the former. Assuming that the cost increment remains constant, the same health technology would be more cost effective under the tariff based on PLE measurements than the tariff based on the SG. Thus, for the more severe conditions, the SG-based tariff is underestimating the true QALY gain. Obviously it can be argued that the difference is not so large, because we are comparing models based on different community preferences. This is true, of course, but as Abellán-Perpiñán et al. [9] point out, this fact does not explain the whole divergence: the different preference elicitation method clearly matters.

The two approaches described in this chapter to eliminate or at least reduce anomalies in health state utility measurement are not difficult to apply, since they basically respect the current way of obtaining preference-based measures. Multi-attribute utility measures like EQ-5D, SF-6D and Health Utilities Index can incorporate PT corrections, as Abellán-Perpiñán et al. [42] demonstrate. Alternatively, new and less biased methods can be used to estimate social tariffs, such as Abellán-Perpiñán et al. [9] did with the SF-6D. All in all, there are means to bridge the gap between power and act, and the available means are feasible.

Conclusions and Recommendations

The gap between traditional measurement methods (VAS, TTO, SG) used to elicit health state utilities and empirical evidence on the biases distorting those measurements can be bridged in two ways. One possibility is to use the same measurement methods and to debias "raw" valuations ex-post, by applying corrective formulae provided by different theories. Examples of quantitative corrections for the SG are prospect theory (PT) formulae proposed by Bleichrodt et al. [11]. Corrections based on Parducci's Range-Frequency theory can be applied to VAS assessments [28].

Another way to avoid biases is to search for new elicitation techniques, less biased than usual methods. In this line, a method such as the probability lottery equivalent (PLE) used by Abellán-Perpiñán et al. [9] to estimate the Spanish SF-6D preference-based scoring algorithm for Spain is a promising procedure. Further research about its validity is needed, but it seems to give more consistent results than the SG.

If we sum the evidence contrary to the SG derived from the application of PT corrections and the evidence favourable to the use of the PLE, a clear message emerges for practitioners and analysts: do not use the SG or if you do use it, do not evaluate responses by assuming expected utility (EU) but PT. If you do not want to apply quantitative PT corrections or the PLE, then, rather than use the SG, it is better to use the TTO. This is because biases that can distort TTO scores go in different directions, in such a way that they may cancel out. In other words, it is sure that the SG is biased upward while biases in the TTO may be balanced. We are not sure about the latter.

Finally, it has to be clear, that the use of different framings to measure positive and negative utilities, as is usual with the TTO and the SG, is problematic. Typical practice of rescaling negative "raw" utilities between 0 and −1 does not solve the problem, since adjusted utilities do not represent in a meaningful way the preference that was originally elicited by means of the TTO and the SG [34]. Therefore, methods that apply a common framing to elicit both positive and negative valuations are preferable. This is the case of the PLE, and also of the lead TTO developed by Robinson & Spencer [39].

This book was supported by an unrestricted educational grant from Celgene.

REFERENCES

1. Bleichrodt H, Johannesson M. An experimental test of a theoretical foundation for rating-scale valuations. Med Decis Making. 1997;17(2):208-16.
2. Bleichrodt H, Pinto JL, Abellán-Perpiñán JM. A consistency test of the time trade-off. J Health Econ. 2003;22:1037-52.
3. Bleichrodt H, Pinto JL, Wakker PP. Using descriptive findings of prospect theory to improve the prescriptive use of expected utility. Management Science. 2001;47:1498-514.
4. Pinto JL, Abellán-Perpiñán JM. When normative and descriptive diverge: how to bridge the difference. Soc Choice Welfare. 2012;38(4):569-84.
5. Garratt AM, Schmidt L, MacKintosh A, Fitzpatrick R. Quality of life measurement: Bibliographic study of patient assessed health outcome measures. British Medical Journal. 2002;324:1417-21.
6. Robinson A, Loomes G, Jones-Lee M. Visual analog scales standard gambles and relative risk aversion. Med Decis Making. 2001;21(1):17-27.
7. Abellán-Perpiñán JM, Pinto JL, Méndez I, Badía X. Towards a better QALY model. Health Economics. 2006;15:665-76.

8.   Abellán-Perpiñán JM, Bleichrodt H, Pinto JL. The predictive validity of prospect theory versus expected utility in health utility measurement. J Health Econ. 2009;28:1039-47.

9.   Abellán-Perpiñán JM, Sánchez FI, Martínez JE, Méndez I. Lowering the floor of the SF-6D algorithm using a lottery equivalent method. Health Economics. 2012;21:1271-85.

10. Starmer C. Developments in non-expected utility theory: the hunt for a descriptive theory of choice under risk. J Econ Literature. 2000;38:332-82.

11. Bleichrodt H, Abellan-Perpiñán JM, Pinto-Prades JL, Mendez-Martinez I. Resolving inconsistencies in utility measurement under risk: tests of generalizations of expected utility. Management Science. 2007;53(3):469.

12. Pinto JL, Herrero C, Abellán-Perpiñán J. QALY-based cost-effcetiveness analysis. Adler MD, Fleurbaey M, (eds). Handbook of well-being and public policy. Oxford University Press, In press.

13. Plott CP. Rational individual behavior in markets and social choice processes. Arrow KJ, Colombatto E, Perlman M, Schmidt C, (eds). The Rational Foundations of Economic Behavior: Proceedings of the IEA Conference Held in Turin Italy. St Martin's Press New York, 1996:225-50.

14. Torrance GW. Measurement of health state utilities for economic appraisal. J Health Econ. 1986;12:39-53.

15. Bleichrodt H, Quiggin J. Characterizing QALYs under a general rank-dependent utility model. J Risk Uncertainty. 1997;15:151-65.

16. Abellán-Perpiñán JM, Pinto JL. Quality adjusted life years as expected utilities. Spanish Economic Review. 2000;2(1):49-63.

17. Pliskin JS, Shepard DS, Weinstein MC. Utility functions for life years and health status. Operations Research. 1980;28(1):206-54.

18. Miyamoto JM. Quality-adjusted life years (QALY) utility models under expected utility and rank-dependent utility assumptions. J Mathematical Psychol. 1999; 43:201-37.

19. Bleichrodt H, Filko M. New tests of QALYs when health varies over time. J Health Econ. 2008;27:1237-49.

20. Feeny D, Furlong W, Torrance GW, Goldsmith C, Zenglong Z, Depauw S, Denton M, Boyle M. Multi-attribute and single-attribute utility functions for the Health Utilities Index Mark 3 System. Medical Care. 2002;40(2):113-28.

21. Brazier J, Roberts J, Deverill M. The estimation of a preference-based measure of health from the SF-36. J Health Econ. 2002;21:271-92.

22. Wakker P, Deneffe D. Eliciting von Newman-Morgenstern utilities when probabilities are distorted or unknown. Management Science. 1996;42(8):1131-50.

23. Pinto JL, Abellán-Perpiñán JM. Measuring the health of populations: the veil of ignorance approach. Health Economics. 2005;14(1):69-82.

24. Bleichrodt H. A new explanation for the difference between time trade-off utilities and standard gamble utilities. Health Economics. 2002;11(5):447-56.

25. Kahneman D, Tversky A. Prospect theory: an analysis of decision under risk. Econometrica. 1979;47:263-91.

26. Tversky A, Kahneman D. Advances in prospect theory: cumulative representation of uncertainty. Journal of Risk and Uncertainty. 1992;5:297-323.

27. Parducci A. Category judgment: a range-frequency model. Psychological Review. 1965;72(6):407-18.

28. Schwartz A. Rating scales in context. Med Decis Making. 1998;18:236.

29. McCord M, de Neufville R. Lottery equivalents: reduction of the certainty effect problem in utility assessment. Management Science. 1986;32:56-60.

30. Camerer C. Recent tests of generalizations of expected utility theory. In utility: theories measurement and applications. Edwards W (ed). Kluwer Academic Publishers: Boston MA; 1992;207-51.

31. Brazier J, Roberts J. The estimation of a preference-based measure of health from the SF-12. Medical Care. 2004;42:851-9.

32. Dolan P. Modeling valuations for EuroQol health states. Medical Care. 1997;35:1095-108.

33. Badia X, Roset M, Herdman M, Kind P. A comparison of United Kingdom and Spanish general population time trade-off values for EQ-5D health states. Med Decis Making. 2001;21:7-16.

34. Patrick DK, Starks HE, Cain KC, Uhlmann RF, Pearlman RA. Measuring preferences for health states worse than death. Med Decis Making. 1994;14:9-18.

35. Devlin NJ, Tsuchiya A, Buckingham K, Tilling C. A uniform time trade off method for states better and worse than dead: feasibility study of the 'lead time' approach. Health Econ. 2011;20(3):348-61.

36. Wakker P. Lessons learned by (from?). An economist working in medical decision making. Med Decis Making. 2008;28(5):690-8.

37. Van Osch SM, Wakker PP, van den Hout WB, Stiggelbout AM. Correcting biases in standard gamble and time tradeoff utilities. Med Decis Making. 2004;24(5):11-7.

38. Doctor JN, Bleichrodt HJ, Lin H. Health utility bias: a systematic review and meta-analytic evaluation. Med Decis Making. 2010;30:58-67.

39. Robinson A, Spencer A. Exploring challenges to TTO utilities: valuing states worse than dead. Health Econ. 2006;15(4):393-402.

40. Pinto JL, Rodríguez E. The lead time trade-off: the case of health states better than death. WP ECON 1110 Universidad Pablo de Olavide, 2011.

41. Parkin D, Devlin N. Is there a case for using visual analogue scale valuations in cost-utility analysis? Health Economics. 2006;15(7):653-64.

42. Abellán-Perpiñán JM, Sánchez FI, Martínez JE, Méndez I. Debiasing Eq-5D tariffs. New estimations of the Spanish Eq-5D value set under nonexpected utility. 2009; CENTRA Documento de Trabajo E2009/06.

CHAPTER 7

What Health Technology Assessment System Do we Really Need? A Critical Review of the Current Situation of Health Technology Assessment in Five European Countries

Juan E. del Llano-Señarís

What is Health Technology Assessment?

What is health technology assessment (HTA) and why is it important? The original intention of the introduction of HTA in the developed countries was to react to three emerging problems: the strong increase of medical costs, an unexplained variability in clinical practice and the incalculable outcome and long-term effects of many health technologies [1].

According to the European network for HTA (EUnetHTA) [2], HTA is defined as: *"...a multidisciplinary process that summarises information about the medical, social, economic and ethical issues related to the use of a health technology in a systematic, transparent, unbiased, robust manner. Its aim is to inform the formulation of safe and effective health policies that are patient-focused and seek to achieve the best value. HTA endeavours to provide a structured, evidence-based input to the policy-making process."* [3]

HTA aims to provide rationality to the launch of new health technologies into the healthcare market thereby prioritising security, efficacy, effectiveness and efficiency.

The final objective of HTA is to be a fundamental instrument for decision making with regard to health policy.

In this chapter we intend to analyse different European HTA systems and propose solutions to improve their current practice.

The Current Situation of the Health Technology Assessment System in Spain

Since the foundation of the first HTA agency in 1992, the HTA system in Spain has come a long way in terms of efficiency and equity. One of the most effective achievements was the installation of a digital platform (Agencias y Unidades de Evaluación de Tecnologías Sanitarias, AUnETS) in 2007, linking the work of the eight Spanish HTA agencies (Table 7-1, page 112) [4].

© Springer International Publishing Switzerland 2015
J.E. del Llano-Señarís and C. Campillo-Artero (eds.), *Health Technology Assessment and Health Policy Today: A Multifaceted View of their Unstable Crossroads*,
DOI 10.1007/978-3-319-15004-8_7

In October 2013, the Ministry of Health, Social Services and Equality (Ministerio de Salud, Servicios Sociales e Igualdad, MSSSI) finally approved the creation of the Spanish Network of Agencies for Health Technology Assessment (Red) aiming to: "... *generate, diffuse and facilitate the implementation of information intended to provide the basis for decision-making in the National Health System (Sistema Nacional de Salud, SNS) through networking and coordination of the different HTA agencies and entities*" [5]. It was created in order to evaluate the content of the benefits catalogue of the SNS as well as new techniques, technologies and procedures [6]. Health technologies (including "Pharmacy" and "Transport, Prostheses and Medical Devices") make up approximately 20% of the public healthcare expenses in Spain (Figure 7-1, page 113) [7]. However, there are remaining challenges.

Governance, organisation and political influence of health technology assessment

The eight HTA agencies in Spain act in a purely advisory capacity and do not participate in the implementation of decisions. They are public institutions linked to health authorities. Their budget is set by the government, but their work is carried out without conflict of interests. The agencies provide non-obligatory assessment upon request to Health Ministry and the Autonomous Communities (CCAA). Therefore, it is mainly the MSSSI and the CCAA who set the agenda. The information shared by the agencies is not binding and thus, usually does not constitute a recommendation even though it contains conclusions. The dissemination of data by the agencies and the basis of political decision making related to HTA are not public. Decision criteria are not defined and primarily follow administrative and political demands. There is an implicit threshold of EUR 30,000 per quality-adjusted life year (QALY). However, the use of thresholds and the monetary valuation of one QALY are the subject of ongoing controversial discussion [8,9].

The remit of the Spanish HTA agencies includes drugs, medical devices, clinical guidelines, activities of healthcare promotion associated with health policy, organisation and management of healthcare services and detection of emerging technologies. The latter is called Horizon Scanning and is carried out by only one agency, Axencia de Avaliación de Tecnoloxías Sanitarias de Galicia (AVALIA-T).

Determination of professionals in charge of HTA – for instance health economists, physicians, epidemiologists – as well as the inclusion of scientific societies, patients, universities and the industry in the evaluation process is part of current reorganisational measures.

Objectives

The aim of HTA in Spain is to evaluate the clinical efficacy of health technologies and the quality of available scientific data. Assessment of efficiency is carried out only by two agencies, Servicio de Evaluación del Servicio Canario de Salud (SESCS) and Unidad de Evaluación de Tecnologías Sanitarias- Agencia Laín Entralgo (UETS-ALE).

The perspective from which a certain evaluation should be conducted is not defined but the agencies tend to prioritise clinical benefits to cost-effectiveness ratios. HTA mainly applies to drugs, although a new European guideline has been recently published claiming the inclusion of other health technologies and any medical intervention [10].

Implementation of the evaluation process

In contrast to other European HTA systems, the Spanish system does not have a standardised evaluation process at present. The agencies point to working methods based on systematic review of qualified scientific evidence; with randomised controlled clinical trials being the most valuable source. Insufficient determination applies to various stages of the evaluation process from selection criteria to basic aspects of evaluation.

Explicit selection criteria – such as burden of disease, impact on resources, political and clinical importance, and relevance of technology and existence of inappropriate variability in clinical practice – have not yet been determined. Certain basic principles of quality similar to those in other countries assuredly exist, but they are not officially recorded. The minimum content of evaluation is not defined. This also applies to basic aspects of evaluation namely transparency, deadlines, revocation and participation of stakeholders.

Thus, neither the procedures and methods nor the different stages of evaluation are public. The agencies solely publish a final report. Aiming to catch up on its delay in transparency and publicity, the Red has recently started to develop respective documents pursuant to standards of the European network for health technology assessment (EUnetHTA) [2]. The agencies do not explicitly regulate revocation nor fix public deadlines with regard to the different stages of evaluation. Intervention of the three possibly affected groups – patients, professionals and the industry – is not determined. Although the agencies indicate that the involvement of these groups is a more or less common practice, there is no document that regulates its implementation and defines the rights of the stakeholders.

As mentioned above, the objective of HTA is to evaluate the clinical efficacy and the quality of available scientific data. This approach entails a major drawback as it emphasises the clinical outcome but usually excludes economic criteria. The Real Decreto Ley 16/2012 was the first bill to take up this important issue. It determines the consideration of economic criteria in the evaluation of the content of the benefits catalogue of the SNS [11]. Some agencies already consider efficiency mainly using cost-effectiveness analyses (CEA). These agencies have, however, not yet established criteria that determine the tools used for the economic evaluation. Most of the analyses define outcome variables and involve subgroup analyses, arising costs and discount rates. The most problematic methodological aspects are related to the respective approach and the absence of sensitivity analyses, incremental analyses and declaration of the source of funding [12]. The significance of QALY within the economic analysis in Spain is lower than in other countries.

Output

The eight Spanish agencies differ as well in the number of total publications (per year) as in the type of publication. Taking into consideration that we are dealing with total numbers relative to staff and budget, the Andalusian agency AETSA is the most productive, making up 28% of the total publications on AUnETS from 2006 to 2012. It is followed by the Galician AVALIA-T (17%), the Catalan AQuAS and the Canarian SESCS (both 13%) (Figure 7-2, page 114) [4]. A certain specialisation of the agencies relating to the type of publication is noticeable. Whereas AETSA has published the majority of data sheets, AQuAS and UETS have produced large parts of clinical guidelines.

The reports published by the agencies on the digital platform AUnETS are only descriptive meaning their contents are not analysed. AUnETS contains all data published by the agencies from 2006 to 2012. The total number of reports published per year increased rapidly from 2007 to 2009, followed by a sharp and continual decline. The economic crisis and the change of government have brought along massive budget cuts and insecurity amongst the HTA agencies, due to changing priorities in health policy.

The agencies produce almost as many scientific articles as HTA reports. These articles are published in journals with middle to high impact factor (1.8 on average) and mostly in Spanish (47.6%). The articles written in English are regularly listed in relevant medical databases and cited by international journals. Conversely, the HTA reports of the Spanish agencies are rarely cited [13]. This is most probably because they are written in Spanish and only contain an English summary.

Summary

There have been useful achievements in the past years regarding the organisation and evaluation process of the Spanish HTA system. The system is nevertheless somewhat prone to inefficiency, mismanagement and conflicts of interest due to lacking transparency, non-standardised evaluation processes and unpublished funding details. The agencies are very productive but the diffusion process of their products (appraisals and reviews) to the clinical scenario needs improvement. The impact of the reports on political and administrative decisions, unfortunately, remains unknown.

Table 7-1. Details about the eight Spanish health technology assessment agencies.

	AETS-ISCIII (Spain)	AQuAS (Catalonia)	OSTEBA (Basque country)	AETSA (Andalusia)
Name	Agencia de Evaluación de Tecnologías Sanitarias- Instituto de Salud Carlos III	Agència de Qualitat i Avaluació Sanitàries de Catalunya	Osasun Teknologien Ebaluazioko Zerbitzua	Agencia de Evaluación de Tecnologías Sanitarias de Andalucía
Competent authority	Ministerio de Economía y Competitividad	Servei Català de la Salut. Departament de Sanitat i Seguretat Social Generalitat de Catalunya	Dirección de Planificación y Evaluación Sanitaria. Departamento de Sanidad del Gobierno Vasco	Junta de Andalucía. Consejería de Salud. Viceconsejería
Year	1994	OTATM: 1991 AATRM: 1994 AIAQS: 2010 AQuAS: 2013	1992	1996
Web	www.isciii.es	www.gencat.cat	www.osanet.euskadi.net/osteba	www.juntadeandalucia.es/salud/servicios/aetsa

	SESCS (Canary Islands)	UETS-ALE (Madrid)	IACS (Aragon)	AVALIA-T (Galicia)
Name	Servicio de Evaluación del Servicio Canario de Salud	Unidad de Evaluación de Tecnologías Sanitarias- Agencia Laín Entralgo	Instituto Aragonés de Ciencias de la Salud	Axencia de Avaliación de Tecnoloxías Sanitarias de Galicia
Competent authority	Servicio Canario de Salud	Viceconsejería de Ordenación Sanitaria e Infraestructuras de la Consejería de Sanidad	Departamento de Salud y Consumo. Gobierno de Aragón	Servicio de Desenvolvemento de Sistemas e Avaliación de Tecnoloxías. Subdirección Xeral de Planificación Sanitaria e Aseguramento da Secretaría
Year	1995	2001	2002	1999
Web	www.sescs.es	www.madrid.org	www.iacs.aragon.es	www.avalia-t.sergas.es

Year = Year of foundation.
Source: Based on information from [1].

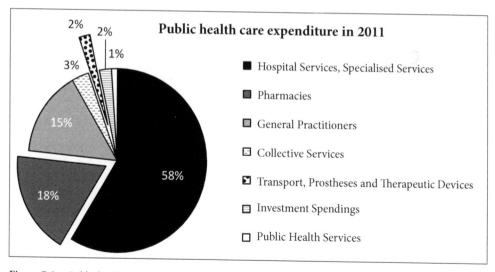

Figure 7-1. Public healthcare expenditure in Spain according to function, 2011.
Source: Based on information from [7].

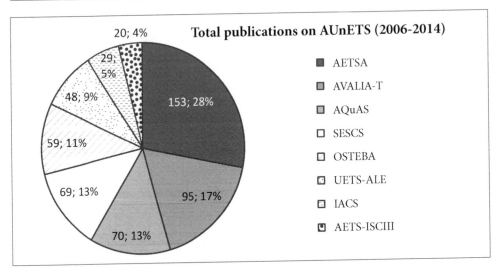

Figure 7-2. Total publications of the different Spanish health technology assessment agencies on the digital platform European network for health technology assessment (EUnetHTA) from 2006 to 2012.
Abbreviations: AETS-ISCIII, Agencia de Evaluación de Tecnologías Sanitarias- Instituto de Salud Carlos III; AETSA, Agencia de Evaluación de Tecnologías Sanitarias de Andalucía; AVALIA-T, Axencia de Avaliación de Tecnoloxías Sanitarias de Galicia; AQuAS, Agència de Qualitat i Avaluació Sanitàries de Catalunya; IACS, Instituto Aragonés de Ciencias de la Salud ; OSTEBA, Osasun Teknologien Ebaluazioko Zerbitzua; SESCS, Servicio de Evaluación del Servicio Canario de Salud; UETS-ALE, Unidad de Evaluación de Tecnologías Sanitarias-Agencia Laín Entralgo.
Source: Based on information from [4].

Health Technology Assessment in England/Wales, France, Germany, Sweden and Spain: Learning From One Another

The intention of this section is not to benchmark HTA in particular countries of the European Union (EU). The proper context of each HTA system, involving for example non-explicit guidelines, idiosyncrasy, history, political interest, professional support, legitimacy, reputation, government, participation and alliances, makes comparison difficult. Furthermore, we herein do not provide information about the budget, equipment and staff of each agency. Thus, how to compare different HTA systems? This question is taken up by one of the most important contemporary experts on HTA, Michael Drummond. In his article *Can we reliably benchmark health technology assessment organizations?* Drummond characterises 15 key points on which HTA and decision making in health policy should be based [14]. First, each agency is embedded in a particular setting impinging on the political scope and importance of HTA and thus on its practice. Second, each key point weighs differently in a particular setting. Therefore, we need to find weighting factors that can be very individual for each agency. These factors can be directly linked to the availability of resources, development of standardised procedures and international reputation.

One possible solution to the problem of comparison would be to focus on a starting point and establish a more-or-less objective process of audit based on Drummond's 15 principles. The audit should approach the problems that have been described earlier using a questionnaire adjusted to the setting of each agency. It should contain direct and polar questions in order to establish an objective evaluation that is comparable at each point. Transparency should thereby always be considered the most important aspect since the objective of comparison is to identify the best practice; and standardise and implement the lessons drawn from it.

The following descriptive evaluation topics selected are based on the book *HTA in five European countries: Learning from one another* [1]. The framework is given by the book *Ensuring value for money in health care – the role of health technology assessment in the European Union*; which was written by Drummond et al. and published by the European Observatory on Health Systems and Policies in 2008 [15].

Governance, organisation, diffusion and political influence of health technology assessment

Three out of five analysed HTA agencies in the EU act in a purely advisory capacity: The French "Haute Autorité de Santé" (HAS) [16], the German "Institut für Qualität und Wirtschaftlichkeit im Gesundheitswesen" (IQWiG) [17] and the Spanish Red. The "National Institute for Health and Clinical Excellence" (NICE) [18] in England/Wales and the Swedish "Statens Beredning för medicinsk Utvärdering" (SBU) [19] additionally have the right to intervene in a regulatory capacity. Both are authorised to take decisions related to the benefits catalogue and reimbursement of public health services. All five agencies are public institutions linked to Health Authorities. They are more or less independent from the Government and most of them dispose of established procedures to avoid conflicts of interest. In Spain the latter are currently developed. Their agenda is set by the corresponding Ministry of Health, as it demands the reports. In France however, the industry is the main contracting entity.

The remit of the agencies includes health technologies such as drugs and medical devices. In Spain and England/Wales the field of action is larger, also containing clinical guidelines, activities of healthcare promotion associated with health policy (Public Health) and detection of uprising technologies (Horizon Scanning). With regard to the latter, NICE pays special attention to interventional procedures. In Spain, organisation and management of healthcare services are also included in the HTA agenda.

All countries, except for Spain, define distinctive roles of representatives that are in charge of the different stages of the evaluation such as health economists, medical professionals and epidemiologists. Moreover, these agencies determine the influence of scientific societies, patients, universities and the industry.

NICE is by far the most transparent of all agencies. This accounts for all levels of the HTA process. Amongst others, the dissemination of data and the basis of political decision making related to HTA are entirely public. With regard to this, Spain is a step behind.

The measure of QALY dominates decision making in England/Wales and Sweden, but is less important in Germany (limit of efficiency) and of minor importance in France and Spain. The importance of weighted QALYs is part of an ongoing discussion, especially in England/Wales. Its use instead of simple QALYs is considered to provide more equity to decision making in health policy.

NICE and SBU stress dissemination of information using for example financial incentives in order to carry the decisions into clinical practice.

Objectives

The majority of agencies aim to not solely evaluate the clinical efficacy of health technologies but also their efficiency explicitly using incremental cost-effectiveness ratio (ICER). Most agencies hereby tend to prioritise clinical benefits. NICE equally considers economic criteria as assessing value for money is one of its core functions.

In France and Spain, the perspective from which the analysis is conducted is not defined. In Sweden and Germany, it is the society. In England/Wales the perspective can be both, the National Health System (NHS) and the society, dependent on the respective health technology. However, NICE is currently changing its point of view. Considerations on value-based pricing and the proportional QALY shortfall are moving the perspective of the assessment more and more towards the society.

In all five countries, HTA mainly applies to drugs; although a new European guideline has recently been published claiming the inclusion of other health technologies and any medical intervention [10].

Implementation of the evaluation process

As described in the last paragraph, the Red does not have a standardised evaluation process. Conversely, NICE and SBU strictly define basic principles of evaluation, such as minimum content and quality criteria, as well as guidelines regarding the applied methods and type of evaluated evidence. They also define selection criteria, as for example burden of disease, impact on resources, political and clinical importance, and existence of inappropriate variability in clinical practice and relevance of technology. In Spain and Germany, these criteria are not explicitly determined. In France, they are not relevant as the industry demands the reports.

NICE has a well-defined organisation including fixed deadlines for the different stages of evaluation. In Spain for instance, public deadlines do not exist. The English/Welsh HTA system is the most transparent, not only with regard to the dissemination and implementation of results but also to the evaluation process itself. The agency publishes almost all documents obtained during the process. SBU for instance, also publishes unpublished data received from the industry. Similar to NICE, the Swedish define explicit deadlines and rules of revocation.

All five agencies conduct systematic reviews of the entire (qualified) scientific data available. SBU stands out as it even standardises the search of unpublished data in order to minimise the bias in publication. All agencies consider randomised controlled clinical trials as the strongest source of evidence with respect to clinical efficacy. IQWiG, HAS and Red base evaluation criteria on the efficacy of the health technology and the quality of the available scientific evidence. SBU and NICE additionally include criteria of efficiency, mainly in form of CEA. These criteria have however, been to some extent adopted by the other agencies.

All agencies define, more-or-less detailed, the type of applied economic analysis. The NICE stands out as it refers to CEA respecting the concept of cost consequence. In doing so, the agency takes into account the complex and multidimensional character of Public Health interventions and programmes. The compared systems are usually selected according to the most used in clinical practice (less in Spain). The Swedish agency compares all approved drugs of a certain therapeutic group. HAS considers all costs of treatments which have been recently added to the positive list. All agencies, except for the German agency, define possible outcome variables and include subgroup analyses, arising costs, discount rates and sensitivity analyses. The evaluation always includes the analysis of incremental or comparative clinical efficacy and ICER.

Output

The total number of publications of the five European agencies strongly depends on the size of the field of action and the contracting authority of each agency. HAS and NICE made up 69% of the total number of publications of all five agencies in 2012 (Figure 7-3). Of the 88 documents published by HAS, 76 are "opinions on drugs". This is probably because its agenda is mainly set by the industry. The subject area of the documents published by NICE is much wider reflecting its large field of action. It contains final HTA reports, clinical guidelines, diagnostic guidelines, Public Health guidelines, interventional procedures guidelines and technology appraisal guidelines.

The distribution relative to type of document is different. NICE for example publishes very few final HTA reports compared to the other agencies (Figure 7-4). However, with regard to the number of total publications of final HTA reports, clinical guidelines and data sheets, NICE and Red are the agencies with the highest output (Figure 7-5).

Summary

Taking into consideration the different setting of each agency, the HTA system seems to work best in England/Wales and Sweden. NICE and SBU have the most transparent and standardised evaluation processes and are involved in political decision making (Table 7-2). The HTA agencies of all five selected European countries are enviable in terms of output. However, its impact on administrative and clinical decision-making has to be considered.

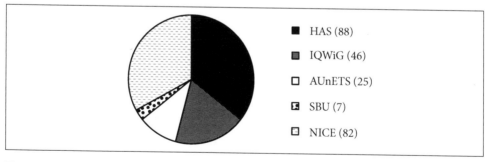

■ HAS (88)

▨ IQWiG (46)

□ AUnETS (25)

▨ SBU (7)

□ NICE (82)

Figure 7-3. Comparison of the total number of publications of five European HTA agencies in 2012. SBU: final HTA reports. IQWIG: final HTA reports, rapid reports, opinions on drugs. NICE: final HTA reports, clinical guidelines, diagnostic guidelines, Public Health Guidelines, interventional procedures guidelines, technology appraisal guideline. HAS: final HTA reports, opinions on drugs, opinions on medical devices. AUnETS: final HTA reports, data sheets, clinical guidelines, technical consult.
Abbreviations: AUnETS, Agencias y Unidades de Evaluación de Tecnologías Sanitarias; HAS, Haute Autorité de Santé; IQWiG, Institut für Qualität und Wirtschaftlichkeit im Gesundheitswesen; NICE, National Institute for Health and Clinical Excellence; SBU, Statens Beredning för medicinsk Utvärdering.
Source: Based on information from [1,4,16–19].

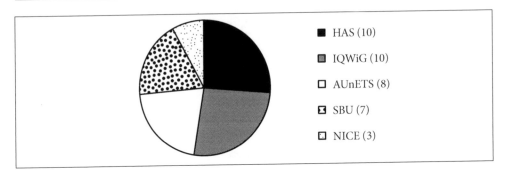

Figure 7-4. Comparison of the number of final HTA reports of five European HTA agencies published in 2012
Source: Based on information from [1,4,16–19].
Abbreviations: AUnETS, Agencias y Unidades de Evaluación de Tecnologías Sanitarias; HAS, Haute Autorité de
Santé; IQWiG, Institut für Qualität und Wirtschaftlichkeit im Gesundheitswesen; NICE, National Institute for
Health and Clinical Excellence; SBU, Statens Beredning för medicinsk Utvärdering.

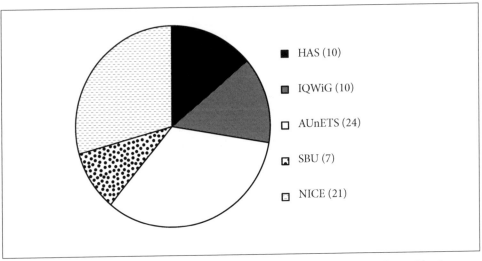

Figure 7-5. Comparison of the number of final HTA reports, clinical guidelines and data sheets of five European
HTA agencies published in 2012.
Source: Based on information from [1,4,16–19].
Abbreviations: AUnETS, Agencias y Unidades de Evaluación de Tecnologías Sanitarias; HAS, Haute Autorité de
Santé; IQWiG, Institut für Qualität und Wirtschaftlichkeit im Gesundheitswesen; NICE, National Institute for
Health and Clinical Excellence; SBU, Statens Beredning för medicinsk Utvärdering.

Table 7-2. Details about the five European HTA agencies.

	Red (Spain)	HAS (France)	NICE (England/Wales)	IQWiG (Germany)	SBU (Sweden)
Name	Red Española de Agencias de Evaluación de Tecnologías Sanitarias	Haute Autorité de Santé	National Institute for Health and Clinical Excellence	Institut für Qualität und Wirtschaftlichkeit im Gesundheitswesen	Statens Beredning för medicinsk Utvärdering
Capacity	Advisory	Advisory	Regulatory	Advisory	Regulatory
Contracting authority	Ministry of Health, Social Services and Equality, Interterritorial Council of the SNS	Independent public entity	Department of Health in collaboration with NICE Board	Ministry of Health, Federal Joint Committee (G-BA)	Ministry of Health and Social Services
Field of action	Drugs, medical devices, new HTs, detection of new HTs, clinical guidelines, organisation and management of healthcare services	Drugs, medical devices	Drugs, medical devices, public health, new HTs, diagnostic/ clinical/ interventional procedure guidelines	Drugs	Drugs, new HTs
Perspective of analysis	Not defined	Dependent on the objective	Reference cases: NHS others: Society	Society	Society
Transparency of decision making	Not available	Input from various health authorities is required. Decisions have to be taken within 1 month. Price negotiations and conclusions are not public	Most information about the evaluation process and decision making is published on the website	Revision and accounting of the decisions by the Federal Joint Committee, independent organisations and BMG	Decisions of the TLV are published on the website including facts on which the decisions are based
Web	www.aunets.isciii.es	www.has-sante.fr	www.nice.org.uk	www.iqwig.de	www.sbu.se

Abbreviations: BMG, German Ministry of Health; HT, Health Technology; NHS, National Health System; TLV, independent government agency (HTA Board).
Source: Based on information from [1].

Valuable Lessons on Health Technology Assessment for the European Union: Operating as a Network of National Bodies?

The first European HTA agency was founded in Sweden in 1987, followed by some of the Spanish agencies (AQuAS, Osasun Teknologien Ebaluazioko Zerbitzua [OSTEBA], SESCS and AETSA) in the early 1990s and NICE in 1999. By 2004, the European Council of Ministers was calling HTA a political priority: *"... the European Council concluded that the exchange of expertise and information through HTA may be enhanced through systematic EU-wide cooperation, in order to assist the Member States to plan, deliver and monitor health services effectively, based on the best available scientific evidence on the medical, social and economic implications of health technology"* [20]. As a result, the project EUnetHTA was created one year later by a group of 35 organisations from all over Europe, with the Danish Center for HTA (DACEHTA) in Copenhagen leading the way. It aims to establish an efficient and sustainable network for HTA across Europe [2]. Its previous activities can be summarised as following:

- support efficient production and use of HTA in countries across Europe
- provide an independent and science-based platform for HTA agencies in countries across Europe to exchange and develop HTA information and methodology
- provide an access point for communication with stakeholders to promote transparency, objectivity, independence of expertise, fairness of procedure and appropriate stakeholder consultations
- develop alliances with contributing fields of research to support a stronger and broader evidence base for HTA while using the best available scientific competence [2].

Ever since then, the interest of the EU in closer collaboration with its different HTA systems remains unabated. Cross-border HTA activities have recently been given more and more legal and financial leverage by Brussels. This acceleration has been driven by several factors, including the financial crisis which has entailed, and still does, massive cuts in the healthcare budget of most European countries (Figure 7-6).

In 2007, the Informal Health Council of the EU brought about a paper stating that the value of access to good quality care, the principle of patient safety and healthcare quality standards across the different health systems in the EU can be improved by HTA [22]. Moreover, the World Health Organization (WHO) of the European Region declared in the 2008 Tallinn Charter that: *"Fostering health policy and systems research and making ethical and effective use of innovations in medical technology and pharmaceuticals are relevant for all countries; health technology assessment should be used to support more informed decision-making"* [23].

Up to date, the most momentous decision was made in 2011 when the European Parliament and Council stipulated, by means of Article 15 of the Directive 2011/24/EU, to (financially) support the cooperation on HTA between the Member States within a voluntary network aiming to: *"...(a) support cooperation between national authorities or bodies; (b) support the Member States in the provision of objective, reliable, timely, transparent, comparable and transferable information on the relative efficacy as well as on the short- and long-term effectiveness of health technologies; (c) support the analysis of the nature and type of information that can be exchanged; (d) avoid the duplication of assessments"* [24]. According to the subsequent Implementing Decision 2013/329/EU of the European Commission, the created European HTA network should be supported by scientific and technical cooperation [25]. This support is carried out by the EUnetHTA until the end of 2015, as decided during the network's first meeting on October 16, 2013 in Brussels [2]. The European HTA network currently consists of 28 HTA agencies from the 28 Member States plus Norway, which is holding the status of an observer member (Table 7-3). Showcasing of different HTA practices by bodies such as the EUnetHTA strives to develop and harmonise the work of HTA agencies since it still covers a wide variety of practices and regulations.

The EU is relatively homogenous and from a global perspective the variety is markedly larger. HTA is being most advanced in industrialised countries and gaining more and more influence in Brazil, Russia, India, China and South Africa (BRICS) countries, especially in Brazil. Other middle-income countries show intermediate levels of HTA development and some are just beginning, as, for example, India and Russia [27]. The International Network of Agencies for Health Technology Assessment (INHTA) includes 57 member agencies from 32 countries covering both developing and developed countries all over the world [28]. These countries inter-exchange on issues related to HTA development. Sometimes wholesale recommendations from leading institutions such as NICE are adopted by countries introducing HTA.

The need for greater value in healthcare has been at the centre of discussion in the recent years driven by the general awareness that traditional healthcare is unsustainable in developed and unaffordable in emerging economies. HTA plays a significant role in this process, particularly in terms of reimbursement and the regulatory approval process. Value-based healthcare is health outcome per cost expended. It aims to maintain the best possible access and quality in healthcare through rationalisation of services. It is important to understand that the patient hereby occupies the centre stage [26]. Adoption rates of value-based healthcare practices differ significantly across Europe. Countries having a large element of outcomes-based purchasing and reimbursement are, for example, the UK and Germany [29]. As mentioned in the last section, we need to view each European country in its particular setting. Hence, it is somewhat difficult to entirely standardise HTA processes inside the EU. The application of value-based HTA across the EU should, at the present point, rather be considered a common approach than a finished recipe. Even though the bodies to inform decisions on reimbursement have more in common with each other than differences, these do exist; for example, different conceptions of 'value' or different market sizes [30,31].

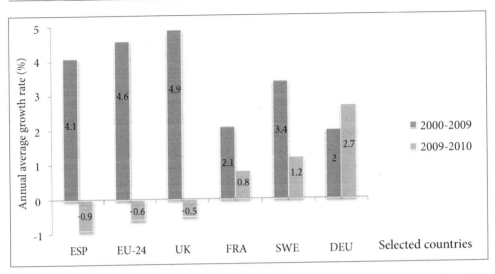

Figure 7-6. Annual average growth rate in health expenditure per capita in five European countries and the EU-24, in real terms.
ESP, Spain; DEU, Germany; EU-24, EU member states, excluding Luxembourg, Latvia, Bulgaria and Croatia; FRA, France; SWE, Sweden; UK, United Kingdom.
Source: Based on information from [21].

Table 7-3. Member states, observer members and observer stakeholders of the European HTA Network as of 15 April 2014.

Members of the European HTA network		
	Austria – Ministry of Health		Italy – Ministry of Health
	Belgium – Belgium Health Care Knowledge Centre (KCE)		Latvia – Ministry of Health
	Bulgaria – National Center for Public Health and Analyses (NCPHA)		Lithuania – State Health Care Accreditation Agency
	Croatia – Agency for Quality and Accreditation in Health Care and Social Welfare		Luxembourg – Inspection générale de la sécurité sociale (IGSS)
	Cyprus – Ministry of Health Services		Malta – Ministry of Health
	Czech Republic – State Institute for Drug Control (SUKL)		Netherlands – Dutch Healthcare Insurance Board (CVZ)
	Denmark – Ministry of Health		Poland – Ministry of Health
	Estonia – Ministry of Social Affairs		Portugal – Autoridade Nacional do Medicamento e Produtos de Saúde (IN-FARMED)

	Finland – National Institute for Health and Welfare		Romania – Ministry of Health
	France – Ministry of Health		Slovakia – Ministry of Health
	Germany – Ministry of Health		Slovenia – National Institute of Public Health
	Greece - National Evaluation Center of Quality and Technology in Health SA (EKAPTY)		Spain – Ministry of Health
	Hungary – Ministry of Human Resources		Sweden – Swedish Council on Health Technology Assessment (SBU)
	Ireland – Health Information and Quality Authority		United Kingdom – Department of Health

Observer member

	Norway – Norwegian Knowledge Centre for the Health Services

Observer stakeholders

Co-chair of the EUnetHTA Stakeholders Forum (SF): EURORDIS, European Organisation for Rare Diseases
Representative of the SF – Professionals: CPME – Standing Committee of European Doctors
Representative of the SF – Providers: MLOZ, Studies & Strategy
Representative of the SF – Patients: EPF – European Patients' Forum
Representative of the SF – Industry: EFPIA – European Federation of Pharmaceutical Industries and Associations

Source: Compiled by the author based on [26].

Foregone Benefits and Future Possibilities of Effectiveness Improvements on Health Technology Assessment Outcomes and Dissemination

In this last section we will address the question posed in the title of this chapter – what HTA system do we really need? The plainest answer to this question is: we need an excellent HTA system. Excellence is a product of constant practice, meaning gradual improvement. In the first paragraph I outlined the strong and weak points of the Spanish HTA system. Subsequently, I analysed the characteristics of five European systems and the collaboration of HTA across the EU. The challenge now is to learn lessons, highlight aspects working well in some countries and establish a roadmap in order to upgrade our (European) HTA systems. Let us start with some theoretical considerations on how to implement excellence in HTA practice.

HTA should involve processes to avoid conflicts of interest. It needs to ensure active participation of different entities such as experts, clinicians, patients and the industry. The assessment of any new health technology should not only include an analysis of efficacy and effectiveness, but also an economic evaluation. Selection criteria should be defined and based on various factors such as burden of disease, impact on resources, political and clinical importance, the existence of inappropriate variability in clinical practice and relevance of technology. Another important methodological aspect is to previously define the perspective of the evaluation. HTA should preferably be conducted from a social viewpoint. In some specific cases however, a more limited perspective as, for example, the perspective of the NHS, can as well be adequate.

Deadlines need to be explicitly defined. They should give sufficient time to publish a report responding to a question asked about the respective health technology. At the same time, they should be appropriate to influence decision making. It is sensible to permit revocation in order to consider the consequences of the evaluation. Also, HTA should comprise a re-evaluation process, including deadlines, which allows for updates of the health technology and its use.

Transparency needs to be at a maximum. This requires a profound definition of procedures during the entire process of evaluation, dissemination and implementation of decisions taken on the basis of the evaluation. The obligatory participation of different stakeholders contributes to the improvement of transparency since it increases the acceptance and legitimacy of the decisions taken by the agencies.

It is important to define the methodology used in the evaluation relative to selection and review of scientific evidence, including strategies to alleviate publication bias. To obtain the best available evidence, the selection of alternatives should be based on established standards and on what is used in clinical practice. The economic evaluation needs to implicitly contain determined outcome variables, such as sensibility analysis, subgroup analysis and discount rate. The introduction of thresholds for acceptability and availability should be considered.

Contribution of experts: the adequacy of the local context

From a practical point of view, these theoretical considerations refer to different parts of the HTA system:

HTA agencies need to work with decision makers from beginning to end. They should cooperate in clarifying objectives, requirements and scope of the application of results. This will ensure that everything, including the deadline of the report, is in accordance with decision making. Future use of products generated by the agencies should be clarified beforehand. Priority setting should be defined and based upon internationally accepted criteria as, for example, the magnitude of problem and the feasibility of solution, impact and volume.

It is critical to define measures to promote transparency and participation of the different stakeholders during the entire HTA process. This starts with the announcement of upcoming assessments and includes the contribution of stakeholders during the evaluation, and ends with procedures to respond to the appeals of stakeholders. A preliminary declaration of interest should be demanded from each agency in order to safeguard the product against bias associated with conflicts of interest. Innovation, research and education should be promoted within the agencies, thus reducing the uncertainty related to decision making; improvement of research methods, scientific modelling and economic evaluation, use of Real World Data (RWD) or Real World Evidence (RWE) on healthcare should hereby be of highest interest.

Furthermore, good HTA practice requires a framework of action for the agencies that facilitate and give incentives to the diffusion of reports and clinical guidelines. This is a crucial step to improve the effectiveness of recommendations and conclusions published by the agencies, and also contribute to re-evaluation and periodic actualisation.

Characteristics to strengthen the health system

Agencies act in an advisory capacity. They should have the right to intervene in decision making related to disinvestment or the introduction of new health technologies. A partial regulatory capacity is very efficient since it merges evaluation and valuation. If there are multiple HTA agencies in one country, they should be embedded in a national network. This network should give answers to the needs of government institutions and, in federal republics, regional institutions in order to accomplish equity in the NHS. HTA should be responsible for new and existing health technologies, such as drugs and medical devices, and healthcare administration and management. The methodological criteria applied to the evaluation process should always be in accordance with internationally accepted standards. The national agencies should further maintain international collaborations with other HTA agencies. Transparency is crucial and ought to be considered during the course of the entire evaluation process. The agencies should deliver a high number of products.

Characteristics to improve the health technology assessment process

The collaboration of HTA agencies with decision makers should be close from the very beginning of the assessment process. They should cooperate in clarifying objectives, requirements and scope of the application of results. This will ensure that everything, including the deadline of the report, is in accordance with decision making. The agencies should dispose of explicit priority setting, adapted to internationally accepted criteria that are based on the magnitude of problem, feasibility of solution, impact and volume. Furthermore, the criteria included in the evaluation, such as effectiveness and cost effectiveness, and all variables that affect them, such as comparative effectiveness, comparison criteria, sensitivity analysis and discount rates, should be explicitly defined.

It is important to determine the methodology of the evaluation and deadlines to re-evaluate the product. The reports should include an economic evaluation conducted from, preferably, a societal perspective. Moreover, official thresholds of acceptability should be established. Transparency and participation of the stakeholders need to be promoted. The agencies should therefore previously declare their interests. A solid framework of action will facilitate and encourage the diffusion of HTA reports and clinical guidelines. This is a crucial step to improve the effectiveness of the implementation of recommendations given by the agencies, their re-evaluation and actualisation.

Conclusions

1. HTA is a series of methods that helps to improve health services functioning through informed decisions. The toughest challenge, however, is not to bring about rea-

sonable improvements, but to implement them appropriately. With regard to the latter, there seems to be a political underuse of HTA reports, but policy implementation is another story not covered in this chapter.

2. HTA reports help to facilitate the access to health technologies that are valuable enough to be publicly funded.

3. HTA agencies work properly, in terms of output. However, reports and guidelines often do not reach individual clinical level. Dissemination is limited in scope and applies in all European agencies. Active participation of clinicians in the HTA process (AVALIA-T) and the strategy of SBU "ambassadors" have made an increased impact. Awareness-building of HTA amongst clinicians should start at university.

4. There are major issues regarding governance, organisation and political influence of HTA. The agencies could be described as "public institutions linked to Health Authorities", with few exceptions. They are not independent because their budget and management are set by the government. Conflict of interests and transparency is something not properly solved.

5. The agencies mainly act in an advisory capacity. Their real participation in the decision-making scenario is sometimes erratic and in practice executive capacity is not addressed, with few exceptions. If some sweeping political conflicts were produced, the agencies would be at risk and consequently might be closed (as happened to the US Office of Technology Assessment [OTA] in 1995). Policy makers need to remember, sometimes, that the absence of evidence of effectiveness is not the same as evidence of the absence of effectiveness.

6. Objectives of HTA agencies mainly include assessment on technical aspects such as efficacy and safety. Perspective of HTA, as claimed by the agencies for a long time, should be more ambitious and include social and economic aspects.

There may be some potential integration between HTA and comparative effectiveness research (CER) that surprisingly has not been explored yet. CER is a main issue in the US since the Obamacare reform has taken place.

7. In contrast to SBU and NICE, the evaluation process of Spanish agencies lacks standardisation and transparency. Regulation of stakeholder participation is indispensable in a transparent HTA system. It also includes revocation mechanisms and how far agencies should go retrieving non-published literature in order to minimise publication bias.

8. European collaboration on HTA could largely increase efficiency of healthcare delivery in the member states. A universal platform or agency in the sense of a "EuroNICE" would avoid generations of many similar studies and reports. It should also include a European HTA committee fixing priorities and assigning responsibility for the production of reports to be done by different national agencies. The French breast implant scandal in 2011 was the first event to awaken the European Parliament to the problem. Ever since then, the EU seems to be making some tangible efforts to bring their HTA systems closer. However, there are no legally binding rules as the participation in the European HTA network remains voluntary.

9. Since public financial resources are limited, their inappropriate use for particular health technologies inevitably impacts on other health technologies making them unavailable or increasing the deficit. In other words, leaving things the way they are means ignoring opportunity costs. HTA interest, at least in Spain, increases in times of hardship. Cuts and disinvestment strategies could be more rational using HTA outputs.

10. Citizens' call for transparency will demand accountability from politicians, professionals and all manner of institutions. This is a major challenge for the HTA community at large; it needs to make the need for transparency understood and clarify each role and place in the collective decision-making process.

11. Electronic clinical data and networks might be some of the most promising innovations in HTA. Digital patients' records, observational studies, pragmatic clinical trials, registries, all under the umbrella of RWD or RWE, will facilitate the acquisition of data on effectiveness (efficacy in clinical practice). It is both a new challenge and a new opportunity for HTA agencies at large. RWD/RWE will help to improve utilisation of permanently short public means that have to meet society's increasing healthcare needs. Agencies will be more effective and useful when they reflect everyday medical practice in their reports. This means that the future role of HTA agencies involving decisions will be broader.

Acknowledgements

I would like to thank Dr Magdalena Kimmich for her valuable contribution to this chapter. I also thank Dr Jordi Gol, for his feedback on the conclusions and Dr Carlos Campillo, for his careful reads.

This book was supported by an unrestricted educational grant from Celgene.

REFERENCES

1. Rivera López-Tello AJ, García López JL, del Llano Señarís JE. [HTA in five European countries: Learning from one another]. Madrid, Spain: Fundación Gaspar Casal; 2013. Available from: http://www.fgcasal.org/publicaciones/Evaluacion_Tecnologias_Sanitarias_en_cinco_Paises_Europeos.pdf.
2. EUnetHTA [Internet]. 2005 [cited 2014 Mar 31]. Available from: http://www.eunethta.eu/
3. Kristensen FB. EUnetHTA and health policy-making in Europe. Eurohealth (Lond). 2006;12(1): 36-8. Available from: http://www.ncbi.nlm.nih.gov/pubmed/10354763.
4. Instituto de Salud Carlos III. AUnETS [Internet]. 2012 [cited 2014 Mar 31]. Available from: http://aunets.isciii.es/web/guest/
5. Orden SSI/1833/2013, de 2 de octubre, por la que se crea y regula el Consejo de la Red Española de Agencias de Evaluación de Tecnologías Sanitarias y Prestaciones del Sistema Nacional de Salud. [Internet]. Madrid, Spain: Ministerio de Sanidad, Servicios Sociales e Igualdad; 2013 p. 6. Available from: http://www.boe.es/boe/dias/2013/10/11/pdfs/BOE-A-2013-10581.pdf.
6. Proyecto de orden por la que se concreta y actualiza la caretera común básica de servicios asistenciales del sistema nacional de la salud [Internet]. Madrid, Spain: Ministerio de Sanidad, Servicios Sociales e Igualdad; 2012 p. 21. Available from: http://www.msssi.gob.es/normativa/docs/Orcarterabasica.pdf.

7. Ministerio de Sanidad Servicios Sociales e Igualdad. Estadística de Gasto Sanitario Público [Internet]. Madrid, Spain; 2011 p. 18. Available from: http://www.msssi.gob.es/estadEstudios/estadisticas/docs/EGSP2008/egspPrincipalesResultados.pdf.

8. Sacristán JA, Oliva J, Del Llano J, Prieto L, Pinto JL. [What is an efficient health technology in Spain?]. Gac Sanit. 2002;16(4):334-43. Available from: http://linkinghub.elsevier.com/retrieve/pii/S021391110271933X.

9. Sanz-Granda A, Hidalgo A, del Llano JE, Rovira J. Analysis of economic evaluations of pharmacological cancer treatments in Spain between 1990 and 2010. Clin Transl Oncol. 2013;15(1):9-19. Available from: http://www.ncbi.nlm.nih.gov/pubmed/23180344.

10. EUnetHTA. JA1 WP5 methodology guideline - Comparators & Comparisons: Criteria for the choice of the most appropriate comparator(s) [Internet]. 2013 [cited 2014 May 14]. p. 24. Available from: http://5026.fedimbo.belgium.be/sites/5026.fedimbo.belgium.be/files/Choice_of_comparator.pdf.

11. Real Decreto-ley 16/2012, de 20 de abril, de medidas urgentes para garantizar la sostenibilidad del Sistema Nacional de Salud y mejorar la calidad y seguridad de sus prestaciones. [Internet]. Madrid, Spain: Jefatura del Estado; 2012 p. 35. Available from: https://www.boe.es/boe/dias/2012/04/24/pdfs/BOE-A-2012-5403.pdf.

12. Oliva J, Del Llano J, Sacristán JA. [Analysis of economic evaluations of health technologies performed in Spain between 1990 and 2000]. Gac Sanit. 2002;16 Suppl 2:2-11. Available from: http://www.ncbi.nlm.nih.gov/pubmed/15826599.

13. C.F. [The HTA agencies sparsely promote their reports]. Diario Medico. Madrid, Spain; 2014 May 21;9.

14. Drummond M, Neumann P, Jönsson B, Luce B, Schwartz JS, Siebert U, et al. Can we reliably benchmark health technology assessment organizations? Int J Technol Assess. Health Care. 2012;28(2):159-65. Available from: http://www.ncbi.nlm.nih.gov/pubmed/22559758.

15. Sorenson C, Drummond M, Kanavos P. Ensuring value for money in health care - The role of health technology assessment in the European Union. Political Science. Copenhagen, Denmark: WHO Regional Office for Europe on behalf of the European Observatory on Health Systems and Policies; 2008. Available from: http://www.ispor.org/congresses/prague1110/documents/PlenaryII-Role-of-HTA-in-the-EU.pdf.

16. HAS - French National Authority for Health [Internet]. [cited 2014 Mar 31]. Available from: http://www.has-sante.fr/portail/jcms/r_1455134/fr/about-has?portal=r_1455081.

17. IQWiG - Institute for Quality and Efficiency in Health Care [Internet]. [cited 2014 Mar 31]. Available from: https://www.iqwig.de/en/home.2724.html.

18. NICE - National Institute for Health and Care Excellence [Internet]. [cited 2014 Mar 31]. Available from: http://www.nice.org.uk.

19. SBU – Swedish Council on Health Technology Assessment [Internet]. [cited 2014 Mar 31]. Available from: http://www.sbu.se/en/.

20. Danish Centre for Health Technology Assessment. Final Tecnical Report EUnetHTA - European network for Health Technology Assessment [Internet]. Copenhagen, Denmark; 2009. Available from: http://ec.europa.eu/health/ph_systems/docs/eunethta_report_en.pdf.

21. OECD. Health expenditure per capita. Health at a Glance: Europe 2012 [Internet]. OECD Publishing; 2012 [cited 2014 Apr 25]. Available from: http://dx.doi.org/10.1787/9789264183896-52-en.

22. Trio Presidency of the European Union. Notes of the Trio Presidency - Health care across Europe: Striving for added value. Informal Health Council. Aachen, Germany: European Union; 2007. p. 6. Available from: http://www.eu2007.de/en/News/download_docs/April/0419-BSGV/090Triopapier.pdf.

23. Danzon M, Maripuu M. The Tallinn Charter: Health Systems for Health and Wealth. WHO European Ministerial Conference on Health Systems: "Health Systems, Health and Wealth". Tallinn, Estonia: WHO Regional Office for Europe; 2008. p. 5. Available from: http://www.euro.who.int/_data/assets/pdf_file/0008/88613/E91438.pdf.

24. Buzek J, Györi E. Directive on the application of patients' rights in cross-border healthcare. Strasbourg, France: European Parliament and Council; 2011. p. 45-65. Available from: http://eur-lex.europa.eu/LexUriServ/LexUriServ.do?uri=OJ:L:2011:088:0045:0065:en:PDF.

25. Barroso JM. Implementing Decision providing the rules for the establishment, management and transparent functioning of the Network of national authorities or bodies responsible for health technology assessment. Brussels, Belgium: European Commission; 2013. p. 71-2. Available from: http://ec.europa.eu/health/technology_assessment/docs/impl_dec_hta_network_en.pdf.

26. Porter ME, Olmsted Teisberg E. Redefining health care: Creating value-based competition on results. 1st ed. Boston, MA, USA: Harvard Business Review Press; 2006.

27. Oortwijn W, Broos P, Vondeling H, Banta D, Todorova L. Mapping of health technology assessment in selected countries. Int J Technol Assess Health Care. 2013;29(4):424-34. Available from: http://www.ncbi.nlm.nih.gov/pubmed/24290336.

28. INAHTA-International Network of Agencies for Health Technology Assessment [Internet]. [cited 2014 Apr 14]. Available from: http://www.inahta.org.

29. Value-based health: the new normal in healthcare. The Economist Intelligence Unit. London, Great Britain; 2014;4-10.

30. Paris V, Belloni A. Value in pharmaceutical pricing. OECD Health Working Papers. 2013. Report No.: 63. Available from: http://www.oecd-ilibrary.org/social-issues-migration-health/value-in-pharmaceutical-pricing_5k43jc9v6knx-en.

31. Rovira Forns J, Gómez Pajuelo P, del Llano Señarís JE. [Value-based pricing of drugs]. Fundación Gaspar Casal, Editor. Madrid, Spain; 2012. http://www.fgcasal.org/publicaciones/Lilly_FGC-Libro_La_Regulacion_del_precio_medicamentos.pdf.

CHAPTER 8

The Final Stretch? How Shared Decision Making Extends Health Technology Assessment to Meet Patient Preference

Stuart W. Grande and Glyn Elwyn

Introduction

Eric Topol, the author of *The Creative Destruction of Medicine*, calls our attention to a quote from Voltaire who wrote, "doctors prescribe medicine of which they know little, to cure disease of which they know less, in human beings of which they know nothing". Topol uses this quote, seemingly, to challenge us to rethink our assumptions about the practice of medicine and how little it reflects what actually matters most to patients.

Consider then, a 1967 statement from the US House of Representatives describing health technology assessment (HTA) as a tool for policy makers: "A policymaker cannot judge the merits or consequences of a technological programme within a strictly technical context. He has to consider social, economic, and legal implications of any course of action." Extending this early definition, today HTA can be seen as a multidisciplinary process that summarises information about the medical, social, economic and ethical issues related to the use of a health technology in a systematic, transparent, unbiased and robust manner. HTA endeavours to provide a structured, evidence-based input to the policy-making process by clarifying the following: what is the nature, function and attributes or characteristics of health technology? [1]. Consequently, HTA offers a process that can effectively manage the costs and process implication associated with new technology, but does not seem interested in the patient's views about the trade-offs between relevant harms and benefits.

Now, more than ever, as technology enters our lives making decision making easier and more efficient, might researchers and policy makers need to consider just how these new technologies are changing the way clinicians make healthcare decisions with patients? If doctors, as Voltaire cynically contends, already misunderstand patients, then might the addition of technology, no matter the width and breadth of available evidence, further amplify misunderstandings? Although the strength of HTA is the evaluation of new technologies for policy makers, might this purely high-level evaluative approach also limit HTA?

© Springer International Publishing Switzerland 2015
J.E. del Llano-Señarís and C. Campillo-Artero (eds.), *Health Technology Assessment and Health Policy Today: A Multifaceted View of their Unstable Crossroads*,
DOI 10.1007/978-3-319-15004-8_8

Advances in medical technology offer more assessment and diagnostic capabilities than ever before allowing doctors to provide life-extending disease therapies. Before these innovations were made available, they were first evaluated and tested for patient safety, cost effectiveness, and clinical efficacy. Notably, however, cost effectiveness is currently limited to pre-approval in a few counties. In this way, HTA exists as a process to help policy makers and providers make decisions about which innovative technologies should be used in clinical medicine. Yet, for all the evaluative strength of HTA, when it comes to allowing patients an opportunity to compare reasonable alternatives, HTA falls short.

At the preference lab we believe shared decision making (SDM), a process where patients and providers discuss options according to most up-to-date evidence to determine the most appropriate treatment, has a distinct role in HTA. In the last 40 years HTA has emerged as a systematic strategy, to evaluate a wide array of technologies to ensure they are safe, effective, and provide the best value for patients. Given this important task of ensuring quality and safety of innovations in medicine, might SDM have a role within HTA? In the following chapter we make the supposition that SDM may, indeed, play an important role in HTA by essentially linking evaluative evidence and what matters most to patients. To do this, we have broken the chapter into several sections explaining what SDM is and how it is currently being applied in practice, and offer examples of how SDM might be applied to HTA.

Shared Decision Making: Definitions, Origins, and Expectations

Definitions

SDM is an approach to patient-centred care, where providers support patients in deliberation, using the best-available evidence on potential treatment options, to build informed preferences that are aligned with what matters most to patients. The earliest concepts of SDM considered the importance of helping physicians to support patients to make more informed decisions that were concordant with patient values.

SDM emerged from work framing different models of decision making between patients and providers, as well as from efforts to better understand patient-centredness, i.e. the thought that focusing assessment on patient experience and clinical indicators impacted patient outcomes. Early contributions to theories of decision making focused a great deal of attention on the idea of the rational decision maker, like the "economic man", a person who has complete information and makes choices based on maximising best alternative [2]. Theories associated with expectancies as Vroom [3] suggests, consider valences of outcomes (i.e. importance or anticipated satisfaction of outcome) by measuring the correlation between an action and an outcome [4]. This process where discrete choices are modelled to compare outcomes based on probabilities, was limited by the amount of evidence available. It was a more prescriptive and logic-based method, highly dependent on assumptions based on the most accurate and up-to-date evidence. Arguably these models were, at best, a proxy for individual patient choice and, at worse, an inaccurate substitute for unique patient experiences. All told, what mattered most to the patient really wasn't being considered.

SDM extends far beyond discrete decisions involving probabilities or models, and requires a much greater conceptual understanding of the relationship between patients and providers. We will explore early concepts of the patient-provider relationship in detail, compare those early concepts to modern ones, demonstrate how new patient roles complement HTA, and provide examples of how including the patient's perspective, lived-experience and preferences with HTA fosters greater long-term potential for ensuring better patient care.

Origins

Rational thinking about the evolution of modern medicine from early humoral theory to modern cell theory leads us to ask whether or not we, as humans, are better off today than we were fifty or one hundred years ago. While recognising our skills at making early diagnosis and providing life-saving surgeries, this thinking is arguably misguided, because it overlooks what many consider the foundation of all medicine, the relationship between physicians and their patients. In fact, some might say the patient-provider relationship has changed very little in the last 500 years and therefore ensures that essential parts of the medical experience have evolved very little.

Ancient philosophers struggled with concepts and ideas pitting the ephemeral, things relating to the spiritual or superstitious, against the observable, things seen, touched, and experienced. It wasn't until Hippocrates suggested that a life-process was a blend of the individual and the environment that ancient thinking recognised the relationship between nature and the individual [5]. Plato wrote about the practice of medicine as a combination of art and science, where art represents the practice of making conjecture based on subjective observations and science is the aggregation of relational experiences into a conceptual "ideal type". King [6] offers the view that Plato conceived the art of medicine as both exalted and mundane, stating that "true art deals with reality," which Plato believed to be the foundation of his philosophy.

Foucault [7] suggested that looking at the patient differently changed the status of patients in society and also the relationship between help and knowledge. By the late 19th century medical education and the medical profession itself began to focus on the physical body and pathology of patients. McWhinney [8] wrote about this change in context, where medical attention focused more on patient pathology rather than the experience, saying "the success of medical technology ha[s] exposed most vividly the limitations of the traditional method." Acknowledging the benefits of innovative technology requires understanding the consequences of its use. As medical practice continued to focus more attention on the "medical" or "pathological" diagnosis of patients, there became more and more of a disconnect between patients being seen as people and patients being seen as objects of disease [9].

This focus on pathology was so strong that medical education seemingly left patients behind, turning its attention to the apparently more scientific and rigorous, clinical origins of illness. McWhinney contends that as a result, the personal experience of the patient was thought unimportant, and overlooked in favour of clinical examinations and the "traditional clinical method" [8]. Essentially, early notions of illness, those aligned with germ theory, were linked inextricably to clinical or measurable data – if we can find the pathogen of origin then we can attribute cause and apply a solution. Yet, as the field of medical sociology expanded, so did thinking about the influence of culture and experience on perceptions of illness. It was in the 1960s when Balint introduced ideas of psychoanalysis as being part of the patient-provider relationship. It was Balint [10] who first presented the idea of patient-centredness, expressing the idea that in order to understand a patient's illness you had to first listen, rather than ask questions [11].

This type of thinking was very new and seemed to be reflective of bigger ideas involving the interaction of both individual experiences and physical manifestations of disease. Von Bertalanffy was one of the first to apply the idea of systems theory to medicine, as a way of making the link between the way individual parts (organs for example) might work together in harmony or disharmony as a system. Engel took this thinking a step further and proposed the biopsychosocial model, which for all intents and purposes redefined how the world would forever think about the link between what it means to be sick or well and how this might affect individuals. Engel [12] makes the connection between culture and perceptions of disease, reminiscent of Zola's earlier work that found groups of immigrants perceived pain and suffering differently based on their cultural backgrounds [13].

In New England around the late 1960s and early 1970s, two researchers who were investigating healthcare utilisation rates uncovered a high degree of unexplained variation in their data. What Wennberg & Gittelsohn [14] found were vastly different rates of tonsillectomy in two neighbouring towns in Vermont. The results of their investigation to explain this variation revealed an uncomfortable truth. The way doctors practiced and the way they made decisions concerning the treatment of their patients, seemed to reflect their individual practice style rather than how sick their patients were [15]. This work would become the cornerstone of unwarranted variation. Broken down into three types, (i) effective care, (ii) preference-sensitive care, and (iii) supply-sensitive care, unwarranted variation became one of the building blocks for conceptualising the way provider practice habits, proven clinical evidence, and large supplies of resources all influence the delivery of healthcare to patients. This work was controversial because it challenged normative assumptions, which held patient demand as the primary driver of service use. In fact, Wennberg's findings showed that much of the variation among patients was due, in part, to events that happened after the physician visit, rather than how sick the patients were before the physician visit. These findings provided some of the first evidence that showed just how little the patient perspective mattered in the course of a clinical diagnosis and how such behaviours affected treatment rates. Therefore, these findings show how evidence, when collected purposefully can be an effective tool for evaluating rates, but less effective for modifying rates if patients' perspectives are ignored.

By the mid-to-late 1970s, other researchers were focusing more on the social context of the medical consultation rather than the epidemiology of service utilisation, realising that patient experiences actually matter when seeking to understand disease. Under the leadership of Ian McWhinney, an interdisciplinary team began to merge the system's thinking of VanBertalanfy with Mechanic's concepts of patient "illness behaviour", believing that diagnosis was a combination of both patient behaviour and the social context of disease [16]. Inspired by visiting South African general practitioner Joseph Levenstein, who thought that determining patient feelings and expectations were essential skills for providers, McWhinney's group had defined "the patient-centred method" as a coupling of the physician's "differential diagnosis" with the patient's "understanding illness experience" [17]. A new focus on provider communication skills and its impact on patient outcomes lead to much of the current evidence that links health outcomes with the relationship between patient and provider

[18]. Consequently, the foundation was built for a deeper assessment of the patient-provider relationship, originally modelled by Szasz & Hollander [19].

McWhinney, Stewart and colleagues showed that when providers developed strong relationships with patients, provided detailed treatment information, elicited patient expectations, supported patients to take an active role, and had mutually agreed on goals, patients were more likely to have successful health outcomes. This framing of patient and provider in partnership was necessary to help navigate clinical situations, where making a treatment decision depends on equivalent evidence, i.e. clinical equipoise. Again, the importance of good evidence, collected and evaluated systematically, aided in the process of determining which treatments were equivalent. Consequently, a way of making the right treatment choice, when "clinical equipoise" was present, could be assessing patient's views about the trade-offs between relevant harms and benefits as defined by the evidence. Thus, establishing patient expectations and goals based on an assessment of trade-offs, through informing and building a relationship are in accordance options and with Balint's earlier concepts of patient-centredness.

In their edited volume profiling SDM, Edwards & Elwyn [20] summarised over three decades of research investigating decision making. They finally agreed that the following statement: "involving the patient in decision making, to the extent they desire" was appropriate (p5). While firmly embedded in the history of health communication, patient-centredness, and medical ethics, the emergence of SDM as a widely accepted term reflects a myriad of historical legacies, without appearing to highlight one perspective over another. The importance of that tradition is critical when trying to understand how SDM fits into current practice, and how much work has been done in the last three decades to support this, still emerging, concept placing the patient perspective at the heart of decision making.

Wennberg would later adopt SDM as part of a solution to the problem of variation, later defined as preference-sensitive care, attributable to instances where two or more equivalent treatment options exist. In association with clinical researchers like Mulley, Fowler, and Barry in Boston, efforts were made to create the first decision aid, a tool to help patients make an informed decision about treatment options [21,22]. Based on principles of prescriptive decision making (using probabilities and utilities to help derive effective treatment decisions), this tool was designed to help patients with benign prostatic hypertrophy (BPH). The decision aid was developed to show differences in preference between two men. Although this remains a controversial area, many patients choose different options based on their symptoms or comfort with the surgical procedure, which happens to be consistent with early thinking about the importance of patient expectations and goals. This underlying principle, allowing patients to base their decisions on what matters most to them, reflects a fundamental shift in approach from more traditional, paternalistic, models of care [23]. Thus, by providing patients with options and giving them the opportunity to weigh the benefits and risks, as determined by the best available evidence, integrates both evidence and preference into the decision process.

What researchers know about SDM is that it puts the patient first allowing for the sharing of preferences based on what matters most, but as shown, the fundamental construct of the clinical encounter has changed very little in 100 years. Consequently, the fact that the patient-provider relationship has not evolved as far as medical technology suggests that the current culture of healthcare prevents the appropriate integration of SDM into routine clinical practice.

Johnson [24] provides some helpful examples to demonstrate how the culture of medical practice has changed over the years, and how this might influence the failure to integrate SDM into routine practice. Johnson segments the changes in modern medicine into three different models from collegial to patronage to mediated. The collegial model represents the emergence of occupational associations formed to define scope of practice and therefore control how a service, in this case health, would be distributed. The patronage model reflects a period of time when consumers were organised around small, unitary, and privileged clientele. In this way, the doctor was not assessed on ability, but rather by social acceptance – priority was given to subjective choice rather than clinical evidence. The mediated model identifies the emergence of state-controlled or -mediated patient-provider relationships. In the mediated model, control of content (scope of practice) rests with the state, which allocates resources based on the principle of being a citizen (being a member of the state), rather than on an individual's ability to pay. Johnson's models, while descriptive, seem limited by a mainly policy level perspective and offer little in terms of the patient's role.

Consequently, there seem to be strong parallels to modern medicine, particularly because the role of the patient seems obscured, once again, by the role of the professional. Arguably, the mediated model comes closest to our modern system where the role of physician, which is no longer controlled by a state, appears co-mediated by insurance and pharmaceutical companies. This co-mediated frame amends the mediated model by recognising the economic influences of advertising, for-profit and fee-for-service incentives, and private-sector lobbyists who pursue policy agendas and perhaps wield more influence in US healthcare than patients and providers combined.

Today, there is a resurgence of a new ruling party, the insurance companies and hospital administrators, where content (information) and care (treatment decisions) are often determined by third-party sources – not the provider or patient. As the emergence of HTA in the 1970s seemed to suggest, this pressure from powerful interest groups had not gone unnoticed, and systematic approaches have been necessary to mediate those influences.

As David Mechanic argues, modified roles and overall changes in medicine reflect ever more structured environments, which are indicative of mediated environments, where technology now casts a much larger shadow. The discipline of medicine, the profession itself, is being pushed into new territory, but where does the patient fit in determining this new frontier?

As technology and innovation have made their way into medicine, there have been remarkable advances in life-saving procedures, and life-extending medications. Despite these advances, unbridled growth in medical care, treatment, and technology have led to what Shannon Brownlee calls over-treatment and misuse of health resources. She further points out that over-treatment reflects a culture of medicine, where aggressive treatment is the norm and where the science of medicine is thought to be capable of fixing any illness. Such a culture supports organisations in the purchase of the newest, biggest, and shiniest equipment at a heavy cost to consumers – once bought, these technologies need to be paid for, and unfortunately the bottom line rests on the shoulders of providers and in the pockets of patients [25]. By evaluating such technologies for cost, HTA helps by considering the medical, social, economic, and ethical impact of new systems, processes, and devices.

Such a process is critical for determining optimal use in a system where consequences of inattention and misuse are high.

In the book, *Limits of Medicine*, Ivan Illich derided the medical system for its flagrant misuse of medical resources to do more harm than good [26]. Illich admits that while his book changed the conversation of medicine at a time when physicians were considered beyond reproach, the book also exposed the realities of a powerful system, co-mediated by large business interests. His ultimate statement was an indictment of medicine and healthcare. By drawing our attention to the dangers of over-treatment, and medically caused illness (iatrogenic), Illich and Brownlee have also opened our eyes to the potential for new technologies to overshadow the preferences of patients in the decision-making process. HTA, in this case, offers a limited solution by only giving companies, organisations, payers and high level authorities evidence that certain technologies are effective, useful, efficient and safe.

In Arthur Frank's *The Wounded Storyteller*, he described the patient illness experience as when "popular experience is overtaken by technical expertise, including complex organizations of treatment" [27]. In many ways technology supports simplification, or increased efficiency of treatment through streamlined organisational and diagnostic processes. Frank seems to suggest that a system, which removes the patient from the diagnostic or treatment process, by putting technology first, fails to account for patient preference or experience. Zola [13] who demonstrated the influence of culture on patient experience, might argue that effective solutions alone aren't enough to meet the needs of the individual patient. There seems to be a need to reinsert the voice of the patient back into the system, in order to balance the diagnostic process. In fact, HTA alone is potentially ill-equipped to address the many individual characteristics that make up patient preference. To determine the optimal treatment choice for patients, evidence alone, presumably, only gets us part of the way there. The remainder of the distance needs to be provided by the patient, and can only be determined with patient feedback; therefore, requiring an additional process that includes assessing the unique features characteristic to the patient experience.

Expectations

To overcome the misuse and overuse of treatment, the evidence-based movement, inspired by Gordon Guyatt and David Sackett, has underscored the need for rigorous and objective evaluations of medicines, technologies, and clinical procedures. Such assessments have been extremely helpful in understanding the clinical impact of drugs, the efficacy of certain treatments, and the long-term success of procedures. While evidence-based medicine (EBM) may get us part of the way towards providing more effective care, where does the patient fit in the evaluation of these treatments and procedures?

Once again, Eric Topol provides some context, where in *The Creative Destruction of Medicine* he discussed the idea of a "surrogate endpoint". He talks about the use of EBM as a means of promoting statins (medicines used to reduce low-density lipoprotein [LDL] [bad] cholesterol) [28]. The surrogate endpoint represents the LDL number, a clinical measure of the amount of cholesterol in one's system – what many providers use as a proxy measure for likelihood of coronary artery blockage. A lower LDL number means your risk for coronary blockage is lower. EBM shows that a statin reduces overall levels of LDL in the blood, yet it neither accounts for independent nor variable patient factors like age, gender, history or response to medication. Consequently, as Topol points out, using evidence alone to promote use of medicine, even strong evidence to support an efficacious, cost effective, and safe medication like statins, can be grossly inappropriate if patient lifestyle, history or reaction to medication isn't considered.

The point where evidence, rigorously collected and tested, falls just short of helping a patient make the most appropriate decision is where SDM finds a definitive role in HTA. The evidence, essentially, only gets the profession so far. As demonstrated, the evolution of the patient-provider relationship recognises the importance of putting the patient first, and highlights the consequences when patient preferences are not taken into consideration. By providing patients and physicians with a clear strategy that integrates evidence, preference, and possible solutions into the clinical encounter, decisions are more likely to be informed, and in line with patient values.

Why Shared Decision Making Matters

As previously stated, SDM is an approach, where (using the best available evidence) providers and patients deliberate to weigh the pros and cons of potential treatment options, to build informed preferences and ultimately treatment decisions. Over two decades ago, Emanuel & Emanuel [23] proposed a new deliberative model of the physician-patient relationship that was marked by informing, sharing and eliciting patient values. A few years later, Charles and colleagues offered further clarified SDM [29]. They suggested that key characteristics of SDM included two participants (physician and patient), sharing of information, building consensus about preferred treatment and agreeing on final treatment choice. Elwyn, Edwards, and Kinnersley [30] showed that SDM fits between the traditional models of care marked by paternalism and the practice of informed choice, making the argument that although technical knowledge rests with providers, the patient is an expert in their own personal preference. Makoul & Clayman [31] reinforced this patient role agreeing that SDM reflects a meeting of experts where both provider and patient bring equally important values and skills to the conversation. Taken together, these models of SDM offer a critical break from the traditional medical model, where the doctor stands as the lone expert and where the patient role is as a passive observer.

SDM has been promoted as more than just a method of deciding between options. Many consider it a consciousness-raising framework to support physicians and patients at the point of care. SDM is considered ethically necessary [32] and a logical next step for ensuring informed consent [33]. The process of SDM considers patient vulnerabilities [34], recognises that physicians are under more and more burden to provide necessary care to patients [35] and values the use of patient-centred communication to improve patient outcomes [36].

One of the ways SDM has found expression in clinical medicine is through the application and use of decision support interventions or decision aids – like the one described earlier for prostate cancer – to assist patients and/or physicians in the decision-making process. These tools have been systematically reviewed [37] and their benefits include: increased patient involvement, satisfaction, knowledge, reduced decisional conflict and increased number of patients who felt their values matched their treatment choice. Consequently, the growth of these tools in the last decade has been exponential, indicating interests at both the practice and policy levels. To manage the growth of these tools in a systematic and controlled manner, a group of leading researchers across the world came together in 2003 and formed IPDAS, the International Patient Decision Aid Standards Collaboration. The IPDAS mandate is to enhance the quality and effectiveness of patient decision aids by establishing standard criteria to improve content, development, implementation and evaluation. With over 500 decision aids currently in use, and many more on the way, there is growing need to ensure that there is a recognisable, measurable, and standard of quality. As the number and quality of decision aids continue to grow, there is still a well-established challenge of integrating them into routine care pathways [38,39].

Although decision aids are designed to be helpful, they are not substitutes for SDM; rather, they support the role of the patient in understanding and/or constructing their preferences. In these circumstances displaying accurate risks and benefits of various treatment options becomes essential, and modifiable depending on the decision aid itself. Consequences of excluding the patient perspective in the delivery of care are dire. Katz explains in *The Silent World of Doctor and Patient* why it is essential to listen to patients' perspectives and values, "patient participation in decision making will not easily become a reality" he says because "the idea of sharing the burdens of decision with patients will create new tensions"[40]. Yet, Kleinman demonstrates that while the old system of communication may be under threat, the new approach, putting patients at the centre of healthcare, can teach us a great deal about their experiences and their health [41]. In many ways, he offers the idea that by listening to what patients need, and hearing their stories, providers fill the void between what patients' need and what providers' treat. The consequences of failing to listen to patient stories are detailed by Williamson in *Towards the Emancipation of Patients*, where she explains how patients, who feel ignored by providers, actively manage their fears and anxieties by organising with others to rebuke the system and seek alternative care solutions [42].

At the preference laboratory we know that integrating what matters most to patients (preferences) with the most up-to-date evidence is essential to providing high quality care. Some have even argued that leaving preferences aside might be an equivalent form of malpractice. One need only consider this patient's story. Upon having her breast removed to eliminate a cancerous tumor, she learned that she could have chosen to keep her breast and receive a lumpectomy instead. Because the potential of her tumor returning was equally likely for both procedures, the only difference between the options was her preference to keep or remove her breast. The failure to adequately inform this patient of her options, and to provide information on the potential risks and benefits of each, seems almost unbearable to comprehend. Indeed, the importance of constructing a "preference" diagnosis to avoid such situations forces many to consider it as a critical step in the process of making SDM an integral part of the clinical process [43]. Perhaps, demanding the integration of preferences with clinical data is the next phase of the medical model. The indisputable truth behind the patient movement and the increase in decision aids is that patients and policy makers understand the value of linking patient preferences with evidence. Patients want transparency and are willing to organise themselves to get it. Providers want patients to be better prepared and more actively involved in their care and find that decision aids can help this happen. Perhaps this is exactly how SDM plays a role in the implementation of HTA.

SDM by definition purports to integrate the individual expertise of the patient and with the clinical expertise of the provider in a way that allows for open deliberation of options based on what matters most to the patient. This approach to the clinical process of communication, acknowledges both the experience of the patient and the scientific or professional knowledge of the provider. One of the ways, as described, to introduce more efficient means of getting patients more prepared to talk with providers about their health is through the use of decision aids. Despite these gains on the decision-making process, there are continued efforts to improve these tools, and many promises being made, heralding their potential to improve patient outcomes, and reduce costs.

How is Shared Decision Making Relevant to Managing Innovative Technology?

In her book, *Overtreated*, Brownlee writes "we spent more on healthcare [2.1 trillion in 2006] than China spend on everything" [44]. One of the largest contributors to growing costs in healthcare is new advances in technology. Brownlee further explains that the US pays greatly for its innovation, essentially supporting an environment where new medical technologies can be invented, piloted, and put into production. While many of these new technologies are incredibly unique, powerful and do save lives, questions remain. Is there a greater cost to developing more specialised devices given they have marginal benefit over previous versions? What about new medical imaging technologies, which give providers clearer and clearer images of bones, soft tissue, muscle and organs? Do these clearer images provide measurable benefits to patients given their costs? These are the types of questions, often not asked of patients, which concern HTA and EBM. What if there were ways to include patients in the process to determine whether a hospital or organisation should purchase some new technology? What if patients were offered the chance to choose between a new "more expensive" technology and current "lower cost" technologies? SDM provides the framework for this kind of patient engagement, where what the patient values is evaluated against possible treatment options. Without allowing patients a role in this process, the potential for overspending on frivolous or unnecessary care treatments is virtually guaranteed.

This is where the Wennberg argument helps to clarify our thinking about how healthcare delivery must rely on including patients in treatment decisions. We know that a portion of unwarranted variation in care is not controlled by what the consumer/patient needs or wants, but rather how providers deliver care. Concurrently, we also recognise how, in a co-mediated system where hospitals pressure providers to deliver care based on a fee-for-service incentive system, often decisions are made independently of the clinical encounter. Think, the more colonoscopies, knee replacements and hip replacements the better. There is also the concept of unnecessary care, which falls in line with consumers not getting what they need, but having it prescribed for them despite little or no clinical necessity.

Ultimately, healthcare can be dangerous, and risky. If treatments are unnecessary then perhaps taking a risk isn't worth it. Determining whether such a decision is made is essentially in the hands of the patients themselves. An argument could be made suggesting that decisions should be made using the best available evidence, in collaboration with the provider, to determine which choice might make the most sense. This is the SDM argument. One example of this might be making a decision to have a knee replacement or steroid injections to alleviate pain. While the long-term outcomes vary, having surgery or an injection to manage pain is highly preference-sensitive.

Knowing there are financial and individual health costs associated with advances in technology (devices, treatments, and medications), SDM may serve as one potential solution to help manage the various cost pressures by linking the appropriate, efficient, and evidence-based medicine to the needs and wants of patients. One attempt to reduce costs in the 1980s came in the form of managed care organisations or HMOs. While they certainly reduced costs, individual choice was limited and for Americans, this meant losing out on what was thought to be the best care or the best care provider. Just north of the US, Canadians have a much more efficient system, but to many in the US, this looks suspiciously like rationing. For many Americans, the single-payer system is too controlling of costs and therefore too limiting on choice. Common refrains heard around the US during Obama's push for a new healthcare system talked about how reviews of patient records by bureaucrats would lead to "death panels" and efforts to restrict Medicare drug benefits by "taking medicines out of grandma's hands". These statements, while provocative, seem to miss the point entirely. The point is to provide what Al Mulley, the Director of The Dartmouth Center for Healthcare Delivery Science says is, "the right amount of care people need and no more, and the right amount they want and no less".

In many ways, SDM puts agency back in the hands of patients, who should be at the centre of any health decision. The SDM process also ensures that checks and balances are in place so that care isn't wildly distributed without regard for rising costs. As discussed, making treatments and choices available, providing transparency, and holding patients and providers accountable for their actions in the clinical encounter allows for more appropriate and legitimate evaluation of medical treatments. HTA and EBM are designed to objectively assess innovative technologies based on effectiveness and cost, but they are not designed to utilise patient preference or values for evaluation.

SDM offers ways of engaging patients at point of care and beyond by being a conduit through which complex and evidence-based information is accessible to patients and their providers. Some have suggested that SDM might work and be more beneficial at the point of care rather than at any other point in the delivery of care process, because of its focus on communication, recognising the expertise of both patients and providers. A more meaningful way to get needed information into the hands of patients requires time and preparation. The creation of shorter decision tools, like Option Grids [45] or Issue Cards [46,47] allows this possibility. There are other technologies too, which might enhance the SDM process at the point of care, and these need to be tested to ensure they are effective and useful.

Technology, in any scenario, has the potential to improve the practice of medicine if patients and providers are supported to deliberate options using best-available data to frame appropriate treatment decisions. The key point, as described earlier, is getting the most up-to-date and accurate evidence into the hands of patients, which means making it accessible, meaningful and relevant. Currently, evidence is so vast and overwhelming that simply getting this information into the hands of providers, then into the decision-making process, can take decades. SDM allows for the appropriate and easily accessible integration of EBM into the care process, by directing providers to elicit patient preferences in response to the evidence. In other words, technology may help overcome the challenges of explaining the most up-to-date evidence to patients and providers by supporting a process of SDM that is neither too complex nor too overwhelming so that it fits nicely in the space of a routine clinic visit.

How Might Shared Decision Making Contribute to Health Technology Assessment?

The benefits of SDM are now widely accepted as necessary in order to deliver appropriate patient-centred care, yet, there is more work needed to accurately measure SDM in the clinical encounter, develop effective and feasible implementation processes/strategies and integrate SDM into routine clinical practice. What this means is holding patients and providers accountable, ensuring that these technologies are feasible and finding ways to elicit patient preferences and integrate them with the most up-to-date evidence.

Technology brings opportunities to patients and providers, if it is managed appropriately and its risks and benefits are made transparent. Transparency in medicine is another way of assuring that information, providers and hospitals are not beyond reproach, that medicine works best when there are systems in place to hold people, organisations and companies accountable. In order for there to be accountability in medicine, there has to be some way to determine whether or not something has occurred. In this case, to determine whether or not a patient has understood a doctor's orders, or if a doctor has adequately outlined the risks and benefits of a medication to the patient, the system needs to hold each accountable. This first means getting the best information to the patient, which means using HTA to set the stage by providing the documentation and authentication necessary for communicating accurate data to patients.

SDM may contribute most to HTA within the clinical encounter, where time is limited and patients often face multiple treatment options. Being required to decide between options with equivalent outcomes, in the presence of clinical equipoise, patients must be allowed to assess the trade-offs between relevant harms and benefits of innovative treatments and/or technologies. SDM gives providers a communication structure, which supports patients and providers to collaborate using the best available evidence (as determined by HTA) to determine the best course of treatment. While decision support interventions (DESIs) have been useful for delivering evidence to patients, there remain implementation challenges [48] despite considerable interest from policy-makers, and is far more complex than merely making decision support interventions available to patients. Few have reported successful implementation beyond research studies. MAking Good Decisions In Collaboration (MAGIC). Notably, HTA findings are critical for patients, providers and policy makers, but often only inform providers and policy makers. Consequently, the communication and feedback processes inherent in the SDM models of care, as discussed previously in this chapter, demonstrate that a collaborative approach to deliberating evidence and informing practice bolster basic evaluation principles of HTA. By extending HTA into the clinical encounter, meeting patients where they are at the point-of-care (via decision tools or technologies), SDM brings immediacy and relevance to HTA, something one might consider as an additional process to engage patients with the best available evidence.

If HTA and EBM assure customers and organisations that new medical technologies are clinically effective, efficacious and efficient, then SDM introduces the patient experience and assures that technologies adequately meet the needs of patients. Although HTA and EBM provide a rigorous assessment process, they do not often include patient concerns, especially at the point-of-care. Part of the strength, we believe, of SDM as a communication framework is the way it contributes in reframing the model of routine clinical practice to allow for much more patient engagement. We also believe that such engagement radically shapes how new ideas get assessed in clinical settings.

One of the criticisms reported by many patient groups across the globe is the need for more access and transparency in data. These include providing more patient-friendly EMRs, patient-portals, open notes, and interfaces where patients can see more of what doctors and nurses are saying about them. It makes sense, when we consider the impact of getting this information wrong. Consequently, making sure that technology does more to further this practice of getting the right information to patients, and making sure they understand it, is exactly how SDM fits into HTA. One recent classification model contends that tools developed for use in the clinical encounter, when compared to other methods to engage patients, are more feasible and potentially have greater likelihood of success [49]; therefore, getting information to patients at the point-of-care is likely the most effective way to ensure a linkage between HTA and SDM.

In the traditional medical model, a provider sits at the centre of care, where the patient assumes the passive role. As circumstances have changed over the past several decades, control of that encounter has fallen to third parties where the presence of insurance companies and hospital administrators is keenly felt. What we're seeing with the advancement of technology are efforts to make systems more user-friendly for patients, and more efficient for providers. Consequently, there is still a very real need to ensure high quality, low costs and high efficacy. In this way, SDM offers technology a point of entry into the clinical encounter.

In many ways, technology is changing the way researchers and clinicians are thinking about healthcare delivery. From avatars, social media and other online systems to bring patients together in novel ways, there are more and more innovations needing to be assessed and evaluated by patients. SDM offers a chance for clinicians and patients to evaluate these tools and technologies for their ability to improve clinical conversations and outcomes.

Conclusions

If the main purpose of HTA is to inform policy makers on how technology might be used to improve patient experience, care and outcomes, then it stands to reason that patients are a key part of that process. Currently, EBM alone and certainly physicians applying technologies in their clinics do not go far enough. In order to go that one necessary step further to make technology safer, more efficient and less costly without hurting patients, SDM can provide a way to do it. It is the communication framework of SDM that supports patients and providers to work together to determine the best course of treatment by integrating what matters most to patients with the best-available evidence. Otherwise, the evidence stands alone leaving patient preferences aside with potentially catastrophic consequences.

As we have already determined, costs of care are rising, and with newly emerging technologies entering our system daily, there is more and more need to evaluate their benefits and risks. With the advent of the Affordable Care Act (ACA) in the US and National Institute for Health and Care Excellence (NICE) in the UK, there are systems in place to try and regulate the amount of technology that enters medical practice. As we know from the work of Wennberg & Gittelsohn, practice patterns have led to overuse, errors, higher costs, and unnecessary suffering. There are ways to ensure that new technologies are tested and evaluated before getting into the routine care, but there are very few systems in place to assure patients that their voice matters in helping to determine which technologies are safest, relevant, and useful.

SDM supports patients and providers with a communication framework that keeps the integrity of clinical expertise and patient autonomy. Ultimately, technology will be the next step in providing patients with better more patient-centred care. But without their input, medicine will continue applying a one-size-fits-all solution and new technologies run the risk of failing to tailor medicine to provide what the patient needs and no more, and what the patient wants and no less.

This book was supported by an unrestricted educational grant from Celgene.

REFERENCES

1. Turchetti G, Spadoni E, Geisler EE. Health technology assessment. Evaluation of biomedical innovative technologies. IEEE Eng Med Biol Mag. 2010;29:70-6.
2. Edwards W. The theory of decision making. Psychol Bull. 1954;51.
3. Vroom VH. Work and motivation. New York: John Wiley & Sons, 1964.
4. Mitchell TR. Expectancy models of job satisfaction, occupational preference and effort: a theoretical, methodological, and empirical appraisal. Psychol Bull. 1974;81:1053-77.
5. Brock A. Greek medicine being extracts illustrative of medical writers from Hippocrates to Galen. London: Dent, 1929.
6. King LS. Plato's concepts of medicine. J Hist Med Allied Sci. 1954;IX:38-48.
7. Foucault M. The birth of the clinic: an archaeology of medical perception. London: Routledge, 1973.
8. McWhinney I. The need for a transformed clinical method. In: Stewart M, Roter D, eds. Communicating with medical patients. Newbury Park, Calif.: SAGE Publications, Inc 1989. p. 25-42.
9. Lown B. The lost art of healing. Boston: Houghton Mifflin, 1996.
10. Balint M. The doctor, his patient and the illness. Par. New York: International Universities Press, 1957.

11. Duggan PS, Geller G, Cooper LA, Beach MC. The moral nature of patient-centeredness: is it "just the right thing to do"? Patient Educ Couns. 2006;62:271-6.

12. Engel GL. The need for a new medical model: a challenge for biomedicine. Science 1977;196:129-36. doi:10.2307/1743658.

13. Zola IK. Culture and symptoms: an analysis of patient's presenting complaints. Am Sociol Rev 1966; 31:615-30. doi:10.2307/2091854.

14. Wennberg J, Gittelsohn. Small area variations in health care delivery. Science. 1973;182:1102-8.

15. Wennberg J. Tracking medicine: a researcher's quest to understand health care. New York: Oxford University Press, 2010.

16. McWhinney IR. Beyond diagnosis. N Engl J Med. 1972;287:384-7.

17. Levenstein JH, McKracken EC, McWhinney IR, Stewart MA, Brown JB. The patient-centred clinical method. 1. A model for the doctor-patient interaction in family medicine. Fam Pract. 1986;3:24-30.

18. Stewart MA, Roter D, editors. Communicating with medical patients. Newbury Park: Sage Publications, 1989.

19. Szasz T, Hollander M. A contribution to the philosophy of medicine. Arch Intern Med. 1956;97:585.

20. Edwards A, Elwyn G. Shared decision-making in health care: achieving evidence-based patient choice. In: Edwards A, Elwyn G, eds. Shared decision-making in health care: achieving evidence-based patient choice. New York: Oxford University Press; 2009. p. 3-10.

21. Barry MJ, Mulley AG, Fowler FJ, Wennberg JW. Watchful waiting vs. immediate transurethral resection for symptomatic prostatism: The importance of patients' preferences. J Am Med Assoc. 1988;259:3010-7.

22. Barry MJ, Fowler FJ, Mulley AG, Henderson JV, Wennberg JE. Patient reactions to a program designed to facilitate patient participation in treatment decisions for benign prostatic hyperplasia. Med Care. 1995;33:771-82.

23. Emanuel EJ, Emanuel LL. Four models of the physician-patient relationship. J Am Med Assoc. 1992;267:2221-6.

24. Johnson TJ. Professions and power. First. Hong Kong: The Macmillan Press Ltd, 1972.

25. Brownlee S, Hurley V, Moulton B. Patient decision aids and shared decision making. The New America Foundation; 2011[cited 2014 May 5]. Available from: http://health.newamerica.net/sites/newamerica.net/files/policydocs/SDM%20primer%20formatted%20FINAL.pdf.

26. Illich I. Limits to medicine: medical nemesis, the expropriation of health. London: Boyars, 1976.

27. Frank AW. The wounded storyteller. Chicago: The University of Chicago Press, 1995.

28. Topol E. The creative destruction of medicine: how the digital revolution will create better health care. New York: Basic Books, 2012.

29. Charles C, Gafni A, Whelan T. Decision-making in the physician-patient encounter: revisiting the shared treatment decision-making model. Soc Sci Med. 1999;49:651-61.

30. Elwyn G, Edwards A, Kinnersley P. Shared decision-making in primary care: the neglected second half of the consultation. Br J Gen Pract. 1999;49:477-82.

31. Makoul G, Clayman ML. An integrative model of shared decision making in medical encounters. Patient Educ Couns. 2006;60:301-12.

32. Drake R, Deegan P. Shared decision making is an ethical imperative. Psych Serv. 2009;60:1007.

33. King JS, Moulton BW. Rethinking informed consent: the case for shared medical decision-making. Am J Law Med. 2006;32:429-501.

34. King JS, Eckman MH, Moulton BW. The potential of shared decision making to reduce health disparities. J Law Med Ethics. 2011;39 Suppl 1:30-3.

35. Mechanic D. Physician discontent: challenges and opportunities. J Am Med Assoc. 2003;290:941-6.

36. Smith MY, DuHamel KN, Egert J, Winkel G. Impact of a brief intervention on patient communication and barriers to pain management: results from a randomized controlled trial. Patient Educ Couns. 2010;81:79-86.

37. Stacey D, Bennett CL, Barry MJ, Col NF, Eden KB, Holmes-Rovner M, et al. Decision aids for people facing health treatment or screening decisions. Cochrane Database Syst Rev 2011. Issue 10. Art. No.: CD001431. DOI: 10.1002/14651858.

38. Uy V, May SG, Tietbohl C, Frosch DL. Barriers and facilitators to routine distribution of patient decision support interventions: a preliminary study in community-based primary care settings. Heal Expect. 2014;17:353-64.

39. Légaré F, Ratté S, Gravel K, Graham ID. Barriers and facilitators to implementing shared decision-making in clinical practice: update of a systematic review of health professionals' perceptions. Patient Educ Couns. 2008;3:526-35.

40. Katz J. The silent world of the doctor and patient. New York: The Free Press, 1984.

41. Kleinman A. The illness narratives: suffering, healing, and the human condition. New York: Basic Books, 1989.

42. Williamson C. Towards the emancipation of patients: patients' experiences and the patient movement. Portland: The Policy Press, 2010.

43. Mulley AG, Trimble C, Elwyn G. Stop the silent misdiagnosis: patients' preferences matter. Br Med J. 2012;345:e6572-e6572.

44. Brownlee S. Overtreated: why too much medicine is making us sicker and poorer. New York NY: Bloomsbury, 2007.

45. Elwyn G, Lloyd A, Joseph-Williams N. Option grids: shared decision making made easier. Patient Educ Couns. 2013;90:207-12.

46. Breslin M, Mullan RJ, Montori VM. The design of a decision aid about diabetes medications for use during the consultation with patients with type 2 diabetes. Patient Educ Couns. 2008;73:465-72.

47. Montori VM, Breslin M, Maleska M, Weymiller AJ. Creating a conversation: insights from the development of a decision aid. PLoS Med. 2007;4:e233.

48. Lloyd A, Joseph-Williams N, Edwards A, Rix A, Elwyn G. Patchy "coherence": using normalization process theory to evaluate a multi-faceted shared decision making implementation programme (MAGIC). Implement Sci. 2013;8:02.

49. Grande SW, Faber MJ, Durand MA, Thompson R, Elwyn G. A classification model of patient engagement methods and assessment of their feasibility in real-world settings. Patient Educ Couns. 2014;95:281-7.

CHAPTER 9

Dissemination of Health Technology Assessment

H. David Banta

Introduction

During recent years, a concern for the efficiency and effectiveness of healthcare systems has been developing [1–4]. Such concerns have been fuelled by the increasing expenditure for healthcare in most countries, especially considering the aging populations that will certainly drive the expenditures higher. At the same time, many questions have been raised about the benefits and risks of healthcare. The main concern might be summarised as assuring "value for money in healthcare" [5].

Health technology assessment (HTA) was developed to support decision making in healthcare, especially policy decision making. The ultimate goal of HTA, as with the health system itself, is to assist efforts to improve health, with attention to costs and efficiency, that is, value for money in healthcare. However, it should always be remembered that the healthcare system of every country is different, depending on the culture and economic status of that country. For HTA to be effective, it must be developed with this fact in mind.

Development of Health Technology Assessment

HTA is now about 40 years old. The early years of HTA in the US, as in the work of the Office of Technology Assessment (OTA), were concerned with methods of HTA and access to information from HTA [6]. These methods were then applied to specific technologies, beginning with such dramatic technology as the computed tomography (CT) scanner, intensive care and coronary bypass surgery. The Swedish Council on Technology Assessment in Health Care was established in 1987 [7], followed by programmes in most Western European countries, Canada and Australia. Although HTA was carried out in other settings, notably in academic institutions, the field was dominated, at least visibly, by the official government agencies. HTA was seen primarily as a form of policy analysis [6].

© Springer International Publishing Switzerland 2015
J.E. del Llano-Señarís and C. Campillo-Artero (eds.), *Health Technology Assessment and Health Policy Today: A Multifaceted View of their Unstable Crossroads*,
DOI 10.1007/978-3-319-15004-8_9

In the 21st century, HTA has continued to expand. Existing agencies have grown and HTA has become a talked-about field in universities and think tanks, in industry, and in some consumer-based organisations. The public form of HTA has expanded internationally. In 2014, the International Network of Agencies for Health Technology Assessment has 57 member agencies throughout the world. Although the agencies are focused in Europe, five member agencies are from Asia, four members from South America, and one from Africa [8].

To reach the goal of improving health, HTA must obviously be used by policy makers. The responsibility of making the decision obviously falls on the policy maker, or any individual or system charged with that responsibility. HTA cannot ever be the only factor in making a decision. The decision maker is prone to many pressures, including patient pressures, industry wishes and media pressure. The resources available in the particular area are an additional important factor the decision maker needs to take into account.

Therefore, HTA is never implemented in isolation of other pressures and financial considerations. HTA, where it exists, is part of the context of decision making. Naturally, those working in HTA wish their conclusions to be seriously considered. This chapter examines some of the issues in assuring full use of the results of HTAs.

Diffusion and Use of Knowledge in Healthcare

The literature on diffusion of knowledge can be considered for its implications for policy. This literature has been examined several times [9,10].

The key point is that dissemination methods must depend on the recipient of the information and how that individual uses information and makes decisions. Different target groups acquire and use information in different ways. Therefore, dissemination methods need to be developed with awareness of such factors. However, most of the research available has been carried out in the US, which makes generalisation elsewhere problematic. Still, some generalisations are possible. For example, efforts to improve scientific literacy can improve the use of HTA results. Policy makers often lack this scientific knowledge. Clinicians may very well have such scientific knowledge, but they often make their decisions based more on the opinions of experts who they know and trust rather than on scientific grounds.

Simple diffusion of information does not change behaviour, or changes it very slowly [9]. Simple diffusion of information refers to the publication of an article or a report hoping that others will read it and use it. Active dissemination of HTA requires contacting the potential users and convincing them of the importance and validity of the information. In other words, advocacy and communication strategies could stimulate the uptake of HTA results by policy makers and others. Such active strategies are described below in the case of Sweden.

Unfortunately, there is little information to indicate that many HTA organisations and agencies pay a great deal of attention to such issues. At the time of the EUR-Assess report, a survey of HTA agencies showed that only 4 of the 18 European agencies surveyed had an explicit strategy for dissemination, implementation and evaluation activities [9].

This finding may be related to the perceived target for reports from the HTA agencies. A survey of *the International Network of Agencies for Health Technology Assessment* (INAHTA) members found that 90% target government policy makers [11]. The second largest category for dissemination was 70% to policy makers in hospitals. The agencies surveyed judged that they had some influence on decisions. Thus, the issue of wide dissemination is probably not a priority consideration for HTA agencies, with such a limited number of targets.

A report from INAHTA suggests appropriate methods of dissemination [11]. The report states that it is necessary to build in a consideration of dissemination needs from the beginning of a report. The report recommends making contact with the primary clients for the report early in the assessment and maintaining dialogue during the course of the assessment.

The European network for Health Technology Assessment (EUnetHTA) project, which involves almost all of the countries in Europe, has examined the use and problems of dissemination of HTA information [10]. Barriers identified concerning the use of HTA included agreement with stakeholders, reaching political interest, funding, and shortage of trained staff. To influence stakeholders, the report recommended adjusting the communication strategy depending on the target group.

With regard to politics, the report recognised the need to strengthen trust between scientists and politicians through dialogue to improve the use of scientific evidence. A problem identified was a frequent lack of appropriate legal framework or regulations. Gaining political interest was recognised as a problem in most countries in Europe. To influence policy makers, the report stated that HTA results must be timely, in line with priorities and consistent with the dynamics of different markets.

Thus, it seems that HTA agencies in Europe, which include most of the most developed agencies in the world, are still struggling with the issue of effective dissemination. The same applies in Canada, where an analysis has shown that the Canadian agencies have no clear vision of dissemination and seldom use active dissemination [12]. A series of articles on HTA in European countries shows that the results of HTA have not been effectively disseminated [13].

A review of the literature, using Google Scholar, finds very few articles on dissemination. A review of the *International Journal of Technology Assessment in Health Care*, the official journal of the international society for HTA (HTAi) shows that almost all articles give detailed and systematic description of methods and findings from HTA, but few mention the dissemination method, and there are almost no articles on the subject of dissemination. There are a number of reports from groups such as INAHTA [11], EUnetHTA [10] and the European Observatory on Health Systems and Policies [14], but while these support dissemination and provide information and frameworks for dissemination, they provide little information to indicate that effective dissemination is actually being carried out or what its impact has been.

HTA is still spreading around the world. The spread has not been so effective in developing countries, but that may be coming. A recent article indicates that a number of emerging economies are developing or have developed public HTA programmes [15]. In January 2013, Malaysia and Maldives presented a draft resolution to the Executive Board of the World Health entitled "Health intervention and technology assessment in support of universal health coverage". The resolution was strongly supported by such countries as Cuba, Lebanon, Nigeria, Panama and South Africa. The general idea is that as countries develop national health insurance systems they must also develop HTA to assure rational technological decision making. This resolution was accepted by the World Health Assembly in May 2014.

Given the experience of Europe, described above, it is not surprising that countries with emerging economies and developing countries have had little success in disseminating HTA. For example, an official of the Pan American Health Organization, WHO for the Americas, stated in 2012 that HTA has had little influence in the health systems of Latin America [16]. This statement can be supported by the experience of Brazil, which probably has the most developed HTA organisations in Latin America. A recent article from Brazil, attempting to examine the impact of HTA activities concluded ". . . (HTA's) impact on Brazilian Unified National Health System remains unclear" [17].

What is the Problem?

HTA is a demanding field of work. The systematic review of the literature has become the main method of HTA. A systematic review is a demanding and time-consuming procedure. The emphasis in HTA programmes, as illustrated by the published literature on HTA, is to present valid and reliable findings. Generally, little energy seems to be given to assuring the use of the HTA results.

Perhaps the reason for this finding is that members of staff of HTA agencies are generally scientifically trained. The scientific norm is to carry out the research, publish the findings and move on. The scientist feels little need to assure that his/her findings are used. The findings become part of the body of scientific knowledge for replication and eventual use. The findings should be accurate and complete, which leads to long reports that take months to complete. One part of being complete is to express the complexity of the situation. There is seldom a clear-cut answer. The report may express probabilities, or simply describe the difficulty of coming to a short definitive answer.

In fact, the articles in the *International Journal of Technology Assessment in Health Care* generally end by expressing the complexity of the situation and calling for more research.

The reports from the agencies, it must be said, attempt to come to a more definitive answer. Still, the complexity of each situation and the weakness of the evidence make it difficult to come to a clear and simple answer.

The audience, usually seen as policy makers, are faced with daily decisions. Surely, they wish for assistance in making these difficult decisions. But the policy maker is not scientifically trained. He/she does not understand probabilities. He/she does not have the time to study a long report that does not have clear conclusions. One approach to this problem is brief reports, often only one page, that sum-up the results of the assessment. The effectiveness of this approach has apparently not been evaluated.

In short, it seems that HTA members of staff, generally, are not deeply motivated to assure use of their findings. Indeed, little is known concerning how such use can be assured. But lessons can be learned from other fields that have experience with advocacy and communication strategies to create change in policies.

The policy or political decision is in the hands of the policy maker. The decisions are complex. He/she is faced with many competing pressures. Patients clamour for new treatments. Patients' organisations pressure decisions. Clinicians also wish for innovations, and not just because they may improve care; they are also likely to enhance prestige and incomes.

Perhaps most important is the role of industry. Industry is not deeply interested in improving health. The goal of industry is to make a profit, to grow as an industry, to satisfy boards and investors. The health industry is very wealthy, and devotes great resources to influencing decisions. The health industry is now one of the largest sectors of the economy in many countries.

The role of industry may be illustrated by its move in 2013 to convince the US trade representative to move against countries that have active HTA programmes [18]. The industry states that HTA is being used more and more as a cost-containment tool, preventing the development and diffusion of useful innovations. In short, industry objects to any development that may impede the diffusion of its products.

What Can Be Done?

The answer seems to be simple. With political will, HTA will find an increasingly important place. Results will be used because they can improve quality of care, and they can often do it at lower cost. Who can argue rationally against value for money in healthcare?

However, such will is lacking. It seems that policy makers do not understand the basic facts of healthcare: that much useless technology finds its way into the healthcare system; that much technology is overused and misused; that industry consciously promotes overuse of technology for financial reasons; that doctors are not trained to make rational choices in healthcare; and that the result is much harm and waste and misuse of scarce healthcare resources.

HTA itself must take part of the blame for the ignorance of the policy makers. As already stated, HTA staff have generally not been actively involved in dissemination. However, in a few cases there has been an active dissemination effort.

In this regard, one can point to the Swedish experience [7]. The Swedish Council on Technology Assessment in Health Care (SBU) has devoted much effort and many resources to dissemination. Not only does SBU publish a newsletter and make its reports freely available, it sponsors regional conferences on selected topics. Notably, SBU has appointed a group of "ambassadors" who work part-time in clinical work, but the rest of the time meet with group of doctors and others to discuss the findings of SBU reports. While these activities have apparently not been systematically evaluated, they do follow general ideas about how to improve dissemination.

Most HTA agencies attempt to determine if they have had influence over decisions [11]. The most commonly used method for such studies is a standardised survey. The HTA agency in Quebec, Canada has carried this method somewhat further [19]. The agency has a routine monitoring system involving a 15-minute telephone interview with selected policy makers to examine the effectiveness of dissemination, satisfaction, utility of the information, and so forth. The agency feels that this approach does give them valuable information on their impact, and also suggestions for improvement.

The Importance of Health Policy

Every country has a structure of health policies that influence health technology. From its beginnings, HTA has focused on these policies, especially policies related to regulation, quality and payment for care, as a target for its work. This is in accord with the definition of HTA as a form of policy analysis. HTA then should develop assessments useful for policy makers and policy making.

Health policies fall into various categories:
-National public health policy (e.g. vaccines)
-Research and development
-Regulation of pharmaceuticals and equipment
-Regulation of number and location of services
-Payment for services
-Quality assurance
-Education and training of providers
-Consumer education

Each of these policies can be influenced by the findings of HTA. HTA can improve the functioning of each policy. In particular, HTA has taken on a strong role in payment decisions. Coverage of health services is often linked to HTA. Lists of covered services based on HTA are commonly found in countries with HTA programmes.

Still, at best HTA has had a moderate impact on the adoption and use of new technologies in the health services. A systematic review on disinvestment on health technologies found little evidence of use or impact of HTA, although noting that the literature is limited and there may be more examples that are not published [20].

One reason, of course, is that these policies are not part of the mandate of an HTA agency. Most agencies end their work with presenting a report of their findings. Perhaps the main problem is that the preoccupation of policy makers has been with costs and not with technology management, or even health outcomes. However, health costs are often more related to the "small ticket" technologies of healthcare such as the clinical laboratory than to the visible technologies such as organ transplantation and computed tomography scanning. That perception seems to make the growing involvement of clinical doctors in the implementation of HTA a necessity.

Implementation of Health Technology Assessment

In recent years, with the relative failure of dissemination efforts in HTA, some attention has been paid to the concept of implementation. Implementation may be defined as an active process, including interventions to reduce or eliminate barriers to behaviour change, and/or activities that promote behaviour change [9]. Implementation efforts typically involve dissemination activities, which are complemented by actions that promote action consistent with the disseminated message. For example, technology assessment results could be disseminated as reimbursement for the technology is changed and the organisation is adapted to deal with the change. The clearest example of implementation of HTA is perhaps in the payment system. Many countries now link insurance or payment coverage to HTA, meaning that technologies should not be covered by insurance until they are shown to be efficacious and perhaps cost effective. This change is undoubtedly beneficial overall, but the decisions are subject to many powerful forces, mentioned earlier.

Implementation has not grown rapidly in HTA agencies [21]. One reason for this may be that HTA agencies are discouraged from becoming very involved in policies. The policy maker is jealous of his/her role. The role of HTA in this view is merely to provide information. The policy maker generally considers that he/she takes responsibility for the actual decision, its politics and its consequences.

One rapidly growing field that can be considered a form of implementation can be termed "performance-based reimbursement" or "value-based insurance design", or other terms [22–26]. In brief, assessment is embodied in the payment system itself. The reimbursement is related to its effectiveness. An effective intervention is reimbursed at a higher level than a less effective one. Although such systems are growing rapidly in some countries, their ultimate effects are not known.

Health Technology Assessment in the Private Sector and Access to Information

As mentioned previously, many private organisations carry out work that is called HTA. As far as is known, this work is not directed to changing health policy. The volume of such work is huge. One indication is most of the articles in the *International Journal of Technology Assessment in Health Care* are by authors not identified as working for a public sector HTA organisation.

This private sector work, for the most part, does end up informing the policy process in healthcare. In the early days of HTA, it was necessary to use indexing systems such as Medline to review the literature, supplemented by using such means as examining reference lists of articles and consulting experts.

The last 20 years have brought a revolution in searching for evidence. The Cochrane Collaboration can serve as an example. Inaugurated in 1993, the Cochrane Collaboration brought together colleagues from all over the world to oversee the preparation and maintenance of systematic reviews of evidence concerning health technologies [27]. In 2007, more than 17,000 participants in more than 100 countries participated in Cochrane Review Groups. The systematic reviews resulting from this enormous body of work are available on-line through the Cochrane Library. In 2008 the Cochrane Database of Systematic Reviews contained 3600 full reviews of interventions. In addition, the Cochrane Library contains approximately 550,000 reports of controlled clinical trials. While the full database is only available to subscribers, the abstracts of the reviews are all available free.

Many other such efforts have been developed in the area of access of healthcare evidence, including health technology assessment reports [28]. The Institute of Health Economics maintains a list of available databases with websites. There are hundreds of such databases covering efficacy, health economics, quality of life, clinical guidelines, and so forth. There are many international sites. One notable site is the Centre for Reviews and Dissemination (CRD), which includes reports from the INAHTA agencies, published economic evaluations of healthcare interventions, database of abstracts of reviews of effects (DARE), and a database of ongoing systematic reviews of healthcare.

It would be difficult to over-emphasise the importance of this development. It is now easy and fast to obtain information on the utility of specific health interventions. There seems little doubt that such information is valuable, but as with all information, change resulting from its availability is generally slow.

Professional Groups

Many professional groups are involved in HTA. It seems probable that these are more credible to physicians than public sources such as HTA agencies. Physicians are generally sceptical of attempts by the government to change their behaviour, and they often doubt that "bureaucrats" can understand the realities of healthcare. The professional organisations, on the other hand, are run by the members and are respected as reliable sources of information.

One example is the Radiation Therapy Oncology Group (RTOG), an organisation set up in 1968 and funded by the US National Institutes of Health [29]. The RTOG has a number of activities related to improving radiation therapy for cancer patients, but a notable one is supporting large controlled clinical trials of radiotherapy for specific cancers. These trials are well designed and carried out and are highly credible among radiotherapists around the world.

Another professional organisation of interest is the International Diabetes Federation (IDF), an umbrella organisation of about 230 national diabetes associations in about 160 countries [30]. The membership is made up of both professionals and lay people active in the field of diabetes. The IDF has a number of activities focusing on improving care for those with diabetes. One related to HTA is a group of clinical practice guidelines for managing diabetes. The IDF also reviews the literature on certain interventions concerning diabetes and publishes the results. For example, the IDF website includes a statement concerning self-management of diabetes, including a review of the effectiveness and cost effectiveness of self-management of diabetes [31]. The care of diabetes has improved greatly in the last years, in accord with the evidence and with the active advocacy of the IDF and its member organisations [32].

Conclusions

HTA, broadly defined, is an increasingly important force in the healthcare world. HTA-like activities are carried out by many groups, both public and private.

Dissemination of the results of HTA is clearly recognised as an important part of HTA, necessary to assure the use of HTA in decision making [11]. HTA is merely information, and must be only a part of the consideration in a policy decision. Any ideas that HTA could be made the determining factor in a policy decision overlook the realities of decision making in a democracy.

Still, dissemination does not seem to receive appropriate levels of interest among the public agencies carrying out HTA. Furthermore, there is little systematic information on the impact of HTA on public policy. Perhaps the main reason for this finding is that HTA agencies perceive that their main client is one public programme or several individual health policy makers. Few publications deal with the efforts by HTA agencies to influence decisions, and statements by organisations such as INAHTA deal with general approaches. Those working in this HTA are reluctant to claim great influence over decision making. Probably rightly so.

Still, there is considerable room for improvement in the public agencies. The INAHTA publications lay out sound principles for development of dissemination methods. Little is known about progress in this area. Perhaps one can hope that there is gradual improvement.

The most interesting aspect of HTA perhaps is not the international growth in public agencies. It seems considerably more interesting that consideration of evidence seems increasingly to be part of decision making at all levels of the health system. The enormous growth in the web-based accessing systems has surely facilitated this development.

Those working in HTA have informally spoken about the "culture of assessment" as the necessary endpoint for the effectiveness of HTA in assuring effective healthcare at a reasonable cost. One gets the impression that this culture of assessment is developing rapidly in much of the world.

This book was supported by an unrestricted educational grant from Celgene.

REFERENCES

1. World Health Organization. The world health report 2000: improving health system performance, Geneva, 2001.
2. Anderson G, Sotir Hussey P. Comparing health system performance in OECD countries. Health Affairs. 2001;20:3219-32.
3. The World Bank. Creating evidence for better health financing decisions. Washington DC, 2012.
4. Squires D. Multinational comparisons of health systems data 2011. Washington DC: The Commonwealth Fund, 2011.
5. Sorensen C, Drummond M, Kanavos P. Ensuring value for money in health care: the role of health technology assessment in the European Union. Copenhagen: WHO Regional Office for Europe. European Observatory Studies Series No. 13, 2008.
6. Office of Technology Assessment. Assessing the efficacy and safety of medical technologies. Washington DC: US Government Printing Office, 1978.
7. Jonsson E. History of health technology assessment in Sweden. Int J Technol Assess Health Care. 2009;25(Suppl 1):42-52.
8. INAHTA website. Accessed April 2014.
9. Granados A, Jonsson E, Banta, HD, Bero L, Bonair A, Cochet C, et al. Eur-Assess project subgroup report on dissemination and impact. Int J Technol Ass Health Care. 1997;13:220-86.
10. EUnetHTA. Facilitation of national strategy for continuous development and sustainability of HTA. EUnetHTA website, November 2011.
11. Hailey D, Babidge W, Cameron A, Davignon L. Health technology assessment agencies and decision makers. An INAHTA guidance document. INAHTA website, May 2010.

12. Lehoux P, Denis JL, Tailliez S, Hivon M. Dissemination of health technology assessment: identifying the visions guiding an evolving innovation in Canada. Journal of Health Politics, Policies and Law. 2005;30:603-42.

13. Banta D, Oortwijn W. Conclusion. Health technology assessment and health care in the European Union. Int J Technol Assess Health Care. 2000;16:626-35.

14. Velasco Garrido M, Kristensen F, Nielson C, Busse R, editors. Health technology assessment and health policy making in Europe. Current states, challenges and potential. Copenhagen: WHO Regional Office for Europe, European Observatory on Health systems and Policies, Observatory Studies Series No. 14, 2008.

15. Oortwijn W, Broos P, Vondeling H, Banta D, Todorova L. Mapping of health technology assessment in selected countries. Int J Technol Assess Health Care. 2013;29:424-34.

16. Lemgruber, A. Presentation to the WHO Global Forum on Medical Devices, Geneva, 23 November, 2012.

17. Novaes H, Elias F. Use of health technology assessment in decision-making processes by the Brazilian Ministry of Health on the incorporation of technologies in the Brazilian Unified National Health system. Cad Saude Publica. 2013;29(Suppl):S7-S16.

18. //:keionline.org/sites/default/files/PhRMA 2014 Special 301 Submission.pdf.

19. Davignon L, Beauchamp S, Martin V. Logic model for improving the impact of public health technology assessment organization in decision making in the health system. Ann Acad Med Singapore. 2009;38(Suppl):S.67.

20. Policena J, Clifford T, Elshaug A, Mitton C, Russell E, Skidmore B. Case studies that illustrate disinvestment and resource allocation decision making in health care: a systematic review. Int J Technol Assess Health Care. 2013;29:174-84.

21. Hailey D. Personal communication. April, 2014.

22. Birstin HR, Conn A, Setnik G, Rucker DW, Cleary PD, O'Neil AC, et al. Benchmarking and quality improvement. The Harvard Emergency Department Quality Study. Am J Med. 1999;107:437-39.

23. Birstin HR. The journey to electronic performance measurement. Ann Int Med. 2013;158:131-32.

24. Carlson J, Sullivan S, Garrison L, Neumann PJ, Veenstra DL. Linking payment to health outcomes: a taxonomy and examination of performance-based reimbursement schemes between healthcare payers and manufacturers. Health Policy. 2010;960:179-90.

25. Chernew ME, Rosen AB, Fendrick AM. Value-based insurance design. Health Affairs. 2007;27:103-12.

26. Fendrick AM, Martin JJ, Weiss AE. Value-based insurance design: more health at any price. Health Serv Res 2012;47:404-13.

27. Starr M, Chalmers I, Clarke M, Oxman A. The origins, evolution, and future of the Cochrane Database of Systematic Reviews. Int J Technol Assess Health Care. 2009;25(Suppl 1):182-95.

28. Institute of Health Economics. IHE report, health technology assessment on the net. Alberta Canada, 2013.

29. Radiation Therapy Oncology Group website. Accessed April, 2014.

30. International Diabetes Federation website. Accessed April, 2014.

31. IDF. Position statement: self-management education. IDF website. April, 2014.

32. ECORYS. DAWN2 follow up health policy analysis - enhancing person centred diabetes care. Final report. Rotterdam. 19 March, 2014.

46281398R00097

Made in the USA
Middletown, DE
27 July 2017